Time and Again

Linguistik Aktuell/Linguistics Today (LA)

Linguistik Aktuell/Linguistics Today (LA) provides a platform for original monograph studies into synchronic and diachronic linguistics. Studies in LA confront empirical and theoretical problems as these are currently discussed in syntax, semantics, morphology, phonology, and systematic pragmatics with the aim to establish robust empirical generalizations within a universalistic perspective.

General Editors

Werner Abraham
University of Vienna / Rijksuniversiteit
Groningen

Elly van Gelderen
Arizona State University

Advisory Editorial Board

Cedric Boeckx
Harvard University

Guglielmo Cinque
University of Venice

Günther Grewendorf
J.W. Goethe-University, Frankfurt

Liliane Haegeman
University of Lille, France

Hubert Haider
University of Salzburg

Christer Platzack
University of Lund

Ian Roberts
Cambridge University

Lisa deMena Travis
McGill University

Sten Vikner
University of Aarhus

C. Jan-Wouter Zwart
University of Groningen

Volume 135

Time and Again. Theoretical Perspectives on Formal Linguistics
Edited by William D. Lewis, Simin Karimi, Heidi Harley and Scott O. Farrar

Time and Again

Theoretical Perspectives on Formal Linguistics

In honor of D. Terence Langendoen

Edited by

William D. Lewis
Microsoft Research

Simin Karimi
University of Arizona

Heidi Harley
University of Arizona

Scott O. Farrar
University of Washington

John Benjamins Publishing Company
Amsterdam / Philadelphia

The paper used in this publication meets the minimum requirements of American National Standard for Information Sciences – Permanence of Paper for Printed Library Materials, ANSI Z39.48-1984.

Library of Congress Cataloging-in-Publication Data

Time and again : theoretical perspectives on formal linguistics in honor of D. Terence Langendoen / edited by William D. Lewis ... [et al.].
    p. cm. (Linguistik Aktuell/Linguistics Today, ISSN 0166-0829 ; v. 135)
Includes bibliographical references and index.
    1. Linguistics. I. Lewis, William D., 1963-.
  P121.T47   2008
410--dc22   2008035987
ISBN 978 90 272 5518 1 (Hb; alk. paper)

© 2009 – John Benjamins B.V.
No part of this book may be reproduced in any form, by print, photoprint, microfilm, or any other means, without written permission from the publisher.

John Benjamins Publishing Co. · P.O. Box 36224 · 1020 ME Amsterdam · The Netherlands
John Benjamins North America · P.O. Box 27519 · Philadelphia PA 19118-0519 · USA

Table of contents

Acknowledgements	VII
Introduction	IX
William D. Lewis, Simin Karimi, Scott O. Farrar and Heidi Harley	

Part I   Syntax and semantics

1. Inverse reflexives   **3**
   Paul M. Postal and John Robert Ross

2. On the nature of the approximative expression NUM-*odd*   **37**
   Sheila Dooley and Ferdinand de Haan

3. Skating along the syntactic verge: Experimental pragmatics and
   understood elements of content   **55**
   Merrill Garrett and Robert M. Harnish

4. Current challenges to the Lexicalist Hypothesis: An overview
   and a critique   **91**
   Frederick J. Newmeyer

Part II   Psycholinguistics

5. On the homogeneity of syntax: How similar do coordinates and
   subordinates look to the comprehension system?   **121**
   Wayne Cowart and Tatiana Agupova

6. The effect of case marking on subject-verb agreement errors in English   **135**
   Janet Nicol and Ines Antón-Méndez

7. First language acquisition of coordination: The mud-puddle study
   and beyond   **151**
   Barbara Lust, Suzanne Flynn, Yuchin Chien and Barbara Krawiec

8. Frequency effects in children's syntactic and morphological development   **177**
   Cecile McKee and Dana McDaniel

9. Abstract linguistic representations and innateness: The development of determiners   **189**
   Virginia Valian

Part III Language as a formal system

10. One-level finite-state phonology   209
    Michael Hammond

11. Biolinguistics today and Platonism yesterday   227
    T. G. Bever

Part IV Standards

12. Linguistics as a community activity: The paradox of freedom
    through standards   250
    Gary F. Simons

13. Sherwin Cody's school of English   251
    Edwin L. Battistella

Index   263

Acknowledgements

First, we would like to acknowledge our enormous debt of gratitude to the authors who contributed to this volume and who so graciously tolerated the numerous revisions and lengthy delays. Likewise, kudos go to the reviewers without whom this volume could not have come to be: Brian Agbayani, David Basilico, Misha Becker, Hagit Borer, Jidong Chen, Venita Dayal, Roland Pfau, LouAnn Gerken, Baden Hughes, Orhan Orgun, Irina Sekerina, Dave Townsend, and Wendy Wilkins. We would also like to thank the many people at the University of Arizona and elsewhere who were champions of this volume in its early stages and encouraged us to continue, including Andrew Carnie, Mike Hammond, Nancy Kelly, and Ben Tucker. But our most heartfelt appreciation, admiration, and gratitude we reserve for Terry Langendoen himself, whose unrivaled brilliance, tireless energy, and extraordinary productivity over the years has been a source of inspiration to us all. *Nos es humilis.*

Introduction

William D. Lewis[a], Simin Karimi[c], Scott O. Farrar[b],
and Heidi Harley[c]

[a]Microsoft Research/[b]University of Washington/[c]University of Arizona

This volume is an effort to pay tribute to D. Terence Langendoen for his significant contributions to various areas of linguistics in a career that has spanned nearly 50 years. Langendoen's influence on the field can be gauged not only by his own unique contributions, but also by measuring his impact on the careers and scholarship of a large number of students, colleagues and collaborators. This volume captures an essence of his career and his impact, containing papers written by scholars who have worked closely with him over the years.

The success of generative linguistics can be attributed in no small part to a number of Chomsky's prolific students, especially to those who began their careers in the "generative revolution" of the 1960s. D. Terence Langendoen is one of those students. He was in fact Chomsky's first PhD student, completing his dissertation entitled *Modern British Linguistics: A Study of its Theoretical and Substantive Contributions* in 1964. Langendoen's eclectic publications have touched on a wide variety of topics in generative linguistics and have echoed its most important trends and themes. Thus, Langendoen's work acts as a testament to the complexity of problems in generative linguistics.

Currently a Professor Emeritus of Linguistics from The University of Arizona, and expert consultant at the National Science Foundation, Langendoen started his first job in the Linguistics Department at The Ohio State University right after his graduation in 1964. He was promoted to Associate Professor in 1968. He then moved to City University of New York in 1969 where he resided till 1988. He was also a member of the Computer Science Department at the same university, and a member of the PhD. Program in Linguistics at CUNY. In 1988, he was hired by the Department of Linguistics at The University of Arizona where he served as the Department Head until 1997, and continued as a professor in the same department until his retirement in 2005. He has been a fellow and a visiting professor in many areas in the world, including China, Holland, and across the US, at a number of prestigious universities.

The importance of Langendoen's contributions can be seen in his own research and in the collaborative research conducted with linguists such as Thomas Bever, Merrill Garrett, Paul Postal, Virginia Valian, and many others. He is the author of a volume entitled *The London School of Linguistics* (1968, MIT Press), *The study of syntax: The generative-transformational approach to the structure of American English* (1969, Holt, Rinehart and Winston), *Essentials of English Grammar* (1970, Holt, Rinehart and Winston), coauthor of *The vastness of natural language* (1984, with Paul Postal, Blackwell Publishers), and co-editor of *Studies in linguistic semantics* (1971, with Charles Fillmore, Holt, Rinehart and Winston), *An integrated theory of linguistic ability* (1976, with Thomas Bever and Jerrold Katz, Crowell Company), and *Optimality Theory: An overview* (1997, with Diana Archangeli, Blackwell Publishers). He has published about 90 journal articles and book chapters, 30 review articles, and has presented numerous talks.

This volume is a collection of papers that highlights some of the recurring themes that have surfaced in the generative tradition in linguistics over the past 40 years. The volume is more than a historical take on a theoretical tradition; rather it is also a "compass" pointing to exciting new empirical directions inspired by generative theory. In fact, the papers show a progression from core theoretical concerns to data-driven experimental investigation.

The editors of this volume include two of Langendoen's colleagues, Heidi Harley and Simin Karimi, both active in the core issues of generative research, and two of Langendoen's recent students, William D. Lewis and Scott Farrar.

This volume consists of the following papers:

Edwin Battistella, in the chapter entitled *Sherwin Cody's famous school*, explores the details of Sherwin Cody's famous correspondence course in the "proper" use of the English language. Battistella discusses the course with respect to the norms of the day, and places the work within an interesting historical context. In the main portion of the chapter, Battistella provides many details of the course, with illustrative examples of pronunciation, practical grammar, grammatical correctness, and other topics that are covered in the course. The author discusses prescriptivism with respect to Cody's work and points out how Cody was dismissive of stigmatized forms. Cody's work is put into context, namely, how the course fit within the context of society in the first half of the twentieth century. The latter portion of the essay indeed deals with how Cody's work was viewed by language experts of the day, e.g., educators and linguists.

Tom Bever explores the ontological status of language, both within a historical and contemporary context in the chapter entitled *Biolinguistics today and Platonism yesterday*. The author presents the ideas of certain New York City grammarians of the 1980s (e.g. Katz, Postal, Langendoen and Bever), including the idea that language has an essential, uncaused structure, that is not the result of human cognition. The author presents these ideas as similar to platonic 'ideal form' and makes a convincing argument using examples from human perception, cognition and mathematics. Bever argues that language structure (like certain properties of numbers) transcends cognition and has properties that existed before humans discovered them. The author discusses three consequences for language acquisition and presents arguments from his earlier work. In essence (as argued by Langendoen/Postal), language is not triggered in the brain, but discovered by the child. The child seems to go through a similar process in discovering number properties. Furthermore, Bever highlights the role of interfaces with respect to this neo-platonic idea. Finally, he points out that the notion of language as an abstract object does not change in light of current theoretical machinery, and in the context of recent work in biolinguistics.

Wayne Cowart and Tatiana Agupova take on what they call the "Homogeneity Thesis" in their paper entitled *On the homogeneity of syntax: How similar do coordinates and subordinates look to the comprehension system?* The assumption of the Homogeneity Thesis is that "coordinates must somehow fall under the same general regime of syntactic principles as apply to non-coordinates" Rather than taking on differing syntactic configurations for the coordination and subordination (see Langendoen's recent work on *Coordinate Grammar* (to appear) for a formalism positing a strong underlying connection between the two), they instead present evidence suggesting different cognitive "systems" involved in processing the two.

In a follow-up to Langendoen's work on approximate numeral expressions with disjunction (*thirty or forty*), **Sheila Dooley and Ferdinad deHaan** consider numerals in combination with approximative -*odd*, as in "twenty-odd years ago". In their paper *On the nature of the approximative expression 'NUM-odd'*, they survey uses of this expression in several corpora, both written and spoken, and document its various permutations. They claim that -*odd* indicates a range of variation bounded on the lower end by the numeral and on the upper end by adding the order of magnitude of the numeral, e.g. in *thirty-odd*, the upper bound is 30+10 = 40; in *five hundred-odd*, the upper bound is 500+100=600. Based on corpus examples showing that -*odd* can occur inside ordinal -*th*, it is treated as a derivational suffix, rather than as a clitic. Syntactically, the distribution of NUM-odd expressions is identical to that of numerals, entailing that they are of the same category. Historically, NUM-*odd* expressions developed out of a use of *odd* to mean 'an unspecified additional amount', as in *thirty-eight degrees and odd minutes;* eventually the second nominal was dropped, in forms like *thirty-eight degrees and odd*, then *thirty-eight and odd degrees*, and finally *thirty-eight-odd degrees*. The last remaining vestige of this additive etymology is the typologically unusual semantic feature of NUM-*odd* approximatives, namely, that the numeral sets a lower bound for the approximation, rather than a central point around which the approximation varies: compare *twenty-odd* with *twenty-ish*—the latter, but not the former, can include values like 18 or 19 within its range.

Coordination has been a central theme of Langendoen's research program for many years, and Barbara Lust's work with him early in her career inspired the line of research described herein. In the broad-ranging article *First language acquisition of coordination: The mud-puddle study and beyond*, **Flynn, Chien and Krawiec** first survey the results on the structure and acquisition of coordinate structures, and then present the results of the first acquisition experiment devoted to non-reducible coordinate structures. The fact that most phrasal coordinations have sentential counterparts (John and Mary left = John left and Mary left) led to the natural notion of 'conjunction reduction': phrasal coordinations are reductions/ellipses of a sentential coordination structure. Results from early childhood studies seem to be consistent with this view, in that children command sentential coordination from very early stages, while phrasal coordination is more variable in its development. However, certain conjunction structures cannot be analyzed as conjunction reductions, since there is no sentential conjunction counterpart with the equivalent semantics; Lust et al. investigated the acquisition of two such types: reciprocals, as in *John and Tom hit each other* (≠*John hit each other and Tom hit each other*), and 'mud-puddle' sentences, such as *Dirt and water make a mud puddle* (≠*Dirt makes a mud puddle and water makes a mud puddle*). Interestingly, children seemed to be insensitive to the semantic anomaly involved in creating sentential conjunctions from sentences of the second type, but they showed a great awareness of the restrictions on the reciprocal type.

In their paper entitled *Skating along the syntactic verge: Experimental pragmatics and understood elements of content*, **Merrill Garrett and Robert Harnish** address elements of communicative content not expressed by overt elements of a sentence. Numerous phenomena, from deletion and ellipsis to trace and PRO provided evidence for unspoken material and mechanisms for recovering it. In the 1970s and 1980s, mostly inspired by the work of Grice, other forms of 'unexpressed elements of content' not contemplated by linguistic theory of the time began to surface under a variety of labels, which the authors collectively call 'impliciture'. They argue that recent experimental work suggests that certain forms of impliciture are tied to language via "standardization" which provides a pragmatic scenario that does not require access to potentially unbounded domains of general background information.

Although **Michael Hammond** in the chapter entitled *One-level finite-state phonology* does not directly address issues regarding the degree to which language can be represented by finite-state processes (see Langendoen 2003 and Langendoen 1981 for discussion and review), he presents an interesting implementation that captures simple phonological generalizations using finite-state automata. Unlike Optimality Theory (Prince & Smolensky 1993, Archangeli & Langendoen 1997), where transduction between input and output does the principal work, Hammond's presentation relies on a "One-Level" phonology built over automata, notably *without* transduction.

Fritz Newmeyer revisits the question of the derivation of nominalizations in English in his paper *Current challenges to the Lexicalist Hypothesis: An overview and a critique*, addressing the question of how much abstract structure is present, an issue which has been addressed repeatedly since Chomsky's seminal 1971 paper, 'Remarks on Nominalizations'. He reviews and rebuts the modern revival (e.g. Fu, Roeper and Borer 2003) of the lexical-semantics notion that event nominals contain a complex verb phrase with argument structure, arguing that such analyses fail to capture the fundamental distributional facts about such nominalizations, namely that they behave, syntactically, exactly like nonderived nominals.

Just as comprehension errors (like those induced by 'garden-path' sentences) can reveal the inner workings of the language processing process, speech errors can reveal the architecture of the language production process. **Nicol and Anton-Mendez**, in their paper *The effect of case marking on subject-verb agreement errors in English*, continue a line of investigation which attempts to pin down the factors influencing the rate of subject-verb agreement errors in a sentence-completion task. In this general paradigm, the head subject noun is separated from the verb by a modifying phrase which itself contains a noun. That second noun, closer to the verb, may differ in number from the head noun. Speakers will sometimes erroneously produce a verb form which agrees with the second noun, rather than the head noun. In the present study, Nicol and Anton-Mendez ask whether case-marked intervening nouns (pronouns like *they, them*) produce the same amount of subject-verb agreement errors as non-case-marked intervening nouns (such as *cats, dogs*). The results show that the agreement error rate is sensitive to case-marking: plural accusative pronouns like *them* produce significantly fewer agreement errors. This result suggests that the part of the production process which determines verbal agreement is sensitive to overt case-marking. The authors consider several ways of implementing this sensitivity in the standard production model, and propose that the explicit presence of case information on the intervening noun makes it easier to filter out speech errors before the utterance is articulated. That is, the differently case-marked NPs induce the same number of errors as case-ambiguous NPs early in the process, but there is a self-monitoring mechanism which filters out production errors if any are detected; detection is easier if the two NPs are grammatically differentiated by case-marking and productions of errors are consequently lower.

Cecile McKee and Dana McDaniel enter into the long standing debate regarding the divide between grammaticality and acceptability in the chapter entitled *Frequency effects in children's syntactic and morphological development*. Drawing inspiration from Langendoen 1970 (*The Accessibility of Deep Structures*), they detail the results of two well-crafted experiments that look at the role of frequency in the syntax and morpho-phonological systems of children, and to what degree their results are predictive of a model where acceptability is predicted by frequency and grammaticality is not.

In their paper entitled *Inverse reflexives,* **Paul Postal and John Ross** address the principles which determine legitimate minimal domain, a simple clause or a nominal phrase, for reflexive forms. The authors criticize the idea that these principles reduce to some elementary statement involving c-command or similar structural relations, and propose a relational account for certain documented constraints.

Gary F. Simons explores the very recent topic of standards within communities of practice in the chapter entitled *Linguistics as a community activity: The paradox of freedom through standards.* This is an issue that has occupied Langendoen throughout much of the second half of his career, for example his involvement with the Text Encoding Initiative (TEI) and the E-MELD (Electronic Metastructures for Endangered Language Data) project. Simons discusses the issue for the field of linguistics by invoking an ingenious analogy with the standardization of time zones in the United States in the late 19th Century. Simons addresses the most current work of Langendoen, his involvement with the development of GOLD, the General Ontology for Linguistic Description (Farrar and Langendoen 2003). Simons emphasizes how this and other related efforts seek to help the linguistics community find wealth in its information.

Virginia Valian in a paper entitled *Abstract linguistic representations and innateness: The development of determiners* addresses the issue of innateness in language acquisition by using the syntactic category of determiner as an example. She states that children show a continuity in acquiring categories; they look as if they are fleshing out the category more fully in time, acquiring more specific details related to it. She concludes that categories, including determiners, are there from the beginning, and the child's task is to find out what the members of each category are in the target language.

PART 1

Syntax and semantics

CHAPTER 1

Inverse reflexives*

Paul M. Postal and John Robert Ross
New York University/University of North Texas

This chapter discusses the principles that determine legitimate minimal domains for antecedents of reflexive forms. It offers novel critiques of the idea that these principles reduce to some elementary statement involving c-command or analogs thereof, and proposes a relational account for certain documented constraints.

1. Introduction

This article considers the principles which determine legitimate minimal domain internal antecedents for reflexive forms. By 'minimal domain' we mean roughly a single clause, but ultimately nominals are also relevant; see note 22. The chapter offers novel critiques of the idea that these principles reduce to some elementary statement involving c-command or analogs thereof and proposes a novel relational account for certain documented constraints.

Turning to actual data, uncontroversially, English examples like (1) are grammatical, while those like (2) are not:

(1) a. Harriet described herself to Arthur.
   b. Harriet was described to herself by Milton.

(2) a. *Herself described Harriet to Arthur.
   b. *Herself was described to Harriet by Arthur.

At issue are the relative positions of a *reflexive* pronoun and its antecedent.[1] What principle determines that (2a, b) are ungrammatical? A rough, initially valid descriptive generalization seems to be, of course, that while a subject can antecede

---

* To Terry, who, in laudable contrast to many, fully understands the difference between linguistics and vaudeville. We are indebted to various anonymous reviewers for a multitude of detailed suggestions and criticisms which have led to great improvements in this paper. Also thanks to Brian Joseph for some input about Greek glosses.

1. The issues raised here about reflexives may well have partially parallel variants involving reciprocals. To avoid unwieldy multiplication of the number of examples though, we limit all citations to reflexives.

a reflexive object in the same clause, an object cannot antecede its clausemate subject. It is now quite broadly assumed (i) that as in our descriptive generalization, (2a, b) are ill-formed *for the same reason*; call this the *uniformity hypothesis* (UH), and (ii) that, moreover, this reason reflects universal principles; call this the *universality assumption* (UVA).

Most common accounts of (2a, b), all variants of Chomsky's (1981, 1982, 1986) so-called *binding theories*, take the UH to follow from, and the UVA to be instantiated by, some variant of Principle A of those theories, which requires that an *anaphor* be bound, that is, c-commanded by, and coindexed with, an expression in the same fixed local domain, whose exact definition need not concern us. The account would depend on the assumption that at least these English reflexive forms are anaphors[2] and on the view that the subject of a clause asymmetrically c-commands all the elements of the verbal phrases of that clause. The number of partially different formulations of binding theories derivative from Chomsky (1981) is now remarkably large, so we make no attempt to cite even a sam-

---

2. A remarkable feature of Chomsky's binding accounts is that notions like 'anaphor' are not defined independently of the binding conditions. This means, minimally, that any testable content to the view depends on the interacting consequences of all the principles. For there is no way to claim independently of them that some form is or is not e.g. an anaphor. Faced with the grammaticality of (i) nothing, for instance, independently blocks analyzing *them* as an anaphor.

    (i)   Most robots$_1$ have wires in them$_1$.

This is at best precluded nontheoretically by the ugly factual consequences of positing an English anaphor shaped *them*, then wrongly not blocked from positions like that in (ii):

    (ii)   *The robots$_1$ placed wires in them$_1$.

A grave undealt with problem about the binding conditions, namely, that they do not properly take into account conjunction, is illustrated in e.g. (iii):

    (iii) a.   Clara$_1$ might, and Stella$_2$ certainly will, strongly defend herself.
          b.   It is HERSELF that Clara$_1$ might, and Stella$_2$ certainly will, strongly defend.

Here, the reflexive form is understood in some sense as linked jointly to both subscripted DPs, since (iii) is equivalent to (iv):

    (iv)   Clara$_1$ might strongly defend herself$_1$ and Stella$_2$ certainly will strongly defend herself$_2$.

But there is no coindexing of the reflexive in (iii) which captures this fact and is consistent with the desired result that the reflexive satisfies Principle A.What then in a Principle A framework could block (vb) and differentiate it from the salvaged (vc) (see section 3.2):

    (v) a.   It is Henry that Audrey thinks might effectively defend himself but Sally is sure will embarrass himself.
          b.   *It is HIMSELF that Audrey thinks might effectively defend Henry but Sally is sure will embarrass Eddie.
          c.   %It is HIMSELF that Audrey thinks might be effectively defended by Henry but Sally is sure will be embarrassed by Eddie.

ple. Common formulations include though that of Larson (1988:336) to the effect that: "Thus reflexives and reciprocals (anaphors) must be c-commanded by their antecedents." and that of Baker (1996:49): "An anaphor must have a c-commanding antecedent within its minimal clause." The differences between various versions are not relevant to the argument of this work, which is that all variations on Principle A are disconfirmed as either (i) universally valid principles governing local antecedence of reflexives or (ii) valid principles governing local antecedence of *English* reflexives. Moreover, this disconfirmation takes a very general form, impugning both the UVA and the UH.

According to the received views, (2a, b) are bad because the reflexives asymmetrically c-command their antecedents, hence are not c-commanded by them and so are not bound, violating Principle A or its analogs. If, further, anything like Principle C of Chomsky's binding theories is adopted, (2a, b) would be independently barred for violating that. This principle claims that a referring expression cannot be bound and the relevant antecedents are referring expressions bound by the reflexives.[3]

Even views *not* appealing literally to Principle A as such, including Pollard and Sag (1992, 1994), Reinhart and Reuland (1993), Bresnan (2000) and others, accept some version of the UH here.

(3) Wilkins (1988:205)

> "There is another apparently syntactic condition on reflexivization which can also be resolved in terms of r-structure. Recall well-known examples such as (29).
>
> (29) *Herself saw Jill.
>
> The fact that reflexives cannot appear in syntactic subject position is generally discussed in configurational terms such as PRECEDE and/or C-command. Actually, this is a syntactic reflex of a certain property of functional structure as discussed by Keenan (1974). An external argument cannot depend on some property of its associated function (= predicate) for its reference."

(4) Williams (1992:195–196)

> "Now the problem at hand is to explain the rather basic contrast between (21a) and (21b):
>
> (21) a. John likes himself.
>   b. *Himself likes John.

---

3. A widespread view, due to Chomsky (1981:193), is that Principle C is the basis for the *strong crossover phenomenon*, illustrated in (i)

(i) *Which activist$_1$ did they persuade him$_1$ the police would soon arrest?

Postal (2004: Ch. 7) argues that this view is unfounded.

John and *himself* are coarguments in both cases, so θ-command by itself cannot distinguish these two. In the theory I will outline it is the presence of the external argument binder on the VP in these examples which rules out (21b) as a sort of violation of condition (10C).

It is of course conceivable that (21b) is ungrammatical because there is a hierarchy of θ-roles, and the antecedent anaphor relation must respect that hierarchy, as proposed in Jackendoff (1972). While there may be such a hierarchy, and such a hierarchy may govern binding, I feel that that is not the correct explanation for the contrast in (21).

Sometimes, when two arguments are internal, either may serve as the antecedent for a reflexive in the other, more or less, as in (22a, b). So if there is a hierarchy, it is partial, or only partially observed by binding rules, for internal arguments. On the other hand, if either argument is made external, then only the external argument may be the antecedent, regardless of which θ-role it is, and the judgments are sharp.

(22) a. The book was given by John to himself.
   b. The book was given to John by himself.
   c. John was given the book by himself.
   d. *Himself was given the book by John.
   e. John gave the book to himself.
   f. *Himself gave the book to John.

Clearly, there is something special about being the external argument, over and above anything having to do with a hierarchy of θ-roles.

(5) Pollard and Sag (1992:266)

The restricted reformulation of Principle A that is required can be stated roughly as follows:

(16) An anaphor must be coindexed with a less oblique argument, if there is one.

Similarly:

(6) Bresnan (2000:218)

This revised version of principle A predicts that reflexive subjects can exist but only when they are bound to an argument of a higher nucleus.

There is then clearly broad current agreement that it is simply impossible for a subject reflexive to be anteceded by some clausemate.[4] Inter alia, this broadly agreed-on view is specifically argued against in what follows.

---

4. Reflexive subjects with higher clause constituent antecedents are, of course, well-known in a variety of languages, e.g. Chinese, Marathi, Korean, Malayalam (see Huang, 2000, Chapter 2.3 for references). Postal (2006) argues that contrary to common assumptions, English also has such reflexives, in fact, several varieties. These are not of direct concern here, although they provide an independent challenge to concepts like Principle A, a challenge much discussed in the now extensive literature on so-called *long distance reflexives*; see e.g. Koster and Reuland (1991), Cole, Hermon and Huang (2001), Huang (2000), Cole, Harmon and Sung (1990) and Cole and Sung (1994) for discussion and references.

Consider next cases in which neither the reflexive nor its antecedent are subjects:

(7) a. Bob described Lucille to herself.
     b. *Bob described herself to Lucille.
     c. The magicians separated Lucille from herself.
     d. *The magicians separated herself from Lucille.

Here also the facts are uncontroversial; apparently, an English direct object can antecede a reflexive (prepositional) object but a reflexive direct object cannot be anteceded by another object of the same clause. Again, it is widely assumed that the badness of (7b, d) follows from the same universal principles that block both of (2a, b). If the theory grounding this view assumes something like Principle A, a structure must be posited in which the reflexive direct object asymmetrically c-commands the PP object.

So far then we have indicated that a broad consensus takes all of (2a, b)/(7b, d) to be blocked by the same universal principle, commonly now taken as some variant of Principle A of Chomsky's binding theory or one of its analogous competitors. The rest of these remarks go beyond these basics to make the following points. *First*, Section 2 claims that crosslinguistic considerations argue that it is impossible for (2a, b)/(7b, d) to be blocked by some universal version of Principle A. Data from several languages argue that nothing like that principle can serve as an instantiation of the UVA for data like (2a, b)/(7b, d). All of the cited data are from Indo-European languages, moreover, those spoken in Europe, and many of them have been available for many years. *Second*, Sections 2 and 3 argue more specifically that it is not possible to viably maintain that a subject cannot be a reflexive anteceded by a clausemate. *Third*, Section 2 also observes that the non-English data exhibit seeming regularity of a sort that nothing like Principle A or its alternatives can capture. A key pattern is that the principles determining the proper distribution of reflexives distinguish *different types of subject*, with types given in a specific way. *Fourth*, Section 3 argues that internal to English itself, considerable evidence both attacks the viability of anything along the lines of Principle A analogs and supports the *same distinction* between subject types reflected in the languages of Section 2. While English does *not* offer direct counterexamples of the same sort provided by the other languages discussed, it does manifest other types of somewhat more complex or indirect counterexamples. *Fifth*, we suggest in Section 4 that a relationally defined notion of *inverse reflexive* is the key to an account of a wider class of reflexives than usually form the basis for choosing between distinct accounts.

2. Non-English facts

2.1 Remark

This section briefly reviews a range of non-English facts which indicate that analogs of Principle A are not the proper mechanism for characterizing the distribution of locally anteceded reflexive forms even in certain Indo-European languages, specifically French, Albanian and Greek.

2.2 French

First, as briefly discussed in Postal (1989:9), while apparently all French speakers accept (8a), some accept (8b) as well:[5]

> (8) a. J'ai décrit Lucille à elle-même.
> 'I described Lucille to herself.'
> b. J'ai décrit elle-même à Lucille.
> 'I described herself to Lucille.'

Each of (8a, b) has a reading in which the reflexive pronominal form is anteceded by the nominal *Lucille*. But no matter how one analyzes the syntax of the verbal phrases in (8), it is not possible under any reasonable assumptions for the antecedent to (asymmetrically) c-command the reflexive in *both* (8a, b). For evidently if the direct object position filled by *Lucille* in (8a) c-commands the indirect object position filled by the reflexive, then that same indirect object position can c-command the direct object position in (8b), as required by Principle A to allow (8b), only if the two positions c-command each other. While that would keep (8b) consistent with a necessary c-command principle, it fails to block the English analog of (8b) or that example itself for the French speakers who reject it. Moreover, mutual c-command in such cases is incompatible with any analog of Principle C, which bars coindexed c-commanded referring expressions, like *Lucille*. In short, if Principle A is *consistent* with data like (8) and their English analogs, it does very little to account for the facts. This conclusion excludes, of course, measures which would claim that (8b) has a radically different verbal phrase structure than (8a), an assumption which would be, as far as we know, unmotivated by anything other than the implications just discussed. Given the clear parallelism between structures like English (7) and French (8), one concludes that the grammaticality of

---

5. Postal (1989:10) noted that the possibility in (8b), though not that in (8a), is limited to third-person nominals.

Chapter 1. Inverse reflexives 9

(8b) argues that no version of Principle A can be the grounds for the ill-formedness of (7b, d) or, for that matter, for the ill-formedness of (8b) for those variants of French in which it is ill-formed.

Of course, the French facts themselves are hardly overwhelming or conclusive, especially given the fact, also noted in Postal (1989:11–12), that while (8b) seems to have a *morphologically* parallel passive, namely, (9b), this lacks a reading involving antecedence, *in accord with* the predictions of a Principle A account.

(9) a. Lucille₁ a été décrite à elle-même₁.
b. *Elle-même₁ a été décrite à Lucille₁.
'HER₁ was described to Lucille₁.'

The string of words in (9b), grammatical but only where the subject pronominal is an emphatic whose denotation is not determined by that of the indirect object.[6]

---

6. Den Dikken (1995:224) cites one Italian informant, Maria Teresa Guasti, as the basis for the following binding judgments:

(i) a. *Ho mostrato Maria a se stessa.
     I-have shown   Maria to herself
   b. Ho mostrato se stessa a Maria.
     I-have shown   herself to Maria
     'I showed Maria to herself.'

This pattern is the opposite of English and partially similar to that variant of French which allows (8b). But unlike the French variant accepting (8b), the Italian of Ms. Guasti is seen not to allow the 'forward' antecedence pattern.

However, we checked these Italian judgments with two Italian subjects, Franca Ferrari and Antonio Gulli (to whom we are indebted). Both reject (ib) while accepting (ia) and hence seem to manifest a reflexive pattern for objects parallel to English. Rendering a c-command-based account of the reflexive facts consistent with both variants of Italian might thus require positing distinct clause structures for cognate clauses in both as well as distinct clause structures for different variants of French. These conclusions are, to say the least, implausible enough to suggest that c-command is not the appropriate feature, a conclusion supported by all that follows.

On the basis of (i) alone, Den Dikken (1995:224 n. 42) concludes that the Italian goal phrase 'must' c-command the direct object. We would quarrel with such a necessity claim, but given the contrasts with our informants and hence either significant dialect variation or unclarity in the data, or both, it would be unwise for us to draw conclusions about Italian at this point.

While we do not know the passive facts for Den Dikken's informant, for the Italian speakers we consulted, the passives of (ia, b) behave like French (9):

(ii) a. Maria e' stata mostrata a se stessa da me.
     'Marie was described to herself by me.'
   b. *Se stessa e' stata mostrata a Maria da me.
     'Herself was described to Maria by me.'

2.3 Albanian

The French-based argument against Principle A is reinforced and extended by the situation in Albanian, as described in Hubbard (1980, 1981). The relevant facts have been discussed in Sells (1988) and Williams (1988), the latter already having raised the issue of their compatibility with binding theories containing Principle A. A background observation is that Albanian has relatively free word order and a rich case system.

Consider first the situation involving reflexive antecedence between direct and indirect objects. Hubbard showed that unlike the variant of French which allows antecedence in either direction, as in (8), and opposite to the situation in English, which allows a direct object to antecede an indirect object but not conversely, Albanian *only* allows the pattern where the indirect object (dative-marked) antecedes the direct object (accusative marked); all the data in (10) and (11) are from Hubbard (1981:43–45). Note that *Drita* is a female name.

(10) a. artisti   i a tregoi veten   Drites.
artist-NOM CL CL show self-ACCUS Drita-DAT
'The artist showed herself$_1$ to Drita$_1$.'

b. artisti   i a tregoi Drites   veten.
artist-NOM CL CL show Drita-DAT self-ACCUS
'The artist showed herself$_1$ to Drita$_1$.'

These examples show that the indirect object can antecede the direct object, regardless of their word order. In contrast, regardless of word order, a direct object cannot antecede an indirect object reflexive:

(11) a. *artisti   i a tregoi Driten   vetes.
artist-NOM CL CL show Drita-ACCUS self-DAT
'The artist showed Drita$_1$ to herself$_1$.'
(irrelevantly ok on reading 'The artist$_2$ showed Drita$_1$ to himself$_2$.')

b. *artisti   i a tregoi vetes   Driten.
artist-NOM CL CL show self-DAT Drita-ACCUS
'The artist showed Drita$_1$ to herself$_1$.'
(irrelevantly ok on reading 'The artist$_2$ showed Drita$_1$ to himself$_2$.')

These facts combine with those from English and French to suggest that either direction of antecedence between direct and indirect object is in principle permitted by universal grammar. If so, languages which restrict the possibilities in one way or another, even under assumptions of mutual c-command between such elements, appeal to distinct principles for that purpose. In short, arguably, in this subdomain, Principle A and its analogs are at best useless for determining the attested range of reflexive form grammaticality.

The facts of Albanian reflexive linkages involving subjects are initially much more in line with those of English and French. In general, a subject can antecede a nonsubject reflexive but *not conversely*. So sets like (12) are typical (data from Hubbard 1981:87, 88).

(12)   a.   Murati i flet   vetes.
            Murati CL speak self-DAT
       b.   vetes   i   flet   Murati.
            self-DAT CL speak Murati-NOM
            'Murati₁ speaks to himself₁.'
       c.   *vetja i flet Muratit
            self-NOM CL speaks Murati-DAT
       d.   *Muratit i flet vetja
            Murati-DAT CL speaks self-NOM
            'Murati₁ speaks to himself₁.'

Again, word order is irrelevant.

However, despite cases like (12c, d), there are two situations in which Albanian allows reflexive subjects to be anteceded within the same clause. First, as Hubbard makes clear, in contrast to either variant of French or English, when a direct object is anaphorically linked to an indirect object, as in (10), under passivization, the only possibility is that the accusative reflexive direct object of the active yields a nominative reflexive subject in the corresponding passive (data from Hubbard, 1980:47–48):

(13)   a.   vetja   i   u tregua Drites   prej artistit.
            self-NOM CL   show Drita-DAT by artist
       b.   *vetes   i   u tregua Drita   prej artistit
            self-DAT CL   show Drita-NOM by artist
            "Drita₁was shown (to) herself₁ by the artist"

Since Hubbard argued independently, on the basis of subject/verb agreement, case marking and the floating of intensive reflexives, that the Albanian passive construction is a personal not an impersonal one, grammatical reflexive subject passives like (13a) seriously threaten accounts of anaphoric relations via any analog of a universal version of Principle A.[7] This challenge is stronger than that from non-

---

7. Woolford (1999:270) describes the Albanian sentence in (i), taken from Hubbard (1980:90), as having a dative subject and a nominative object (which controls verb agreement).

(i)   Vetja   iu   çudit   Agimit.
      self.NOM CL.DAT surprise.3.SG.PST.NONACT Agim.DAT
      'Agim surprised himself.'

subject data, as it is less plausible (hence much less tempting) to posit symmetrical c-command between subjects and nonsubjects than between pairs of nonsubjects. But without that, cases like (13a) represent counterexamples to claims that subject reflexives cannot be internally anteceded by cooccurring objects.

Hubbard also shows that Albanian allows reflexive subjects in one other construction, which he analyzed in relational grammar terms as involving *inversion*, that is, demotion of a subject to indirect object in a non-passive clause where the direct object advances to subject. Thus there are pairs like these (data from Hubbard, 1980: 84):

(14) a. Agimi e   kujton   kengën.
          Agimi-NOM remembers song-the-ACCUS
      b. Kenga   i kujtohet   Agimit.
          song-NOM CL remembers Agimi-DAT
          'Agimi remembers the song.'

That is, some transitive clauses with nominative subject and accusative direct object have intransitive alternatives in which the nominative subject corresponds to a dative surface object and the accusative object appears as a nominative subject.

Strikingly, when the two nominals of the intransitive variant are anaphorically linked, the reflexive form must appear as the nominative subject, regardless of word order (data from Hubbard, 1980: 90–91):

(15) a. vetja iu çudit   Agimit.
          self-NOM surprised Agimi-DAT
      b. *Agimi iu   çudit   vetes.
          Agimi-NOM surprised self-DAT
      c. *vetes iu çudit   Agimi.
          'Agimi$_1$ surprised himself$_1$.'

In Hubbard's terms, there is a clear generalization: reflexive subjects are possible in Albanian only if the subject is an initial direct object (hence a 'derived' subject, in one terminology) and is anteceded by an indirect object. Hence a non-derived subject, that is, one in an active clause, cannot be a reflexive anteceded by an indirect object, as already in effect shown by the contrast between (12a, c). Moreover, even a passivized direct object reflexive is bad if not anteceded by an indirect object; see note 8. We claim that Hubbard's demonstration that local antecedence of

---

She does not argue for this view, which conflicts with Hubbard's (1980, 1981) treatment, accepted here, that the nominative form is the final (in relational terms) subject. The gross properties just cited, e.g. having nominative case and determining verbal agreement are, of course, diagnostic properties of final subjects in Albanian, as in many other languages.

subject reflexives depends on the fact that the subject is 'derived' is a critical aspect of the phenomenon under discussion. That is, the failure of Principle A type accounts and their kin to reference a distinction between inter alia 'derived' and 'non-derived' subjects is a key to their failure to properly characterize the local antecedence possibilities of reflexives.[8]

2.4 Greek

Greek data support the conclusions drawn from the Albanian facts cited by Hubbard. Our sources are Anagostopoulou and Everaert (1995, 1999), Everaert and Anagnostopoulou (1996), and a very kind personal communication of September 25, 2000 from Elena Anagnostopoulou to PMP.

First, Everaert and Anagnostopoulou (1996) and Anagnostopoulou and Everaert (1999) show, although with few examples, that Greek has certain instances of nominative subject reflexives with clausemate antecedents. These seem to be possible largely in cases parallel to those Albanian sentences analyzed by Hubbard as instances of relational inversion. These authors refer to the relevant clauses as involving 'inverse-linking psych verbs'.

(16)   O eaftos tu tu aresi tu Petru
       the self his-NOM CL-DAT like the Peter-DAT
       'Peter$_1$ pleases himself$_1$.'

Agnagnostopoulou and Everaert (1999: 109) note that such nominative subjects are not possible in ordinary transitive clauses, as in (17), and state a key generalization parallel to that seen to hold of Hubbard's treatment of Albanian (which they do not cite), namely: "Our analysis correctly predicts that the Greek nominative anaphor is licensed solely in derived subject positions."

(17)   *O eaftos tu   ton antipathi ton Petro.
       the self   his-NOM CL   dislikes   the Petros-ACCUS
       'Himself$_1$ dislikes Petros$_1$.'

Agnagnostopoulou's private message further specified that:

---

8. The failure of a reflexive object in Albanian to yield a grammatical nominative reflexive in a passive except in indirect object cases like those already cited is illustrated in (i), where the subject reflexive is anteceded by the agent phrase.

(i)   Hubbard (1980: 50)
      *Vetja   u ftua   prej kapedanit.
      self.NOM CL invited by   captain
      'Himself was invited by the captain.'

(18) The sentences where a nominative anaphor can be found without any
problem in Greek are based on experiencer object verbs. Not only cases
where the antecedent is a dative but also cases where the antecedent is an
accusative, that is, 'preoccupare'-type verbs, which in English and Italian
license anaphors inside NPs (picture-NPs).

She gave the example:

(19) O eaftos tu   ton   provlimatizi/apasxoli/enoxli ton Petro.
      the self his.NOM CL.ACC puzzles/worries/bothers   the Peter.ACC
      'Peter puzzles/worries/bothers himself.'

She also stated that other well-formed examples are found with certain unaccusative verbs, illustrating with one verb of existence:

(20) Tu Petru   tu   apomeni o eaftos tu.
      the Peter.GEN CL.GEN is-left-3SG the self his.NOM
      'All Petros has left is himself.'
      (literally, 'His self remains to Petros.')

This is significant if, as the specification 'unaccusative' suggests, this is also a case
where the nominative subject is a 'derived' subject, and thus in accord with the
generalizations already seen for Albanian.

    Turning to passive cases, Agnagnostopoulou informed us that well-formed
nominative reflexive examples are difficult to find, but that (21) is "more or less,
ok":

(21) ?[O eaftos tu]ᵢ   [tu]ᵢ   perigraftike [tu Petru]ᵢ apo ton
      the self his.NOM CL.GEN was.described the Peter.GEN by the
      psychiatrist with the most lively   colours.
      psichiatrome ta   pjozoira xromata
      'Peterᵢ was described to himselfᵢ by the psychiatrist with the most lively
      colors.'

    One notes that in this case, the reflexive is anteceded by the indirect object.
Antecedence by the passive agent is totally impossible:

(22) *O eaftos tu   katigorithike apo ton Petro.
      The self his.Nom was.accused by the Peter
      'Peterᵢ was accused by himselfᵢ.'

The key point is that while (21) may be marginal, it nonetheless contrasts with the
totally impossible (22). This we take to indicate further that in Greek, as in Alba-

nian, internally anteceded reflexive subjects are in principle possible if they are 'derived subjects', subject to other conditions, e.g. indirect object antecedence but not passive agent antecedence.

A final piece of Greek support for this conclusion derives from analogs of the English raising to subject (e.g. with *seem*) construction. Everaert and Anagnostopoulou (1996) note that in the Greek analog of this construction, the subject cannot antecede the experiencer, contrary to the situation in English:

(23) *O   Petros fenete   s-ton eafto tu eksipinos.
     the Peter   seems to the   self his clever
     'Peter₁ seems to himself₁ (to be) clever.'

This raises the question of whether the inverse situation with the experiencer anteceding the subject is possible. Anagnostopoulou specified that the answer involves a complication. Specifically, she noted that sentences like (24) are never very good in Greek, for independent reasons.

(24) ?*O   Petros fenete sti   Maria eksipnos.
      the Peter   seems to-the Mary intelligent
     'Peter seems intelligent to Mary.'

While a PP-experiencer is not good in such examples, a genitive clitic doubled experiencer is:

(25) O   Petros   tis   fenete tis Marias   eksipnos.
     the Peter.nom cl.gen seems the Mary.GEN intelligent
     'Peter seems intelligent to Maria.'

Anagnostopoulou then observed that genitive anaphors in Greek are not good (see Agnagnostopoulou and Everaert, 1999). This renders it difficult to find a way to test for the key issue here. The question reduces to whether there is a contrast between (23) and:

(26) O   eaftos tu   tu   fenete tu Petru   eksipnos
     the self   his.NOM CL.GEN seems the Peter.GEN intelligent
     'Peter seems intelligent to himself.'

Her judgment was that "I think this is not bad, it is certainly much better than (23) above."

Thus we conclude that *despite* the marginality of some relevant examples, in three distinct respects, (inversion cases, passive cases, raising cases), Greek supports the idea that a reflexive subject anteceded by a clausemate is possible, but only if that subject is 'derived'.

3. English

3.1 A *and only* B

A rather unusual English formation whose previous discussion if any we are unaware of will be referred to it as the [A$_i$ and ONLY B$_i$] construction. Some examples appear in (27).

(27) a. Valerie$_i$ and ONLY Valerie$_i$ complained.
 b. *Valerie$_i$ and ONLY Michael$_j$ complained.
 c. Valerie$_i$ and ONLY she$_i$ complained.
 d. *She$_j$ and ONLY Valerie$_j$ complained.
 e. We fed gorillas and ONLY [gorillas/*orangutans].
 f. Some gorilla and ONLY [some/*a certain] gorilla escaped.
 g. She and ONLY she/*her complained (compare: Joe and her complained).

When identity of denotation is impossible, as in *(27b), the construction is ill-formed. The nominal in the B position can be a pronominal anteceded by that in the A position, but not conversely (Cf. (27b) vs. *(27c)).[9] It appears that the essential points made in what follows for [A and ONLY B] cases hold as well for [A but not ONLY B] ones; but we ignore these in the text. The capitalization of the word *only* indicates that it must be contrastively stressed, so that expression B cannot be (e.g. *Valerie$_i$ and only VALERIE$_i$ said anything).

From the present perspective, the key point is that a reflexive can appear in the B position if it also appears in the A position:

(28) Abigail praised herself and ONLY herself.

One asks then what principles control the distribution of [A and ONLY B] expressions in cases when A and B are reflexives. Certain clear constraints seem to parallel those for simple reflexives.

(29) a. Fred praised himself (and ONLY himself).
 b. *Himself (and ONLY himself) praised Fred.
 c. The book was assigned to Mary by herself (and ONLY herself).

---

9. Some speakers allow the B nominal to be a nonpronominal which shares denotation with A, as in (i):

(i) a. Valerie$_i$ and ONLY [that courageous voice]$_i$ said anything.
 b. %Valerie$_i$ and ONLY [the mother of your children]$_i$ complained.
 c. %I and ONLY [I/yours truly/*you/*they] will be allowed to play the xylophone.

d. *Significant praise was received from herself (and ONLY herself) by Mary.

e. The book was assigned by Mary to herself (and ONLY herself).

But more relevant to present goals is that, despite parallels like (29), the distribution of reflexive [A and ONLY B] structures is *less* constrained than that of simple reflexive forms.

(30) a. *Himself was described to Otto by Francine.
b. Himself and ONLY himself was described to Otto by Francine.[10]

(31) a. *Francine described himself to Otto.
b. Francine described himself and ONLY himself to Otto.

(32) a. *The book was assigned to herself by Mary.
b. The book was assigned to herself and ONLY herself by Mary.

(33) a. *Tom discussed herself with Barbara.
b. Tom discussed herself and ONLY herself with Barbara.

There are then for [A and ONLY B] reflexive cases two sorts of subenvironments of those contexts where simple reflexives are *barred*. In one type, illustrated by e.g. (29b, d), the [A and ONLY B] cases are equally impossible; but in another, illustrated by (30)–(33), [A and ONLY B] reflexives are grammatical for us in contexts where simple reflexives are not.

We propose to distinguish these two classes of subenvironments terminologically as follows. Contexts where [A and ONLY B] reflexives are as ungrammatical as simple reflexives will be referred to as *strong antireflexive contexts*, while those where [A and ONLY B] reflexives contrast with ungrammatical simple reflexives and are grammatical will be called *weak antireflexive contexts*.

So the subject context in sentences like (29b) and the prepositional object context in (29d) are strong antireflexive contexts, since the [A and ONLY B] reflexive is as ungrammatical in these positions as the simpler one. But the subject context in sentences like (30b), the direct object contexts in (31a), (33a) and the prepositional object position in (32a) are weak antireflexive contexts, since the [A and ONLY B] reflexive is grammatical although the simpler one is not. Of course, this is a simplification since what is really at tissue are not DP contexts per se but rather relations between antecedent/reflexive pairs. But the simplification should generate no confusion.

---

10. One notes the singular verb agreement property in examples such as (30b), raising the issue of which coordinate DPs are singular, which plural, and according to what principles.

Moreover, we also find that the following subject positions are weak antireflexive contexts:

(34) a. *Herself seemed to Stella to be wise.
      b. Herself and ONLY herself seemed to Stella to be wise.

(35) a. *Herself was really interesting to Stella.
      b. Herself and ONLY herself was really interesting to Stella.

Viewed in isolation, the division between strong and weak antireflexive contexts might not be of much significance. But it takes on importance because of two kinds of parallels between English weak antireflexive environments and other facts. The first involves a partial connection between the English [A and ONLY B] data and that documented for reflexives in French, Albanian and Greek. The latter data revealed that a variety of contexts permit reflexives in positions where grammaticality is either inconsistent with Principle A and its analogs or at best part of patterns which such principles provide no basis for. Those included (some) object positions and 'derived' subject positions. Notably then, all the English subject positions which are weak antireflexive contexts are arguably 'derived' subject positions; see Section 4.1. The implication is then that weak antireflexive positions are contexts *not* ruled by any analog of Principle A.

The second reason for suspecting the importance of the distinction between weak and strong antireflexive contexts involves phenomena distinct from [A and ONLY B] structures. For the next section argues that there is a feature of English which differentiates even simple reflexives in such a way as to correlate with the weak/strong difference.

3.2 Salvageability

Recall now basic reflexive data like that in (2)/(7), which reveals patterns of contrasting grammaticality and ungrammaticality:[11]

---

11. Constraints on reflexives parallel to those seen in (2)/(7b, d) arguably hold for cases in which the reflexive word is a conjunct:

(i)   a. [*Bob and herself/*Herself and Bob] described Harriet to Arthur.
      b. [*Bob and herself/*Herself and Bob] were described to Harriet by Arthur.
(ii)   *Bob described [Arthur and herself/herself and Arthur] to Harriet.

These contrast with the coordinate analogs of (1) and (7a):

(iii) a. Harriet described [Bob and herself/herself and Bob] to Arthur.
       b. Harriet was described to [Bob and herself/herself and Bob] by Milton.

Despite the obvious parallelisms, the principles usually invoked for (2)/(7b, d), Principle A or its analogs, are in general not shown to block (i) and (ii). Such an attempt might be successful if

(36) a. Harriet described herself to Arthur.
　　b. *Herself described Harriet to Arthur.
　　c. Harriet described Arthur to himself.
　　d. *Harriet described himself to Arthur.
　　e. *Himself was described by Harriet to Arthur/to Arthur by Harriet.

While all of (36b, d, e) are definitively ungrammatical, one can consider the interaction of such examples with various extraction constructions like clefting, topicalization, pseudoclefting, etc.[12] These have the property of being able to take reflexive forms as arguments. But the results of taking the images of clauses like (36b, d, e) under the extractions turn out not to be uniform.
Consider first clefting:

(37) a. It was HERSELF that Harriet described to Arthur.
　　b. *It was HERSELF that described Harriet to Arthur.
　　c. It was HIMSELF that Harriet described Arthur to.
　　d. %It was HIMSELF that Harriet described to Arthur.
　　e. %It was HIMSELF that was described by Harriet to Arthur.

Examples (37a, c) simply illustrate that in English it is sometimes possible to grammatically cleft from clausal position P a reflexive which is grammatical in P. Case (37b) illustrates that it is sometimes impossible to grammatically cleft from clausal position P a reflexive which is ungrammatical in P, evidently the expected results.

However, unexpectedly then, (37d, e) reveal at least marginally grammatical clefting from a configuration in which an unclefted reflexive is ungrammatical. That is, in these cases of a direct object reflexive anteceded by the object of a PP, (37d), and a *passive subject* reflexive anteceded by a passive *by* phrase, (37e), clefting of the reflexive yields improved grammaticality, although it *fails* to do that for

---

it appealed to something like the conjunction reduction approach of early transformational accounts. Under the latter, e.g. (ia) could have conjoined underlying structures of the form (iv) in which a Principle A analog could properly fail to be satisfied in one conjunct:

(iv) [Bob described Harriet to Arthur and herself described Harriet to Arthur]

12. Some previous treatments of examples like (36b, e) have claimed that they are ungrammatical because English lacks a nominative form for reflexives. Bresnan (2000:218) made a proposal to this effect, and Woolford (1999:262) cites Brame (1977), Koster (1978), Anderson (1982) and Maling (1984) for the idea that languages may lack nominative anaphors. But even if correct, this perspective is irrelevant, because the patterns illustrated in (36b, e) are replicated in nonfinite constructions in which subjects are not even *allowed* to be nominative, e.g.:

(i) a. For me/*I to describe Harriet to Arthur would be silly.
　　b. *For herself to describe Harriet to Arthur would be silly.
　　c. *For herself to be described by Harriet to Arthur would be silly.

the non-passive subject reflexive in (36b). We will say that violations of the constraint in the former, whatever it is, are *unsalvageable* by clefting, while the ungrammaticalities in (36d, e) are (to some extent) *salvageable* (for some speakers).

Clearly, if something like Principle A or more generally some kind of single UVA-based condition were responsible for all of (36b, d, e), it would be quite mysterious that clefting would salvage one reflexive but not the others. How could a uniform cleft construction interact with different types of ungrammatical antecedent/reflexive pairs putatively all ungrammatical for the *same* reason and yet salvage only some? Moreover, the contrast between (37b) and (37e) also challenges the UH.

The argument from clefting is strengthened by the fact that asymmetric salvaging of ungrammatical antecedent/reflexive pairs is (i) found with other extractions besides clefting and (ii) manifests in parallel ways; that is, these other phenomena can salvage just those cases which clefting can. So, consider topicalization, with respect to which, one finds, alongside (36), the parallel (38).[13] Here and below capitalized reflexives again represent strongly stressed forms:

(38) a. HERSELF, I learned later that Harriet had described to Arthur.
      b. *HERSELF, I learned later had described Harriet to Arthur.
      c. HERSELF, I learned later that Harriet had described Arthur to.
      d. %HIMSELF, I learned later that Harriet had described to Arthur.
      e. %HIMSELF, I learned later had been described by Harriet to Arthur.

Patterns essentially parallel to those in cleft and topicalization constructions are seen in copular/focus cases.

(39) a. The one who Harriet described to Arthur was HERSELF.
      b. *The one who described Harriet to Arthur was HERSELF.
      c. The one who Harriet described Arthur to was HIMSELF.
      d. %The one who Harriet described to Arthur was HIMSELF.
      e. %The one who was described by Harriet to Arthur was HIMSELF.

And the same thing appears in regular and inverse pseudoclefts, as in (40) and (41):

(40) a. What Harriet compared to Arthur was HERSELF.
      b. *What compared Harriet to Arthur was HERSELF.

---

13. For one of the authors, topicalization does indeed behave in the relevant respects in a way parallel to e.g. clefting. For the other, however, topicalization seems to lack the ability to salvage the relevant bad reflexive cases, meaning that the facts in (38) represent the judgments of only one author. We have no account of this crossidiolectal contrast.

> c. What Harriet compared Arthur to was HIMSELF.
> d. %What Harriet compared to Arthur was HIMSELF.
> e. %What was compared by Harriet to Arthur was HIMSELF.

(41) a. HERSELF was what Harriet compared to Arthur.
    b. *HERSELF was what compared Harriet to Arthur.
    c. HIMSELF was what Harriet compared Arthur to.
    d. %HIMSELF was what Harriet compared to Arthur.
    e. %HIMSELF was what was compared by Harriet to Arthur.

Even if the constructions cited so far exhausted those which yield reflexive violation salvageability, they would represent a prima facie nonnegligeable challenge to received ideas about reflexive antecedence.[14]

---

14. Complex Shift and Right Node Raising constructions probably have some salvageability features. The former yields patterns like:

(i) a. I believe to have described herself to Arthur in great detail [THAT NURSE].
    b. *I believe to have described that nurse to Arthur in great detail HERSELF.
    c. I believe that nurse to have described to himself in great detail [the man she loved]
    d. %I believe that nurse to have described to [the man she loved] in great detail HIMSELF.
    e. %I believe to have been described by that nurse to those very frail patients in great detail HERSELF.

The latter construction determines:

(ii) a. Irving may believe to have described herself to Arthur in great detail and probably does believe to have described herself to Arthur in great detail [THAT NURSE].
    b. *Irving may believe to have described that nurse to Arthur in great detail and probably does believe to have described that nurse to Arthur in great detail HERSELF.
    c. Irving may believe that nurse to have described to himself and probably does believe that nurse to have described to himself [THAT MAN]
    d. %Irving may believe that nurse to have described to [the man she loved] in great detail and probably does believe that nurse to have described to [the man she loved] in great detail HIMSELF.
    e. %Irving may believe to have been described by that nurse to Arthur in great detail and his friends probably do believe to have been described by that nurse to them in great detail HERSELF.

While (id, e) and (iid, e) are hardly lovely, we have some sense that whatever is wrong with them is significantly independent of the reflexive linkages. And it appears that both (id, e) and (iid, e) improve when <u>and Xself</u> is added to the extracted reflexive. That is, e.g. (iii) is better than (id):

(iii) %I believe that nurse to have described to [the man she loved] in great detail himself and ONLY himself.

Moreover, in support of the salvageability property of Complex Shift, we note that Williams (1994:188–189) cited (ivb) as perfect, while starring (iva):

Summing up so far, we see that despite the UH, English ungrammatical reflexives divide into at least two classes, roughly characterizable as in (42):

(42) a. *Unsalvageable* ungrammatical reflexives: when such reflexives are clefted, topicalized, 'focused', etc., their ungrammaticality is unaffected.
 b. *Salvageable* ungrammatical reflexives: clefting, topicalization etc., of such reflexives in some cases renders the result grammatical.

So far, we have cited only one sort of unsalvageable reflexive, subjects of an active clause anteceded by some other phrase of the clause, and two sorts of salvageable reflexives, subjects of passive clauses and objects anteceded by following phrases. There are further exemplars of each type.

A salvageable reflexive subject violation independent of passivization is found in Subject Raising structures like (43):

(43) a. *Herself seemed to Audrey to be quite lovely.
 b. It was HERSELF that seemed to Audrey to be quite lovely.
 c. %HERSELF, I am sure seemed to Audrey to be quite lovely.
 d. The one who seemed to Audrey to be quite lovely was HERSELF.
 e. What seemed to Audrey to be quite lovely was HERSELF.

And another salvageable reflexive subject violation is seen in psychological adjective cases like (44).

(44) a. *Himself was interesting to Cardoza.
 b. %It was HIMSELF that was interesting to Cardoza.
 c. %HIMSELF, I am sure was interesting to Cardoza.
 d. %The one who was interesting to Cardoza was HIMSELF.
 e. %What was interesting to Cardoza was HIMSELF.

Finally, paradigm (45) reveals a salvageable nonsubject reflexive violation in (45c), and an unsalvageable one in (45d):

(iv) a. *I recommended himself to John.
 b. I recommended to John HIMSELF.

Williams (1994: 189) took such facts to suggest the following reflexive antecedence principles:

> If this is correct, then the distribution of reflexives comes down to two separate factors: the antecedent must c-command the reflexive, and the antecedent must precede the reflexive if the reflexive c-commands it.

This account is not, of course, consistent with the salvageability facts involving left extractions. For instance, in (37d), even if one grants that the antecedent c-commands the reflexive form, that is, the preextraction position of that form, the former obviously does not precede the latter.

(45) a. The book was assigned to Mary by herself.
b. The book was assigned by Mary to herself.
c. *The book was assigned to herself by Mary.
d. *The book was assigned by herself to Mary.
e. It was HERSELF that the book was assigned to deliberately by Mary.
f. *It was HERSELF that the book was assigned by deliberately to Mary.[15]

The next section considers the implications of the salvage phenomenon in the context of the earlier discussion of crosslinguistic patterns of reflexive antecedence which are at best unexpected in currently received terms.

4. Conclusions

4.1 Correlations

While some of the English data of Section 3.2 may be problematic, we believe that overall section 3 nonetheless supports important theoretical conclusions. Because beyond whatever the [A and ONLY B] cases and the salvage cases might show *in isolation*, their implications are strengthened by two types of correlation. First, the two independently characterized phenomena are themselves significantly parallel:

(46) a. If an internally anteceded [A and ONLY A] subject reflexive in context P is grammatical, an internally anteceded simple subject reflexive in P is salvageable.
b. If an internally anteceded [A and ONLY A] object reflexive in context P is grammatical, an internally anteceded simple obbject reflexive in P is salvageable.
c. If an internally anteceded [A and ONLY A] PP reflexive in context P is grammatical, an internally anteceded PP reflexive in P is salvageable.

The following paradigms briefly reillustrate these generalizations; (47)–(49) document (46a).

---

15. Despite the ungrammaticality of (ic), no direct evidence is available that the reflexive violation in (ib) is unsalvageable.

(i) a. The book was assigned Mary by herself.
b. The book was assigned *herself/them/Jack by Mary.
c. *It was herself that the book was assigned by Mary.
d. *It was them/Jack that the book was assigned by Mary.

For while both authors are in the dialect which accepts (ia), the indirect object in this construction is unextractable independently of all considerations of reflexive antecedence.

(47) a. *Herself was praised by Jane.
    b. %It was HERSELF that was praised by Jane.
    c. Herself and ONLY herself was praised by Jane.

(48) a. *Herself appeared to Ruth to be a strong candidate.
    b. %It was HERSELF that appeared to Ruth to be a strong candidate.
    c. Herself and ONLY herself appeared to Ruth to be a strong candidate.

(49) a. *Herself was interesting to Ruth.
    b. %It was HERSELF that was interesting to Ruth.
    c. Herself and ONLY herself was interesting to Ruth.

Paradigm (50) supports (46b):

(50) a. *Nadine described himself to Farouk.
    b. %It was HIMSELF that Nadine described to Farouk.
    c. Nadine described himself and ONLY himself to Farouk.

And, finally, paradigm (51) supports (46c):

(51) a. *The letters were sent to himself by Larry.
    b. %It was HIMSELF that the letters were sent to by Larry.
    c. The letters were sent to himself and ONLY himself by Larry.[16]

Recalling terminology introduced earlier, all these cases can be summed up by saying that if a simple English reflexive is salvageable in context P, then P is a weak antireflexive context.[17] This English-internal correlation evidently supports the idea that the properties differentiating weak from strong antireflexive contexts are

---

16. There is a clear contrast between the paradigm in (51) and that in (i):

    (i) a. The letters were received from Tom/*HERSELF recently by Sandra.
       b. *It was HERSELF that the letters were received from recently by Sandra.
       c. *The letters were received from herself and ONLY herself recently by Sandra.

While we have no account of the unacceptability of (ib, c), the correlation between the failure of salvageability and the impossibility of the [A and ONLY B] reflexive supports our view that these are strictly connected.

17. We have so far entirely ignored simple *only* + reflexive phrases. It is natural to ask how these fit into the patterns that have been registered. The answer seems to be that this phrase type behaves more like a simple reflexive than like an [A and ONLY B] reflexive one, with certain extra restrictions. So we judge:

    (i) a. Fred praised only himself.
       b. *Only himself praised Fred.
       c. *The book was sent (to) only (to) herself by Mary.
       d. ?*Francine described only himself to Otto

nonaccidental. This claim is reinforced by the fact that all the English-internal evidence from subject reflexives arguably reveals a further more specific positive generalization:

(52)   If R is a grammatical internally anteceded reflexive subject, R is a 'derived' subject.

That English passive subjects and subject-raised ones are 'derived' should be un-controversial. The case of the reflexive subjects of psychological adjectives is less clear. But they also fall into the category of 'derived' subject reflexives if an inversion analysis (in relational grammar terms) of such cases with e.g. *interesting, astonishing*, etc., is correct, that is, one in which the *to*-phrase represents an initial subject, and the final subject an initial direct object.[18]

But such phrases can serve to further illustrate the existence of salvageability, since they participate in the negative fronting extraction:

(ii)   a.   *Only himself did Mary believe to have praised Fred.
       b.   Only himself did Mary believe to have been praised by Fred.
       c.   Only himself did Mary believe Francine to have described to Fred

Thus it would appear that here too, salvaging is possible from weak antireflexive contexts.

18. While it is a complex matter to argue for an inversion analysis of the relevant constructions, two supporting observations deserve mention. First, what such an analysis would take to be a demoted subject is not a possible target for the object raising construction. So in (i), a clear noninversion structure, such targeting is possible. But in plausible inversion cases like (ii) and (iii) it is not:

(i)   a.   Maureen spoke to Greg.
        b.   Greg was difficult for me to imagine Maureen speaking to.

(ii)   a.   Maureen mattered to Greg.
        b.   *Greg was difficult for me to imagine Maureen mattering to.

(iii)   a.   Maureen was astonishing to Greg.
        b.   *Greg was difficult for me to imagine Maureen being astonishing to.

This is possibly due to a generalization barring (inter alia) object raising of an underlying subject, clearly seen in passive cases:

(iv)   a.   Maureen has been hired by Laura.
        b.   *Laura was difficult/impossible for Maureen to have been hired by.

Second, the object raising contrast between e.g. (ia) and (iia) correlates with a passivization contrast:

(v)   a.   Greg was spoken to by Maureen.
        b.   *Greg was mattered to by Maureen.

That is, the putative inversion structure manifests a well-known resistance of clauses with 'derived' subjects to passivization.

Second, and more specifically, the fact that the apparent role of the notion 'derived' subject in the description of English reflexive antecedence stems from a genuine principle is naturally further buttressed by the fact that to a significant extent, English subgeneralization (46a) parallels the facts in Albanian and Greek. Hence one sees the existence of clear parallels for passives between English (47), Albanian (13a) and Greek (21), for subject raising cases between English (48) and Greek (26),[19] and for psychological predicates between English (49), Albanian (15a) and Greek (16).

Of course, (52) can only subsume both simple and [A and ONLY B] reflexives if there is a notion of *reflexive DP* which covers both simple reflexives (herself) and complex phrases of e.g. the form *herself and ONLY herself*. However, it is difficult to see how the distribution of the more complex forms could reasonably be described in the absence of such a characterization, given the distributional parallels between the simpler and more complex types.[20] But if it is correct that [A and ONLY B] reflexives instantiate a notion of *reflexive DP*, then, as well as the indirect evidence based on salvageability, English provides more direct evidence that standard conceptions of the antecedent/reflexive relation are flawed.

The consequences of (52) can be spelled out further. First, what we called the UH in Section 1 cannot be maintained. The principles which determine that non-'derived' subject reflexives cannot be internally anteceded, see Section 4.2, must be in part distinguished from those which determine that *some*, but as we have argued here, only some, 'derived' subject reflexives also have this property. Second, simply on the basis of the subject generalizations, any principle which entails that no subject can ever be internally anteceded is not tenable. For (52) means, of course, that:

---

19. We are aware of no Albanian data indicating the interaction of subject raising and subject reflexive antecedence.

20. Given the partial string identity relations which hold between A and B in [A and ONLY B] constructions, some sort of reduplication analysis might be motivated. That would treat (ia) as involving reduplication of the non-*only* part of (ib):

(i)   a.   Janet and only Janet
        b.   Only Janet

Such an analysis is additionally attractive as the implication that (ia, b) have the same meaning is plausible. To work out such an approach, presumably cases like (ib) would have to be regarded such that *Janet* was a DP and *only Janet* a distinct one. Further, it would be necessary to have a view of anaphoric relations such that cases (like e.g. (27c) in the text) in which A and B do not fully match but rather B is an anaphoric expression anteceded by A could be taken to operate on more abstract structures in which A = B. Actually constructing an analysis with these properties is thus far from straightforward and it would be hazardous to guess that it is possible.

(53)   An English reflexive DP1 can be anteceded within its own minimal clause
        by a distinct DP which not only fails to c-command DP1 but which is in
        fact asymmetrically c-commanded by it.

Hence Chomsky's Principle A in any of its variants, and other views which have
been designed to have many of the same consequences, in particular, the consequence that a subject reflexive can *never* be properly anteceded by another element
of its own minimal clause, must be rejected.[21]

The conclusion that reflexive form antecedence is not governed by an invi-
olable principle along the lines of Principle A or its analogs casts new light on
the limited evidence from French, English and Albanian, to the effect that certain
nonsubject reflexives can have internal antecedents which at best do not asymmetrically c-command them. Given the general untenability of a c-command constraint, there is no a priori basis for assuming that the relevant object reflexives are
c-commanded at all by their antecedents. If viable, this conclusion partially calls
into question a broad range of work which has been driven in part by the idea
that whenever grammatical local domain reflexive antecedence between objects
or PPs is grammatical, the antecedent must c-command the reflexive.[22] Whatever
else can be said about reflexive antecedence, it cannot provide a definitive basis for
conclusions about c-command relations between constituents.

---

21. It also follows of course that specifically because of cases like e.g. (47b, c), (48b, c) and (49b, c),
Principle C is untenable even for the domain of reflexives, even for English.

22. The facts of English *nominal* domains may also be problematic to Principle A and its analogs. Consider:

(i)   a.   Felicia's continuing criticism of herself
       b.   this continuing criticism by Felicia of [herself/HERSELF]
       c.   this continuing criticism of herself by Felicia
       d.   this continuing criticism of Felicia by [herself/HERSELF]

Case (ia) is the sort which is most clearly in accord with Principle A. Ignore the well-known fact
that to render cases like (ib) equally consistent requires the grammar to somehow be indifferent
to the fact that the antecedent is embedded in a PP. The key issue is how Principle A can also be
consistent with both (ic, d)? This would seemingly require mutual c-command, raising minimally issues of how [criticism of DP] can then be a constituent, how requirements that all branching be binary can be met, etc. To our knowledge, such questions have not been systematically
addressed; but see Collins (2005) for relevant remarks.

   Williams (1994: 188–189) notes some cases parallel to (ic), judging them only with two
question marks. While not basically disagreeing with his judgments, we believe they depend
significantly on his choice of examples, rather than on fundamentals of the construction.

4.2 A possibly inviolable antecedence constraint on subject reflexives

The negative conclusions just reached, implying that UVA principles like Principle A and analogs must be rejected, create a series of problems. For without such principles, a multitude of in fact ungrammatical reflexives would appear to be in general unblocked by known conditions. Even though nothing in principle then precludes, for instance, *any* clause-internally anteceded reflexive subjects, the known examples inconsistent with such a claim appear to involve exclusively 'derived' subjects, those which would arguably owe their subject status to *movement* in transformational terms and to what are called *advancements* in relational grammar terms.[23]

One reasonable hypothesis which can, though partially, fill the lacunae is that it is truly impossible in natural languages for what relational grammar accounts roughly regard as an *initial subject* reflexive to be anteceded from within its own clause. Very informally:

(54) An initial reflexive subject cannot be anteceded by another DP in the same minimal clause.[24]

Since (54) says nothing about 'derived' subjects of any kind, it fails to indicate that they cannot be locally anteceded reflexives, and, unlike Principle A type views, it is consistent with the sort of data cited earlier from Albanian, Greek and English.

---

23. In the framework of Johnson and Postal (1980), Postal (1989, 1992 1996), 'derived' subjects would be those in which the arc defining subject status is a successor, possibly always a local successor.

24. A precise version of such a claim would have to take note of the facts for passives. Clearly, the constraint at issue does not hold for passive agent reflexives, since the status of (ia, b, c) is entirely distinct from that of (ii), in ways which cannot be attributed to the sort of distinct considerations discussed presently in the text.

(i)   a.   *Himself/HIMSELF characterized Monroe quite critically.
      b.   *I believe himself/HIMSELF to have characterized Monroe quite critically.
      c.   *I believe to have characterized Monroe quite critically HIMSELF.

(ii)   ?Monroe was characterized quite critically by himself/HIMSELF.

That is, passivization of an impossible reflexive initial subject seems to yield a largely grammatical result. But in relational terms, cases like (ii) are analyzed in such a way that the passive *by*-phrase DP is a non-derived subject, a view long ago argued for in e.g. Perlmutter (1984); see also Postal (2004: Chapter 8). It would appear then that the proper version of the constraint would have to reference initial subjects *which are also superficial subjects.*

4.3 Constraints on inverse reflexives

Despite what we have taken to be the existence of grammatical locally anteceded (noninitial) subject reflexives, and despite principle (54), multitudes of other such cases are also not well-formed, including the unsalvaged English simple reflexive cases. Just so, while it has been argued that there are grammatical locally anteceded direct object reflexives not anteceded by subjects, many such cases are also ungrammatical, e.g the unsalvaged simple reflexive objects in English. These ungrammaticalities must thus be attributed to principles distinct from (54) or various versions of Principle A, seemingly principles of considerably less generality.

It would be tempting to suggest initially for English and possibly many analogous languages that the relevant principles are word-order based. One might claim that English simply excludes simple reflexives which precede their antecedents. This view is in accord with the conclusions of Jackendoff (1990), a quite lonely voice over recent decades, arguing for the role of word order in anaphora and against overwhelming reliance on notions like c-command; see also Williams (1994: 188–189).

However, while we see no theoretical objection to reflexive antecedence constraints which appeal to word order, such constraints do *not* underlie in particular the ungrammaticality of English salvageable but unsalvaged reflexives. First, there are grammatical instances of English simplex reflexives preceding their antecedents, some already cited:

(55) a. I proved to have contradicted themselves at least once those foreign reporters over there.

  b. THEMSELVES, I proved those foreign reporters to have contradicted at least once.

One difference between these cases and the earlier ones where a reflexive cannot grammatically precede its antecedent is that in the latter *both* antecedent and reflexive are in unextracted positions, so-called *A(rgument)-positions* in one framework, while in the former, at least one is not. If one adopts this terminology for its familiarity, the generalization might appear to be:

(56) If a simple reflexive expression R and its antecedent AT are both in superficial A-positions, then AT precedes R.

However, principle (56) is not an adequate approach to salvageable simple reflexives.

Consider the ungrammatical but salvageable subject reflexive violations in (57a) and the ungrammatical but salvageable direct object reflexive violations in (58a):

(57) a. *He believes herself to have been praised by Melissa.
b. %HERSELF, he believes to have been praised by Melissa.
c. *Melissa, he believes herself to have been praised by.
d. *By Melissa, he believes herself to have been praised.

(58) a. *He believes them to have never described herself to Melissa.
b. %HERSELF, he believes them to have never described to Melissa.
c. *Melissa, he believes them to have never described herself to.
d. *To Melissa, he believes them to have never described herself.

While (57c, d) and (58c, d) all satisfy (56), they are clearly as ungrammatical as the unsalvaged cases in (57a) and (58a). These data reveal a fundamental, previously ignored asymmetry with respect to the salvaging phenomena. Namely, this turns out to be achievable by the salvage constructions only if the 'target' of those constructions is the illicit simple reflexive form; it is not achieved if the 'target' is the antecedent. But a word-order principle like (56) predicts exactly a nonexistent *symmetrical* salvaging situation.[25]

Moreover, other types of extractions which effect the word order of antecedent/salvageable reflexives but do not involve extraction of the reflexive form also yield salvageable structures which satisfy (56) but remain ungrammatical. That is, extraction of a phrase containing the antecedent also fails to contribute to salvaging.

(59) a. *They believed himself to be astonishing to Joe.
b. %It was HIMSELF that they believed to be astonishing to Joe.
c.   Astonishing to himself though they believed Joe to be,
d. *Astonishing to Joe though they believed himself to be,

---

25. This discussion might raise the question of whether Principle A can be defended against the implications of the English salvaging data by some sort of revision to the effect that an anaphor only needs to be bound by a c-commanding element *if it is in an argument position*. This might be momentarily attractive, since all of the troublesome salvage cases involve extracted reflexives, hence those not in argument positions. However, such a revision is nonetheless hopeless. For the good cases would thereby be rendered consistent with a revised Principle A only at the price of a failure to block impossible ones like (i), where the italicized form is a copy-trace:

(i)   *It was HIMSELF that I am sure praised Jerome.

Moreover, internal to the now popular view that extractions in general yield traces which are *copies* of the extracted elements (see e.g. Chomsky, 2003: 306–307; and Postal, 2004: Chapter 7 for critical remarks), the proposal fails even for grammatical cases like (iia), which then have structures like (iib):

(ii)   a. %It was HIMSELF that I am sure was praised by Jerome.
       b. [It was HIMSELF that I am sure *HIMSELF* was praised by Jerome].

For in (iib), the highlighted form is an unbound reflexive in an argument position, which would be wrongly barred unconditionally even by the hypothetical revision of Principle A.

Chapter 1. Inverse reflexives   31

One must then search for a different principle to account for (57c, d) and (58c, d) and to provide a reconstruction of the circumstances under which extractions actually salvage ungrammatical simple reflexives. Our best guess is that the right principle will be relational, in the sense of appealing to notions like subject, direct object, indirect object, etc.. We adopt the relational grammar notation of numerical abbreviations for the names of these relations, each name viewed as the label of an arc in the formal structure representing the relations.[26]

(60)   subject (1), direct object (2), indirect object (3), …

We also appeal to a ranking of these relations based formally on a ranking of the symbols (arc labels) taken as their names, specifically, at least that of (61):

(61)   Arc A *outranks* arc B if and only if A's label precedes B's label in the sequence: 1, 2, 3, X (X ≠ 1, 2, or 3)

One can then informally define the notion of *inverse reflexive*, as in (62):

(62)   Definition
       A reflexive expression R is an *inverse reflexive* if and only if the last central arc headed by R outranks the last *central* arc headed by the local antecedent of R.[27]

This says in effect that R is an inverse reflexive if it is a final 1 locally anteceded by a final 2, 3 or X, a final 2 locally anteceded by a final 3 or X, or a final 3 locally anteceded by a final X. Notably, the reflexives in (57a) and (58a) are then inverse reflexives, instantiating antecedence of a 1 by an X and of a 2 by an X, while the ill-formed variant of (63) instantiates, we suggest, antecedence of a 3 by an X:[28]

---

26. For basic accounts of arcs, their labels as names of grammatical relations, hierarchies of such, etc., see Johnson and Postal (1980), Postal (1989, 1992, 1996, 2004, in preparation).

27. Very roughly, Central arcs specify the class of nominal grammatical relations defining core clauses. See Johnson and Postal (1980), Postal (in preparation). This class excludes those nominal relations relevant to extractions, that is, those defining topicalization, interrogative extraction, etc. Hence inter alia, definition (62) claims that the latter phenomena are irrelevant to the characterization of the concept inverse reflexive.

28. The view that (63) involves a final 3 and that the reflexive antecedent is not a final 2 (but a final instance of a distinct relation, call it 4, with no traditional name) assumes conclusions of Postal (in preparation). Moreover, that analysis has the proper consequences for (i):

       (i)   *I offered himself the slave.

Under a traditional view in which the superficial relation of the reflexive object is 3, that of its antecedent 2, the reflexive would not be an inverse reflexive and nothing so far would block the example. But under the analysis of Postal (in preparation), the relations are respectively 3 and 4. This can characterize the reflexive as inverse if the relation 4 is added to the hierarchy in (61)

(63) The book was sent Jack/*herself by Melissa.

With this notion in hand, and adopting an informal terminology which takes the 'target' of one of the salvage constructions to have been extracted, one can account for the relevant data with the following *parochial constraint*:

(64) A simple inverse reflexive in English must be extracted.[29]

Plausibly, the same notion can be used to describe facts in other languages. So, the dialects of French which allow (8b) but ban its corresponding passive might involve a constraint entailing minimally that an inverse reflexive has to be a final direct object; Albanian might manifest a constraint that an inverse reflexive must be a direct object (passivized or not) anteceded by an indirect object, and other languages might simply ban all inverse reflexives.

4.4 Generalizing the results

We have recognized a notion of inverse reflexive to describe a variety of facts from English which were argued to clash with the implications of any universal principle designed to imitate the consequences of Chomsky's Principle A. Evidently, Principle A is only one element of a group of related principles in the same tradition which appeal principally to the notion c-command to describe relations between pairs of DPs. Other such principles have been invoked to describe triggering of negative polarity items, binding of pronominal forms, etc. We *suspect* that in

---

between the 3 and X positions. Salvaging would then be in principle possible but is in fact not because of the constraint independent of reflexivization issues which does not, in our dialects, permit 3s of any sort to be extracted; see note 15:

(ii) *It was Joan that he offered __ the slave.

29. In a framework having *argument position* as a precisely defined construct, (64) might well be stated along the lines of (i):

(i) An inverse reflexive cannot be in a surface argument position.

An issue then is the grammaticality of cases like (ii):

(ii) HIMSELF was what was shown to Joe on the monitor.

These might be taken to attack not only the idea mentioned earlier that English lacks nominative anaphors but also the generalization putatively stated as in (64) or (i). Our suspicion is that such cases fail to conflict with the principle barring finite clause reflexive surface subjects because HIMSELF in (ii) is not a subject of the main clause but a subpart of a subject whose other parts are invisible. It might be noted that verbal agreement in such cases is not what would be expected of a subject.

(i) THEMSELVES ?was/*were what was shown to those guys on the monitor.

Chapter 1. Inverse reflexives   33

many such cases, evidence similar to that appealed to here will show that c-command is not an adequate basis for the facts and suggest that an analog of the inverse reflexive relation may be relevant. While space precludes serious discussion here, it is worth mentioning one case.

It has often been claimed that a pronominal form anteceded by a *quantified DP* antecedent must be c-commanded, hence bound, by the antecedent; see e.g. Barss and Lasnik (1986), Aoun and Li (1993), Baker (2001). This is normally taken to be the basis for facts like (65):

(65) a. Every student$_1$ respects his$_1$ teacher.
　　　 b. *His$_1$ teacher respects every student$_1$.
　　　 c. They convinced every foreign student$_1$ that the professor respected her$_1$.
　　　 d. *They convinced her$_1$ that the professor respected every foreign student$_1$.

Such claims are seemingly attacked by perfectly grammatical cases like (66), in which c-command does not hold between antecedent and pronoun and yet a bound variable interpretation is unproblematic.[30]

(66) Every professor's$_1$ neighbor respects her$_1$.

More directly relevant to the present inquiry are cases like (67) and (68):

(67) a. Every professor$_1$ praised his$_1$ relatives.
　　　 b. *His$_1$ relatives praised every professor$_1$.
　　　 c. $^?$His$_1$ relatives were praised by every professor$_1$.

(68) a. They described every professor$_1$ to his$_1$ neighbors.
　　　 b. $^?$They described his$_1$ neighbors to every professor$_1$.

---

30. One proposed solution to such problems is to claim, as in Hornstein (1995: 26–27), that quantifier expressions are extracted at a level of Logical Form and that the c-command condition holds at that level. So a good case of variable binding like (ia), where surface c-command does not hold properly, is taken to be due to a Logical Form like (ib), in which the quantifier expression does c-command the pronominal form interpreted as a bound variable.

　　(i) a. No gorilla's$_1$ trainer ever beats it$_1$.
　　　　 b. No gorilla$_1$ [1's trainer ever beats it$_1$]

This approach then requires that the impossibility of variable binding in (iia) be attributed to a crossover constraint applying to the (result of) movement at Logical Form:

　　(ii) a. *His$_1$ trainer beat no gorilla$_1$.
　　　　　b. No gorilla$_1$ [his$_1$ trainer beats$_1$]

Such claims are undermined if the data to follow in the text are valid.

The pronouns in cases like (67c) and (68b), although not c-commanded by their quantifier antecedents and in fact c-commanding them in surface forms, seem to us to be reasonably acceptable on a bound variable reading and thus to sharply contrast with the truly impossible (67b).

Moreover, any doubts about (67c) and (68b) vanish in correspondents where the pronominal DPs are extracted:

(69) a. His$_1$ affinal relatives, I am sure were praised by every professor$_1$.
      b. His$_1$ next door neighbors, I am sure they described to every professor$_1$.
      c. It was his$_1$ affinal relatives that I am sure were praised by every professor$_1$.

On the contrary, extraction seems to do nothing to improve e.g. (67b):

(70) a. *His$_1$ next door neighbors, I am sure praised every professor$_1$.
      b. *It was his$_1$ next door neighbors that I am sure praised every professor$_1$.

In short, it appears that in the environments we took to define inverse reflexives, there is at worst a possibility of salvaging (in an obvious sense) quantifier DP/pronominal antecedence cases which are commonly taken to require a c-command relation. This is as unexpected in received terms, e.g. those which appeal to the crossover explication of note 30, as the reflexive salvagings discussed earlier. And just as the reflexive data undermine Principle A style accounts, the bound variable data undermine straightforward appeals to c-command combined with crossover accounts.

Clearly then, a general investigation of such matters in terms which take into account the inverse relation is suggested, as this concept may be of potential relevance to antecedence by quantifier DPs just as it is to the antecedence of reflexives.

References

Aoun, J. & Yen-hui A. Li. 1993. *Syntax of Scope*. Cambridge MA: The MIT Press.

Anagnostopoulou, E. & Everaert, M. 1995. How exceptional are nominative anaphors? A case study of Greek. In *Actes du deuxième colloque de langues & grammaire*, L. Nash, G. Tsoulas & A. Zribi-Hertz (eds). Paris: University of Paris 8.

Anagnostopoulou, E. & Everaert, M. 1999. Toward a more complete typology of anaphoric expressions. *Linguistic Inquiry* 30: 97–119.

Anderson, S. 1982. Types of dependency in anaphors: Icelandic (and other) reflexives. *Journal of Linguistic Research* 2: 1–22.

Baker, M. C. 1996. *The Polysynthesis Parameter*. Oxford: OUP.

Baker, M. C. 2001. Phrase structure as a representation of 'primitive' grammatical relations. In *Objects and Other Subjects*, W. D. Davies & S. Dubinsky (eds). Dordrecht: Kluwer.

Barss, A. & H. Lasnik. 1986. A note on anaphora and double objects. *Linguistic Inquiry* 17: 347–54.

Brame, M. 1977. Alternatives to the tensed S and specified subject conditions. *Linguistics and Philosophy* 1: 381–411.

Bresnan, J. 2000. *Lexical-Functional Syntax*. Oxford: Blackwell.

Chomsky, N. 1981. *Lectures on Government and Binding*. Dordrecht: Foris.

Chomsky, N. 1982. *Some Concepts and Consequences of the Theory of Government and Binding*. Cambridge MA: The MIT Press.

Chomsky, N. 1986. *Knowledge of Language*. New York NY: Praeger Scientific.

Chomsky, N. 2003. Reply to Pietroski. In *Chomsky and His Critics*, L. M. Antony & N. Hornstein (eds). Oxford: Blackwell.

Cole, P., Harmon, G. & Huang, C.-T. J. 2001. *Long-Distance Reflexives, Syntax and Semantics* 33. New York NY: Academic Press.

Cole, P., Harmon, G. & Sung, L.-M. 1990. Principles and parameters of long-distance reflexives. *Linguistic Inquiry* 21: 1–22.

Cole, P. & Sung, L.-M. 1994. Head movement and long-distance reflexives. *Linguistic Inquiry* 25: 355–406.

Collins, C. 2005. A smuggling approach to the passive in English. *Syntax* 8: 81–120.

Den Dikken, M. 1995. *Particles*. Oxford: OUP.

Everaert, M. & Anagnostopoulou, E. 1996. Thematic hierarchies and binding theory: Evidence from Greek. Ms, Utrecht University & Tilburg University.

Hornstein, N. 1995. *Logical Form*. Oxford: Blackwell.

Huang, Y. 2000. *Anaphora*. Oxford: OUP.

Hubbard, P. L. 1980. The Syntax of the Albanian Verb Complex. PhD Dissertation, University of California at San Diego.

Hubbard, P. L. 1981. Dative clitics in Albanian: Evidence for syntactic levels. In *Proceedings of the Seventh Annual Meeting of the Berkeley Linguistic Society*. Berkeley CA: BLS.

Jackendoff, R. 1972. *Semantic Interpretation in Generative Grammar*. Cambridge MA: The MIT Press.

Jackendoff, R. 1990. On Larson's treatment of the double object construction. *Linguistic Inquiry* 21: 427–56.

Johnson, D. E. & Postal, P. M. 1980. *Arc Pair Grammar*. Princeton NJ: Princeton University Press.

Keenan, E. 1974. The functional principle: Generalizing the notion of 'subject of'. In *Chicago Linguistic Society 10*, M. W. La Galy, R. A. Fox & A. Bruck (eds), 298–310. Chicago IL: CLS.

Koster, J. 1978. *Locality Principles in Syntax*. Dordrecht: Foris.

Koster, J. & Reuland, E. 1991. *Long Distance Anaphora*. Cambridge: CUP.

Maling, J. 1984. Non-clause-bounded reflexives in Modern Icelandic. *Linguistics and Philosophy* 7: 211–41.

Larson, R. 1988. On the double object construction. *Linguistic Inquiry* 19: 335–91.

Marantz, A. P. 1993. Implications of asymmetries in double object constructions. *Theoretical Aspects of Bantu Grammar*, S. A. Mchombo (ed.). Stanford CA: CSLI.

Perlmutter, D. M. 1984. The inadequacy of some monostratal theories of passive. *Studies in Relational Grammar* 2, D. M. Perlmutter & C. G. Rosen. Chicago IL: The University of Chicago Press.

Pollard, C. & Sag, I. A. 1992. Anaphors in English and the scope of binding theory. *Linguistic Inquiry* 23: 261–303.

Pollard & Sag, I. A. 1994. *Head-Driven Phrase Structure Grammar*. Chicago IL: The University of Chicago Press/CSLI.

Postal, P. M. 1974. *On Raising*. Cambridge MA: The MIT Press.

Postal, P. 1990. French indirect object demotion. In *Studies in Relational Grammar* 3, P. M. Postal & B. D. Joseph (eds). Chicago IL: The University of Chicago Press.

Postal, P. M. 1989. *Masked Inversion in French*. Chicago IL: The University of Chicago Press.

Postal, P. M. 1992. Phantom successors and the French *faire par* construction. In *The Joy of Grammar: A Festschrift for James D. McCawley*, D. Brentari, G. N. Larson & L. A. MacLeod (eds). Amsterdam: John Benjamins.

Postal, P. M. 1996. A glance at French pseudopassives. In *Grammatical Relations, Theoretical Approaches to Empirical Questions*, C. S. Burgess, K. Dziwirek & D. B. Gerdts (eds). New York NY: CSLI & CUP.

Postal, P. M. 2004. *Skeptical Linguistic Essays*. Oxford: OUP.

Postal, P. M. 2006. Remarks on English long-distance anaphora. *Style* 40(1–2).

Postal, P. M. In preparation. *Edge-Based Model-Theoretic Syntax*.

Reinhart, T. & Reuland, E. 1993. Reflexivity. *Linguistic Inquiry* 24: 657–720.

Sells, P. 1988. Thematic and grammatical hierarchies: Albanian reflexivization. In *Proceedings of the Seventh West Coast Conference on Formal Linguistics*. Stanford CA: CSLI.

Wilkins, W. 1988. Thematic structure and reflexivization. In *Thematic Relations, Syntax and Semantics* 21, W. Wilkins (ed.). New York NY: Academic Press.

Williams, E. 1992. θ-theory as binding theory. In *Syntax and the Lexicon, Syntax and Semantics* 26, T. Stowell & E. Wehrli. New York NY: Academic Press.

Williams, E. 1994. *Thematic Structure in Syntax*. Cambridge MA: The MIT Press.

Williams, K. 1988. Exceptional behavior of anaphors in Albanian. *Linguistic Inquiry* 19: 161–8.

Woolford, E. 1999. More on the anaphor agreement effect. *Linguistic Inquiry* 30: 257–87.

CHAPTER 2

On the nature of the approximative expression NUM-*odd**

Sheila Dooley and Ferdinand de Haan
University of Arizona

In this paper, the morphology, syntax, semantics, and diachrony of expressions like *twenty-odd* are described, based on the results of a corpus study which considers data from the British National Corpus, the Oxford English Dictionary, and Google. The -*odd* suffix appears most frequently with *twenty*, and in collocations with temporal nominals such as years, days, etc. Distributionally it appears to be a derivational suffix on numerals, occurring inside additional suffixation such as ordinal -*th*. It originated from the use of *odd* to denote a surplus or remainder, which usage has existed for several hundred years. It is distinct from other English approximatives, and approximatives in other languages, in that -*odd* expresses an indeterminate range above the cardinality of the modified numeral, but not below it, while other approximative expressions (like *about*) include the possibility that the actual number might be either above or below the reference number.

1. Introduction

The linguistic expression of numerals is one topic which has received much attention and which shows a great deal of cross-linguistic similarities (Greenberg 1978; Hurford 1975, 1987; Gvozdanović 1992; Heine 1997, and others). Such studies usually confine themselves to cardinal (counting) numerals, however, and do not treat other more peripheral numerical expressions such as ordinals (*fourth, fifth*, etc.), fractions, or imprecise expressions of estimation such as *two or three*. The last type of numerical expression, which may be classified formally as an approximative (Plank 2004a, b) is particularly interesting linguistically for many reasons. First, it overlaps semantically with expressions usually categorized as quantifiers such as *many, few*, or *some*, but does not show the same behavior as these quantifiers. Secondly, its form (at least in the English example given above) may be that of a disjunctive *or*-expression, which is subject to particular constraints of its

---

* We would like to thank the editors of the volume and an anonymous referee for helpful comments. All errors are our own. Our heartfelt thanks to Terry Langendoen for consistent encouragement, inspiration, and good humor from across the hall.

own (Langendoen 2006). Thirdly, even within one language approximatives can be used in different ways.

Given that Terry Langendoen taught at the University of Arizona from 1988 until 2005 (i.e. seventeen years), it is tempting to use the numeral *twenty* with an approximative measure, as in (1):

(1) a. Terry taught at the University of Arizona for *twenty or so* years.
b. Terry taught at the University of Arizona for *some twenty* years.
c. Terry taught at the University of Arizona for *twenty-odd* years.

Although (1a) and (b) are perfectly fine, there is a problem with (1c): it seems unnatural to use the expression NUM-*odd* when referring to a number below NUM. The present paper is a study of the NUM-*odd* expression.

This expression may seem like a very infrequent type of phrase in contemporary English, but a corpus study shows that this is an illusion. Section 2.0 reports the findings of a corpus study of NUM-*odd* expressions in written and spoken English. Section 3.0 addresses questions about the identity of the NUM-*odd* expression in the grammar of English. For example, what is the morphological status of the -*odd* element? Also, what is the syntactic status of NUM-*odd* expressions? Should they be regarded as quantifiers? Section 4.0 extends the discussion along the typological and diachronic dimensions, showing indications from the corpus study that the NUM-*odd* expression is undergoing another stage of grammaticalization to become an all-purpose approximative marker and hedge in English. The paper ends with a summarization of our findings and our conclusions about the nature of the NUM-*odd* construction.

2. A corpus study of NUM-*odd* expressions

Data for the NUM-*odd* study was taken from the British National Corpus (BNC), the Oxford English Dictionary (OED), and from Google searches on the web (WWW). The source materials therefore included both spoken and written material, and many different genres of text within the written materials (for example letters, novels, newspaper articles, and scientific texts). Google searches of contemporary English will be especially relevant to our discussion of proposed ongoing developments in the behavior of the NUM-*odd* construction in Section 4.2.

2.1. Semantics of -*odd*

The semantics of NUM-*odd* as evidenced from the corpus data show some variety. The prototypical use of NUM-*odd* is one in which NUM is a round number. In such

Chapter 2. The approximative expression NUM-*odd*   **39**

instances, NUM-*odd* establishes a range in which the expression can felicitously be used. That is, this expression sets an explicit lower bound, namely NUM itself, and an implicit upper bound, which is dependent upon the level of the numeral. If NUM is a decade, the implicit upper bound will be NUM + 10, if NUM denotes a multiple of 100, the upper bound will be NUM + 100, etc. Thus:

(2)   Approx   Range
      twenty-odd   from 20 to 30
      two hundred-odd   from 200 to 300
      two thousand-odd   from 2,000 to 3,000

An example from the BNC is given in (3), where the expression *20-odd* is used to refer back to *23 seasons*.

(3)   Arsenal lead the table on 79 years, followed by Everton (41) and surprise, surprise Coventry City on 40. The biggest surprise still is in sixth place good old Hartlepool United who've not gone down anywhere for 23 seasons. It illustrates, says chairman Garry, that we have been the most successful North-East club over the past 20-odd years.

That NUM-*odd* can refer to items close to the upper bound can be seen in the next BNC example, where *thirty odd* is used to refer to 37 or 38 years of age:[1]

(4)   We were saying that Ron in number four he was a builder. He had his own business, van, the whole lot. He had staff working for him. And he hurt his back last year and the doctor said well you'll either be dead within six months. You've gotta give up the building work. He's only thirty odd, thirty seven, thirty eight.

Round numbers are obvious targets for -*odd* to be attached to as they are highly salient numbers, cognitively speaking. Such numbers participate in other expressions of approximation such as disjunctive *fifty or sixty* (see Langendoen 2006) and *twenty-something*. They are in and of themselves prototypes for their respective range, and it is not surprising that NUM-*odd* expressions with non-round numbers are exceedingly rare.

In certain domains, however, it is perfectly natural for NUM-*odd* to occur with a non-round number, if that number acts as a round number within that domain and is capable of being the prototype for a range. This can be seen in example (5) from the OED, where the numeral *six* can act as a round number in the context of height, as it establishes a range with six (feet) as the explicit lower bound and seven (feet) as the implicit upper bound:

---

1. On the presence vs. absence of the hyphen before *odd* see sections 2.3 and 4.1.

(5) He gazed at six foot odd of gorgeousness, as represented by Sir Percy Blakeney, Bart.[2] (Baroness Orczy, *Scarlet Pimpernel* (1905))

In rare cases, non-round higher numbers can be used with -*odd*, if it is considered suitable as a lower bound in the context:

(6) I mean she's been living off what seventy three odd quid has she? [i.e. between 73 and 74 pounds]

The noun *dozen* can be used with -*odd* and functions as a round number:

(7) I dedicate this essay to the two-dozen-odd people whose refutations of Cantor's diagonal argument … have come to me either as referee or as editor in the last twenty years or so.

When dealing with higher order numerals the situation becomes less clear. Higher order numerals are themselves already less precise, so that adding -*odd* typically yields a type of approximation in which NUM in NUM-*odd* refers to an approximate middle point, rather than an explicit lower bound.

(8) twenty thousand-odd days walking under the sun seems like much, but it's not – you'd barely just begun oh … another golden one who's gone too soon (and i'm missing you) (www.theworryknot.com/lyrics.html)

Perhaps surprisingly, this same type can also be found in expressions where NUM is a low numeral (less than 10). Examples from the WWW are:

(9) a. Public opinion has gone in and out like the tides on Said's book since I first read it some six odd years ago.
(Book review by Earl Hazell, Amazon.com)
b. If someone would've told me that the best action game of the last five-odd years was going to come from a previously unknown company located in Germany …

This obviously does not set a range but rather conveys the idea of *about six years*. Interestingly, the typical use of this type of approximative seems to be tied to points of time in the past. Most uses of low numerals plus *odd* refer to times before the present.

There is syntactic variation in the use of -*odd* with higher level numbers (typically numbers above 10,000) to encode semantic distinctions.[3] There are two ways

---

2. For the reason why *odd* follows the word *foot* rather than preceding it see section 4.1 below.

3. There are a small number of occurrences of the pattern NUM-*odd hundred*. For example:

(i) Out of the **three-odd hundred freestyles** i've personally had my hands on i've only experienced trouble with five. (www.pbreview.com/forums/t312367)

Chapter 2. The approximative expression NUM-*odd* **41**

in which -*odd* can be combined with a number like *thirty thousand*, namely:

(10) a. thirty-odd thousand
[[thirty-odd] thousand]
b. thirty thousand-odd
[[thirty thousand]-odd]

These are not free variations, as there is a difference in meaning. A phrase like *thirty-odd thousand*, with *thirty-odd* having scope over *thousand*, puts the approximation with the *thirty*, and therefore gives us a range between 30 and 40 (thousand). *Thirty thousand-odd* with -*odd* attached to *thousand* puts the range much closer to 30,000, indicating something like between 30,000 and 31,000. In other words, *thirty thousand-odd* is more precise than *thirty-odd thousand*. The structural analysis of *thirty thousand-odd* is arguably one involving -*odd* attached to a single NUM unit, whatever status this unit may have. The numeral *thirty-odd thousand* is then analyzed as [[NUM-*odd*] NUM].[4]

Examples from the BNC are shown in (11). The range shown in (11a) is relatively broader than that of (11b). While (11a) can refer to numbers between 20,000 and 30,000, the range alluded to in (11b) is comparatively narrow, as evidenced by the use of the phrase *just over a hundred million* in the immediate context. The phrase *a hundred million odd* cannot be used to refer to numbers closer to 200,000,000.

(11) a. Well, she was saying. Yeah. They wouldn't give you one [mortgage] on your wages! Yeah! They'd give you one for twenty odd thousand, where you gonna get a house for twenty odd thousand?
b. erm and yeah, er but that was his specialty er so it's so of that four hundred and sixty million er a hundred million odd er just over a hundred million has been recovered …

(ii) She was a minute girl, trembling at the attention of **five-odd hundred** eyes. Her haunted gaze scanned the crowd owlishly before she took a seat on the stool … (www.gonga-ga.com/utter/ms2.htm)

The meaning of NUM-*odd* here is one of approximation rather than range. This fits in with the findings of the combination of -*odd* with lower numerals. See ex. (9) and the accompanying discussion.

4. There is an analogy here with the ordinal suffix -*th*, which can also attach to either NUM unit with a concomitant difference in meaning. For example:

(i) Under the provisions of the law, the rate on the twentieth thousand of earned incomes is 5 per cent. The rate on the taxed at one-fourth of one per cent… (books.google.com/books)

The expression *twentieth thousand* has a different and more precise meaning than that of *twenty thousandth*.

2.2 Collocations

This section discusses the most important contexts in which the expression NUM-*odd* occurs. While there is in principle no restriction on the following NP (beyond the fact that it must contain a count noun), there are some categories of nouns that are especially prone to occur with NUM-*odd*.

By far the most common noun is *year(s)*. Examples are shown in (12):

(12) a. In fifty-odd years of high regard for Englishwomen and awe of the forti-
tude and grace he saw in them, he had never accepted their defiling
hats.

b. Sam Barr, supreme breeder of top class performance horses for
twenty-odd years …

If the accompanying noun is omitted, *years* is usually implied:

(13) Over the passing years, time had been kind to Caduta Massi. Over the
passing years, time had been cruel to nearly everybody else. … Now, at
forty-odd, she could still play the right kind of romantic lead, given a suf-
ficiently elderly and/or bisexual co-star.

As is the case with other combinations of NUM-*odd* and *years* (see (12) above), the intended meaning tends to be 'an elapsed period of NUM-*odd* years', rather than 'NUM-*odd* years of age'. About 85% of all such collocations have a meaning closer to (12a–b) than to (13).[5]

Other frequent collocations are with nouns denoting measurements and with monetary terms.

(14) a. They were now thirty-odd miles away from the Manchester slums where
they had been brought up …

b. It is very difficult to cover all the possible eventualities in the forty-
odd hours of the PPL course …

c. The ones you want are the long ones aren't they? And thermal? Your
hands are really warm, I know and they're thirty odd quid.

---

5. This contrasts with the use of -*something* in e.g., *twentysomething*. When the intended mean-ing is *twentysomething years* (with *years* usually omitted), an age is meant:

(i) Yes, ever been in a car! Yeah. But the kids have got more confidence haven't they? … They
must have when you're twentysomething, you know, they've got less fear.

However, *twentysomething* tends to be used more with dates and monetary items than with *years* even when the noun is omitted. This is a marked difference from NUM-*odd*.

Chapter 2. The approximative expression NUM-*odd*   **43**

2.3 Spoken versus written language variants

The NUM-*odd* construction occurs both in spoken and written English, and actually appears in the BNC in four different forms, illustrated in (15a–d) below.

(15) a. Hyphenated: twenty-odd
      b. Unhyphenated: twenty odd
      c. Digital Hyphenated: 20-odd
      d. Digital Unhyphenated: 20 odd

It was found that in the written corpus of the BNC the hyphenated NUM-*odd* forms (a) and (c) were used, while in the spoken corpus the unhyphenated forms (b) and (d) were used.

This appears to be an artifact of transcription conventions used in constructing the corpus, but does help to track the use of the -*odd* expression in the two registers. Table 1 gives figures for the frequencies of all four variants of the NUM-*odd* expression, comparing spoken to written registers.

Table 1. NUM-*odd* frequency of use: spoken versus written registers

	Hyphenated (=written)	Non-hyphenated (=spoken)
NUM	89	258
Digital NUM	37	14
TOTAL	126	272

As Table 1 indicates, NUM-*odd* expressions are more frequent in the spoken register both absolutely and relatively (given that the spoken part of the BNC is far smaller than the written part).

A closer look at the frequencies for the use of the approximative -*odd* with individual numerals is more interesting, since not all cardinal numerals occur with -*odd*. Table 2 shows the frequencies of use of individual numerals with -*odd*.

Counts for *hundred, thousand, and million* as NUM include higher denomination numerals with these as the final element before the -*odd*, such as *nine-hundred-odd*. Figures for the other NUM expressions in the table do not include these in larger denominations. So, the entry for *forty* only includes the number of occurrences of 40 and not, say, those of 140 or 540.

Instances of other NUM appearing only once in the corpus are not included in the table as they only occur once each. An example is (16).

(16) I went out next. No, you were all in here at the time. On the phone. Oh, were you? Oh, you might have been … I … but most of you were certain-

Table 2. NUM-*odd* frequency of use: individual numerals

NUM	Hyphenated	Non-Hyphenated	Digital Hyphenated	Digital Non-Hyphenated	TOTAL
Twenty	19	50	12	5	86
Thirty	15	48	11	4	78
Forty	15	22	8	2	47
Fifty	7	23	4	0	34
Sixty	12	19	0	0	34
Hundred	8	16	0	0	24
Eighty	4	18	0	1	22
Seventy	4	16	0	1	21
Ninety	2	16	0	1	19
Thousand	1	17	0	0	18
Million	2	3	0	0	5
Fifteen	0	0	2	0	2

ly here. Got as far as you could only use five hundred and forty odd or something …

As discussed earlier in Section 2.1, round numbers are clearly the ones functioning as NUM in NUM-*odd* approximatives, with the cardinal number *twenty* being the most frequent. This is followed fairly closely by the other decade numbers up to *sixty*.

2.4 Summary

The corpus study described above confirms that the NUM-*odd* expression, in both its hyphenated and unhyphenated variants is used quite often in contemporary English, with the expression *twenty-odd* being the most frequent incarnation. We may thus consider *twenty-odd* to be the exemplar or prototype for this construction, and *twenty-odd years* to be the most common collocation. The approximative -*odd* element does not combine freely with any English cardinal numeral, but is instead constrained to appearing in combination with those that can be defined as 'round numbers'. The concept of the round number in approximative expressions is discussed in Wachtel (1980) and Channell (1980). Both researchers point out that 'round number' status is determined contextually rather than numerically.

The collocational possibilities of the NUM-*odd* construction in its capacity as modifier are not strictly constrained, but do follow fairly strong tendencies. It appears most frequently before nouns denoting unit measures of time, money, weight, or distance such as *years, days, hours, dollars, pounds* etc. However, it is not restricted to such expressions, and has been found before a wide variety of countable concrete and abstract nouns, including animates as well as inanimates such as *passengers, plants, sites*, and *replies*. The noun always occurs in its plural form. This is exactly what we would expect of an approximative, given its semantics as an imprecise quantificational expression.

3. Analysis: What is the structural status of *-odd*?

The previous section assumes broadly that the NUM-*odd* expression is a nominal modifier. The class of nominal modifiers includes rather diverse categories such as determiners, quantifiers, adjectives, numerals, and possessives. This section attempts to arrive at a more specific categorial classification of the NUM-*odd* expression, as well as to answer some basic structural questions about the status of the *-odd* element itself. We will start with the latter.

3.1 *-odd*: clitic, suffix, or free morpheme?

The *-odd* element is homophonous with the lexical adjective *odd* meaning 'strange' or 'uneven'. The existence of unhyphenated forms of NUM-*odd* approximatives thus give rise to superficially ambiguous forms like *twenty odd years*, with two hypothetically possible meanings as shown in (17a–b), one being approximative and the other merely descriptive.

(17) a. twenty odd years
     = 20 or so years (i.e. approximative)
  b. twenty odd years
     = 20 strange years (i.e. descriptive)

However, there is no true ambiguity in this expression, at least in the spoken language. English speakers clearly distinguish the two by means of stress placement. In the descriptive (17b), both the numeral and the adjective *odd* receive full word stress, while in the approximative (17a) it is the numeral which receives primary stress and the *odd* element which receives a secondary stress. In other words, the *odd* element in the approximative is clearly forming a structural unit together with the numeral and does not have the status of an independent word. This is analogous to the behavior of compounds in English, as shown in a version of a well-known compound example given in (18). The second member of the expression, which otherwise would receive full word stress as in (a), is de-stressed when compounded in (b).

(18) a. We saw a BLACK BIRD sitting in the tree, not a red one.
  b. We saw a BLACKbird sitting in the tree, not a cardinal.

This allows us to conclude that the *-odd* element in approximative expressions is not an independent word but is functioning as some part of a larger unit together with the preceding numeral.

Should NUM-*odd* expressions then automatically be classified as compounds morphologically? We think not, in spite of the superficial similarity in stress placement. Although the NUM-*odd* expressions show the same stress pattern and the same orthography as English compounds (hyphenated or unhyphenated), there are two important differences, both involving meaning. First, the *-odd* element is not able to occur independently of the preceding numeral and retain its approximative meaning. Any independent occurrence of the form *odd* is always given the descriptive meaning of 'strange' or 'uneven'. This indicates that the approximative *-odd* element is a different lexical item from the descriptive *odd*, and is a bound morpheme rather than a free one. Second, the interpretation of *-odd* approximatives does not conform to the compositional pattern of meaning found in standard endocentric English compounds, in which the right-hand member of the compound is the head of the compound. (Williams 1981a,b). Thus *blackbird* is a kind of bird, *light green* is a shade of green, and *music teacher* is a kind of teacher. However, the interpretation of *twenty-odd* is not a compositional variation on the basic meaning of the lexeme *odd*. Instead, it seems more plausible to construe *twenty-odd* as a left-headed construction, at least in terms of meaning, with *-odd* functioning instead to vary or adjust the basic meaning of the numeral *twenty*. Therefore, we conclude that *-odd* must be a suffix or a clitic rather than the second member of a true compound. (We will examine the relationship between approximative *-odd* and descriptive *odd* further when we discuss the diachronic development of the approximative marker in section 4.)

Although Spencer (1991: 375ff) notes that there are unresolved difficulties in distinguishing clitics from words and affixes, he cites Klavans (1982, 1985) for a generally accepted principle that clitics attach to hosts that are phrasal. In other words, we would expect to find clitics forming the outer edge of a phrase, as the first or last element in a phrase. This does not seem to hold true of *-odd,* which does not necessarily appear at the edge of a structure. Specifically, approximative *-odd* may co-occur freely with another recognized English affix, the ordinal suffix *-eth/-th*, as in example (19b, c):

(19) a. twentieth
      b. twenty-oddth
      c. While I am spouting mad theories about national characteristics, I would like to expound here my theory that German sides' tendency to win big games right at the end, and often unjustly, is connected

with the way German speakers have to wait for the main verb at the end of a sentence, thus developing habits of patience and concentration. That characteristic German goal in the 80-oddth minute is a verb. (London Review of Books Vo. 24 no 13 11 July 2002)

Expressions like (19b) might seem unusual, but we have found that they are surprisingly common, especially in the contemporary register of internet discourse, from which (19c) is taken. Interestingly, *-oddth* expressions are not novel, but have been documented as far back as Jespersen (1942:440).

In a discussion of the allomorphy of *-eth/-th*, Manaster-Ramer (1987) begins with the statement that this morpheme is a regular derivational suffix in English used to create ordinal forms from cardinal numerals. Since approximative *-odd* always occurs closer to the numeral root when used in combination with *-eth/-th*, it cannot be a clitic but must be a suffix. In addition, it must also be considered a derivational suffix, if we accept the general wisdom that derivational affixes always occur closer to the root than inflectional affixes.

3.2 NUM-*odd* expressions: derived numerals

We have just concluded that approximative *-odd* is a derivational suffix which attaches to numeral stems. Does *-odd* then change the syntactic category of the stem? The classic tests for determination of category membership include meaning, substitution, and distribution. We applied those tests to the NUM-*odd* expression to determine which pre-nominal modifier category it should be identified with.

The results exemplified partially here in examples (20)–(22) indicate that the NUM-*odd* expression still behaves like a numeral modifier, which is perhaps not surprising. It continues to occupy the same position as the numeral in syntax, which can be seen in (20) where multiple pre-nominal modifiers of different types (determiners, adjectives, and possessives) are combined. Substitution is modeled in examples (20b) and (20c), where the numeral and NUM-*odd* are interchangeable.

(20) Multiple modifiers:
    a. Those few fifty-odd muddy miles before we arrived were the worst.
    b. Our last twenty-odd happy years together passed by all too quickly.
    c. Our last twenty happy years together passed by all too quickly.

A classification of numeral is further supported by example (21), which shows that the NUM-*odd* expression cannot be combined with another numeral modifier in the same phrase. Only one numeral modifier is allowed.

(21) Multiple Numeral modifiers:
     *thirty-odd thirty-eight years[6]

Finally, the behavior of NUM-*odd* with quantifiers and determiners follows the same pattern as bare numerals with these categories. That is, there are constraints governing the use of certain quantifiers with numerals. The addition of -*odd* to a numeral does not affect the acceptability of its use with a quantifier, which suggests that -*odd* does not alter the core meaning and categorial features of the numeral.

(22) Quantifiers and Determiners:
    a. *few twenty years/*few twenty-odd years
    b. every twenty years/every twenty-odd years the codes must be renewed
    c. *each fifty men/*each fifty-odd men
    d. All fifty men/all fifty-odd men passed the physical.
    e. ?many hundred miles/?many hundred-odd miles
    f. Some twenty years/some twenty-odd years had passed since they last met.
    g. These forty applications/these forty-odd applications were then processed.

In view of these results, the co-occurrence of -*odd* and ordinal -*eth*/-*th* noted above in Section 3.1 is to be expected. If the ordinal suffix regularly attaches to cardinal numerals, then approximative NUM-*odd* expressions are just a subclass of cardinal numerals.[7]

We conclude then that -*odd* is a derivational suffix which attaches consistently to cardinal numerals in English. It does not, however, affect the categorial status of the numeral. Its purpose is solely to introduce an approximative meaning into the basic meaning of the cardinal numeral. In this sense, its function is analogous to a derivational diminutive suffix, which introduces a diminutive meaning when added to nouns, but does not alter the categorial status or other syntactic features of the noun. The derived NUM-odd numeral is still free to participate in further derivation to become an ordinal with the addition of the suffix -*eth*/-*th*.

---

6. This is only possible as a repair or recast in conversation.

7. Kayne (2005: 15–18), in discussing the French approximative suffix -*aine* as in *centaine, douzaine*, etc, claims that there is no overt English equivalent. In the sense that -*aine* does change the categorial status of French cardinal numerals to transform them into nouns, while -*odd* does not, -*aine* and -*odd* are not equivalent. However, the approximative function of the two derivational suffixes is the same.

4. Origin and typology of -*odd*

In this section we will have a look at the etymology of NUM-*odd* as well as the place of NUM-*odd* within the typology of approximatives. It will be shown that the behavior of -*odd* can be satisfactorily explained by taking the origin and typology into account.

4.1. Etymology of -*odd*

The origin of the suffix -*odd* is, unsurprisingly, the word *odd*, denoting a surplus of remainder (OED entry for *odd*, lemma 3a). This use dates back to the 14th–15th century. Based on the OED examples, its earliest uses were with monetary items and with terms denoting weights and measures, but by the 17th century this use had broadened to include other count nouns as well. The structure of such examples is still NUM-*odd*-N, where *odd* is an adjective.

(23) The Mexicans divided the yeare into eighteene moneths, ascribing to each twentie dayes, so that the five odde dayes were excluded.
(*Pilgrimage*, by S. Purchas (1613–4))

Quite soon after the use described above, *odd* became used in constructions of the type NUM N1 (*and*) *odd* N2, where N2 is a count noun of lower rank than N1 (OED lemma 3b,c). The meaning of the adjective *odd* is still one of 'surplus', 'extra'.

(24) a. Than leveth there 38 degrees and odde minutes.
(Chaucer, *Treat. Astrolabe* II §25, 48 (1590))
b. The Moons Month … that is twenty seven daies and odd minutes.
(Sharp, *Midwives Bk.* V.x.297 (1671))
c. Thirty-eight thousand odd hundred infantry, two thousand odd hundred cavalry. (Wilson, *Private Diary* I. 434 (1813))

Soon N2 can be omitted and elliptically understood, giving a general sense of surplus without exactly specifying the surplus (OED lemma 4a).

(25) a. Distant sixtie miles and odde. (Herbert, *Relation Trav.* 134 (1634))
b. Bradbury and Evans's account for the half year is £1100 and odd.
(Dickens, *Let.* (30 Aug. 1846))
c. They were eyes that saw everything, that had been trained to see everything through all his twenty years and odd in the ring.
(London, *Piece of Steak* (1911))

Since the phrase *and odd* denotes a surplus of the same kind (though of lower denomination) as N1, it becomes possible to shift the *and odd* phrase to a position immediately preceding N1, yielding the construction NUM *and odd* N1 (OED lemma 4b).

> (26) a. Now wee so quietly followed our businesse that in 3 monthes, we made 3 or 4 Last of Pitch, and tarre, and sope ashes; ... of 3 sowes, in one yeare increased 60 and od pigges.   (Symonds, *Proc. Colony* xi. 85 (1612))
>
> b. Having ridden post day and night fourscore and odd miles ... (Kenrick, *Falstaff's Wedding* I.v.5 (1760))
>
> c. A man ... weighing two hundred and odd pounds.   (Faulkner, *As I lay dying* (1930))

Finally, the *and* is omitted and *odd* becomes suffixed to the numeral (OED lemma 4c and paper above). This use dates from the 16th century, based on OED examples.

> (27) a. Eightie odd yeares of sorrow haue I seene.   (Shakespeare, *Richard III* IV. i. 95 (1597))
>
> b. Hendrick, the Indian who went out ... to annoy the French in their Out-Settlements at Canada, with thirty odd Indians.   (Boston Newsletters, 16 July 1747)
>
> c. He gazed at six foot odd of gorgeousness, as represented by Sir Percy Blakeney, Bart.   (= (5) above)

The meaning of *-odd* can still be 'surplus', i.e., above numeral but not below. However, it is now apparently also possible to use *-odd* as a general approximative, i.e. as meaning 'about'.

4.2 Typology of approximatives

In this section we will consider *-odd* from a typological perspective and how well it fits with other expressions of approximation in the world's languages. The non-*odd*-related data here are based on Plank (2004b).

There are many ways in which approximation can be expressed, both syntactic and morphological. Some examples of syntactic approximation include:

– inversion of numeral and noun, Russian:

> (28) a. pjat' knig   b. knig   pjat'
>   five book.GEN.PL   book.GEN.PL five
>   'Five books'   'About five books'

Chapter 2. The approximative expression NUM-*odd*   **51**

– using two numerals to express a range (very common):

(29)   English: five to ten books

(30)   Dutch: tussen de tachtig en negentig kippen
                'between 80 and 90 chickens'

Morphological strategies include, among others:

– reduplication, Fongbe:

(31)   ðégbà   'four thousand'
       ðégbàðégbà   'thousands'

– special affixes

(32)   English: six-ish 'about six'
                 twenty-odd

(33)   Italian: una trent-ina di polli
                 'about 30 chickens'

(34)   Dutch: een dertig-tal kippen
                 'about 30 chickens'

(35)   Finnish: kolm-isen vuotta
                 three-APPROX year
                 'about three years'

Therefore, from the point of view of morphology, *-odd* is fairly unremarkable. What sets this suffix apart from other morphemes such as English *-ish* or Italian *-ina* is the fact that it sets an explicit lower limit (the numeral to which *-odd* is attached) and an implicit upper limit (the next level depending on the level of the preceding numeral, i.e. whether it is a numeral based on 10, 100 or 1,000). See (36), repeated from (2) above.

(36)   Approx   Range
       twenty-odd   from 20 to 30
       two hundred-odd   from 200 to 300
       two thousand-odd from 2,000 to 3,000

Based on Plank (2004b) this use is decidedly unique and no doubt rooted in the fact that *-odd* derives from a word meaning 'surplus'. There are of course words such as English *at least* or Dutch *minstens* 'at least' which give an explicit lower limit, but these words do not give an upper limit. The expression *at least 200 chickens* does not give us a range but merely tells us the lower limit.

Approximatives in other languages typically either give an explicit range (examples (29) and (30) above) or, when they occur by themselves, they denote more or less a "middle" point rather than a lower bound. It is probably still the case that NUM-*odd* when combined with lower level numbers (the 'tens') expresses a range with NUM as the lower limit, especially when combined with nouns such as *year* (the prototypical instance). However, at higher levels, such as *two thousand-odd* the NUM-*odd* construction is turning into a true approximative and can be used in the sense 'about'.

5. Conclusions

In these twenty-odd manuscript pages we have presented our findings on the use, semantics, structural status, etymology, and typological place of the English approximative expression NUM-*odd*. We can now say that the derivational affix -*odd*, which originates in the adjective *odd*, is added to round numerals in English to produce approximatives which delimit a lower bound for a range. In this sense, it is unique typologically among approximative expressions.

References

Channell, J. 1980. More on approximations: A reply to Wachtel. *Journal of Pragmatics* 4:461–76.
Greenberg, J. 1978. Generalizations about number systems. In *Universals of Human Language,* Vol 3, J. Greenberg, (ed.), 249–95. Stanford CA: Stanford University Press.
Gvozdanović, J. (ed.). 1992. *Indo-European Numerals*. Berlin: Mouton.
Heine, B. 1997. *Cognitive Foundations of Grammar*. Oxford: OUP.
Hurford, J. R. 1975. *The Linguistic Theory of Numerals*. Cambridge: CUP.
Hurford, J. R. 1987. *Language and Number: The Emergence of a Cognitive System*. Oxford: Basil Blackwell.
Jespersen, O. 1942. *A Modern English Grammar on Historical Principles,* Part VI: *Morphology*. Copenhagen: Munksgaard.
Kayne, R. S. 2005. Some notes on comparative syntax. In *Oxford Handbook of Comparative Syntax*, G. Cinque & R. S. Kayne (eds), 3–69. Oxford: OUP.
Klavans, J. 1982. *Some Problems in a Theory of Clitics*. Bloomington IN: IULC.
Klavans, J. 1985. The independence of syntax and phonology in cliticization. *Language* 61:95–120.
Langendoen, D. T. 2006. Disjunctive numerals of estimation. *Style* 40:46–55.
Manaster-Ramer, A. 1987. –eth. *Folia Linguistica* 13:355–62.
Plank, F. 2004a. Inevitable reanalysis: from local adpositions to approximative adnumerals, in German and wherever. *Studies in Language* 28:165–201.
Plank, F. 2004b. How to disclaim precision about numbers. Handout of paper read at the Leipzig Numerals Workshop, March 2004.

Spencer, A. 1991. *Morphological Theory*. Londohn: Blackwell.

Wachtel, T. 1980. Pragmatic approximations. *Journal of Pragmatics* 4:201–11.

Williams, E. 1981a. On the notions 'lexically related' and 'head of a word'. *Linguistic Inquiry* 12: 245–74.

Williams, E. 1981b. Argument structure and morphology. *The Linguistic Review* 1:81–114.

CHAPTER 3

Skating along the syntactic verge

Experimental pragmatics and understood elements of content

Merrill Garrett and Robert M. Harnish
University of Arizona

This chapter discusses elements of communicative content that are not expressed by overt elements of a sentence. In the 1970s and 1980s, mostly inspired by the work of Grice, forms of 'unexpressed elements of content' not contemplated by linguistic theory of the time began to surface under a variety of labels, collectively called 'impliciture' here. It is argued in this chapter that recent experimental work suggests that certain forms of impliciture are tied to language via "standardization" which provides a pragmatic scenario that does not require access to potentially unbounded domains of general background information.

1. Introduction

When we understand language, we are, by conventional construal of the process, reconstructing the speaker's thought. The physical elements of an utterance are data that listeners use to identify and represent the relevant thought of the speaker. But, that is not all the 'data'. Indispensable additional information resides in the context of utterance and in background information in the mind of the listener. The dynamic combination of these two information sources with the physical form of the utterance determines the outcome of the comprehension process.

The notion that the explicit form of an utterance is the primary driver of language processing is often described as a kind of 'bottom up' priority for language comprehension, and there is much in the experimental literature on language processing to support some version of that idea. One does, after all, want some defense against wholesale hallucination. But, one does not march very far into the web of language use before encountering equally strong evidence for constraints derived from the projection of several kinds of background information onto the acoustic (or orthographic, or signed) data stream. These range from the sublimely metaphoric to the most mundanely literal. How is the balance struck between form-driven and knowledge-driven processing in a way that combines veridical perception with our fluent appreciation of the force of an unexpected turn of phrase, a bit of whimsy, or a creative metaphor? We are inclined to the view that the answer lies in the multi-systems approaches that have emerged in many cognitive domains over the past couple of decades. Wherever the research probe has been stuck — memory, human judgment and decision making, mathematical reasoning, social reasoning, and so on, we find a collection of specialized systems from whose interaction the fabric of performance in that domain emerges. We will return to this issue.

The infrastructure of phonetics, phonology, morphology, and phrasal syntax are the conservative focus of bottom up analysis approaches to language. Processes based on such structures deal in a sharply limited range of information, and their real-time application to the analysis of a signal is, while complex, demonstrably manageable. Matters become more difficult as syntax becomes more complex and as information not explicitly represented in standard grammar is required for capturing interpretive options. The difficulty is, as Fodor (1983) outlined the matter in his monograph on modularity, that the range of facts to which interpretation of a sentence is potentially responsive is open. This complicates enormously the computational problem that must be solved in real time. It is the limitation on access to information that motivates the informational encapsulation move in modularity theory. And, it is the unencapsulated nature of information relevant to the interpretive nexus of utterance, speaker and context that makes the pragmatic problem so acutely compelling. We know that people can solve this problem and that they can do it in a time frame captured by the rhythms of normal conversational interaction.

The phenomena we discuss encompass examples of plausibly bounded application of non-linguistic constraint to linguistic decision. Indeed, there is controversy about whether some examples should be dealt with within syntax or in some "pragmatic" way. Thinking about these problems invites an experimental pragmatics that usefully broadens basic psycholinguistic processing theory. A variety of related phenomena identifiable from early to recent studies can be linked to pragmatic theory at several points. We will take note of these in following sections.

2. Understood elements of content

The idea that there are "understood" elements of content associated with sentences (and fragments of sentences) has been an important part of linguistic theory since at least the early work in transformational grammar. We look briefly at some examples of these and their treatment over the ensuing years.

Syntactic Ellipsis: Famously (and notoriously), early transformational grammars posited a variety of operations that removed surface pronounceable aspects

Chapter 3. The syntactic verge: Experimental pragmatics   **57**

of underlying[1] (syntactically categorized and semantically interpreted) material on condition of "recoverability".[2] Many of these went under the label of "syntactic" ellipsis, and the operations had labels such as:[3]

Gapping	Mary hit the hay and John the bottle.
VP Deletion	The man who didn't leave saw the man who did.
Comparative Deletion	Mary found more counterexamples than John found.
PP Deletion	Mary is at the door and Betty is too
Subject–Verb Gapping	John ate dinner last night, and breakfast this morning.
Sluicing	Mary is at the door and I wonder why.
Stripping	Mary likes to surf but not Betty.[4]

Pragmatic Ellipsis: The syntactically motivated cases contrast with "pragmatic" ellipsis. Here, information is understood not because it is in the sentence and not pronounced, but because it can be assigned a place in the sentence from context; i.e., immediate context can fill out the content. Sometimes this is verbal:

> *Do you ski? Yes (I ski)*

Sometimes it is situational or perceptual:

> We both notice Hulk Hogan entering the room: *(That guy is) Big!*

Interestingly, there appear to be eliptical processes which must be syntactically controlled and cannot be pragmatically controlled.[5] So, compare (28) and (29); (31) and (32) (original numbers)

Stripping:

(26)   Alan likes to play volley ball, but not Sandy

(28)   *Hankamer*: Listen, Ivan, he's playing the William Tell Overture on the recorder.
       Sag: Yeah, but not very well.

---

1. 'Underlying' is supposed to be neutral between "deep" structures, "d" structures and anything else syntactic, but not surface structure.

2. See e.g. Akmajian and Heny (1975: ch. 7). This included identity with material left behind, as well as identity to material in the rule itself (see below).

3. See e.g. Williams (1977) and Sag and Hankamer (1977) for discussion.

4. Note that it is not easy to see the elliptical version as simply missing the elliptical parts: *Mary likes to surf, but not Betty likes to surf. Rather: Mary likes to surf, but Betty does not like to surf.

5. These examples are from Sag and Hankamer (1977). See also Stainton (1995, 1997), Elugardo and Stainton (2005) for more discussion of the distinction between syntactic and pragmatic ellipsis.

(29) [Sag plays William Tell Overture on a recorder] Hankamer: *Yeah, but not very well.

Gapping:

(30) Erlichman duped Haldeman, and Nixon, [duped] Erlichman

(31) *Hankamer*: Ivan is now going to peel an apple.
Sag: And Jorge, an orange.

(32) [Hankamer produces an orange, proceeds to peel it, and just as Sag produces an apple, says:] *And Ivan, an apple.

Lexically Specified Deletion: There were also cases of understood elements associated with specific transformations, whose condition of recoverability was that the operation "mentioned" particular lexical items. Consider, for instance, the Imperative Transformation of Akmajian and Heny (1975, 236), which deletes the lexical items 'you' and 'will':[6]

$$you-Tense-will-VP \Rightarrow VP$$

A variant of the imperative case used abstract syntactic and semantic units which "surfaced" in radically different forms. For instance, Katz and Postal (1963), implementing the idea that transformations can't "change" meaning (as the Imperative Transformation above does), posited underlying morphemes 'IMP' and 'Q' that received a "performative" semantic interpretation,[7] were never pronounced, and caused the syntactic changes characteristic of imperatives (no subject) and interrogatives (inversion, rising intonation). So, we get derivations such as:

Q the book is where $\Rightarrow$ The book is WHERE?, Where is the book?
IMP You will leave the room $\Rightarrow$ Leave the room!

In each case, Q and IMP are deleted (in some cases along with other material), but are recoverable from characteristic surface features of the sentence.[8]

Empty Categories and Null Elements: More recent linguistic theory changed the categories and operations involved, both eliminating and explaining them, but

---

6. See also the Dative Movement (184), and Agent Deletion (247) transformations for more of the same.

7. To IMP "we can assign the sense of 'the speaker requests (asks, demands, insists etc.) that'" (76), and to Q "I request you to answer ..." (89).

8. The Higher Performative Hypothesis of Generative Semantics is clearly a variant on Katz and Postal --just replace the IMP and Q morphemes with their (e.g. English) paraphrases.

the idea of understood elements of content remained. For instance, GB theory recognized a variety of elements that are unspoken (and unspeakable) at their underlying location and hence have unspoken occurrences:[9]

> NP-trace: The story$_i$ was fabricated e/t$_i$ by the re-election committee,
> The re-election$_i$ committee seems e/t$_i$ to have fabricated the evidence
> Wh-trace: Who$_i$ does Mary think I like e/t$_i$?

And, at least one element (in English) does not involve simply being an unspoken occurrence, but is unspoken *simpliciter*:

> PRO: PRO to vote for Bush is PRO to vote for war.

In GB theory, these null elements have different linguistic properties,[10] but share the property that they are not pronounced at all (PRO), or not pronounced at the "null" occurrence(s).

Argument Structure: Finally, both early transformational grammar and more recent versions have a lexicon as a (or the) repository of idiosyncratic, unsystematic elements in the language, and this seems to include the number and nature of arguments of e.g. a verb,[11] which in English (and perhaps other languages) can range from one to three:[12]

> 1 (intransitive): to sneeze (Sx)
> 2 (transitive): to hit (Hxy)
> 3 (ditransitive): to give (Gxyz)

In GB theory, argument places are associated with two other pieces of information: (i) their subcategorization, and (ii) their thematic or theta roles. There is wide variation how this information is represented. For instance subcategorization can be represented:[13]

---

9. See Sells (1985) and Haegeman (1991) for introductory surveys.

10. In general, a wh-trace is [-a, -p], and a NP-trace is [+a, -p], PRO is [+a, +p]. Here +a = anaphor and so is governed by principle A of Binding Theory (bound in its Governing Category), and +p = pronominal and so is governed by principle B of Binding Theory (free in its Governing Category). PRO, having contradictory properties if having a Governing Category, consequently has no Governing Category in GB theory.

11. We leave the question of the number and nature of arguments for adjective, prepositions and nouns open.

12. See Jackendoff (1987) and Dowty (1991) for discussions of thematic relations in general, not just in GB theory.

13. See Haegeman (1991, chapter 3) for a discussion of argument structure in GB theory.

smile: verb, 1-NP
kill: verb, 1-NP 2-NP
give: verb, 1-NP 2-NP/PP 3-NP

And theta structure can be represented in a thematic (or theta) "grid" (we collapse the grid — the subscripts should be under the NPs):

kill: verb AGENT-NP$_i$ PATIENT-NP$_j$

Sometimes the information is merged (where angles indicate subcategorization, and underlining indicates external argument or subject):[14]

smile: V, (<u>Agent</u>)
kill: V ⟨NP⟩, (<u>Agent</u>, Theme)
give: V, ⟨NP, PP⟩, (<u>Agent</u>, Theme, Goal)

It has been argued (Perry (1986), et al) that some verbs surface as one-place syntactic relations, but are semantically two-place relations:

It is raining $(R(t,p))$

It has also been noted (Bach 2001: s. 5.4), Recanati (2004: 98-99)) that some verbs with very similar meanings, at least on a reading, and hence presumably very similar underlying argument structure, have different surface argument structure[15] (* = ungrammatical, @ = grammatical, but not the right content, and parentheses mark understood content):[16]

> *finished* (Fx,y): John finished the novel, John finished (something) vs
> *completed* (Cx,y): John completed the novel, John completed (*0, something)
>
> *eat* (Ex,y): John ate dinner, John ate (something) vs
> *hear* (Hx,y): John heard the car, John heard (@something, something from context)
>
> *attempt* (Ax,y): John tried three times vs *John attempted three times

---

14. See Sells (1985).

15. This appears to conflict with intuitions that argument structure and thematic roles are semantically determined. For instance Haegeman (1991, 35) "Whether a verb is transitive or not is not a matter of mere chance; it follows from the type of action or state expressed by the verb, from the meaning".

16. And perhaps: John put it on the table (*John put it) vs John set it down on the table (John set it down).

Such argument structure is a potential source for understood elements of content.

Overall, we have numerous sources of understood elements of content (UECs) — elements that (i) are associated with specific locations in sentence structure, and (ii) are not pronounced or written. Some UEC are "understood" occurrences (syntactic ellipsis, movement: NP, Wh traces) where the missing material can be linked to the content of (other) overt material in the sentence. Call these cases "Linked" UECs. Still others are understood simpliciter, and their content cannot be traced to other overt material. Call these "Unlinked" or "Free" UECs. Free UECs can be associated with the underlying structure of the sentence (PRO, argument structure), or can supplement overt material that is fragmentary to make a whole content (pragmatic ellipsis).[17] Against this background of linguistically oriented cases, we turn to pragmatics and to recently emphasized types of understood content that go under a variety of labels. Part of the challenge is to uncover the nature of the data, as well as in the mechanisms proposed to account for them. It is an open question to what extent these data are distinct from the free UECs just surveyed.

3. Implicature and impliciture: pure pragmatics

Recent pragmatics has uncovered a category of content that is putatively non-Gricean, i.e. is not a part of the meaning of the sentence, is not a part of what Grice would have called what is said, and is not a part of what is traditionally considered a (particularized) conversational implicature.[18] We will steal a term from Bach (1994) and call this class of understood elements of content 'implicitures'. We will represent this information in square brackets. This content, or the process of providing it, has various labels: 'default heuristic', 'unarticulated constituent', 'explicature', and 'impliciture'. This variety suggests a family of conceptually distinct but overlapping phenomena, though the relations among them have not been sorted out. Indeed, as we will see, there is good reason to distinguish subtypes among these examples.

---

17. We leave open the question of "whole" contents — i.e. whether they are or must be complete propositions, or whether they can be "propositional functions" — contents that become propositions when supplemented. A problem with this idea is that any bit of content is a propositional function in the sense that a proposition could be built out of it. Frege (who spoke of "concepts") and Russell (from whom we get the above term) solved this problem by tying the notion to predication.

18. Harnish (1976) argues, in effect, that Grice had the category, but not a label — his label was "Group A" implicatures, where no maxim is flouted.

Here is a brief review of the main categories of, and/or mechanisms of providing, information that is communicated, but (i) it is not said, and (ii) it is not a particularized conversational implicature (i.e involving the flouting and exploitation of a maxim).

Grice (1975) introduced generalized conversational implicature (GCIs) to mark off a class of implicatures with the distinctive feature that uttering the expression involved would "normally" carry the implicature, unlike "particularized" conversational implicatures that require special circumstances to be understood:

> 'He's meeting a woman [not his wife, mother, sister, or close Platonic friend] tonight.'
> 'He went inside a [someone else's] house and found a tortoise.'
> 'He broke a [his] finger.'

Perry (1986) introduced the term 'unarticulated constituent' (UC) for an element of thought expressed in an utterance not linked to items in the sentence uttered (and hence "unarticulated"). He did not propose any specific mechanisms for recovering this constituent in communication:[19]

> 'It is raining.' [here, in X]
> 'Everyone [in domain D] came to the party.'
> 'Bill is tall.' [relative to X]

Sperber and Wilson (1986) introduced the term 'explicature' for similar phenomena (see also Carston, 1988, 2002) and proposed that they be explained with mechanisms of enrichment (spelled out in terms of relevance theory):

> 'I've had breakfast.' [today, on X]
> 'It will take us some [longer than expected] time to get there.'
> 'He went to the edge of the cliff and jumped.' [off the cliff]

Recanati (1989, 1993, 2004) agreed with most of this data, but introduced some of his own terminology. He distinguished between what he called (i) "primary" pragmatic processes, devoted either to building a proposition from a non-proposition using procedures of "saturation" or building an enriched proposition using procedures of "strengthening", "loosening, and "metonymical (semantic) transfer",

---

19. The idea that there are such constituents has recently been challenged by Stanley and Szabo (2000) and Stanley (2000), but defended by Bach (2000) and differently by Recanati (2002, 2004). More recently, Borg (2004) and Capellen and Lepore (2005) have argued against purely pragmatic UECs. Expect a host of replies to Capellen and Lepore.

Chapter 3. The syntactic verge: Experimental pragmatics   **63**

and (ii) "secondary" pragmatic processes, mostly devoted to traditional conversational implicature.

Bach (1994) also agreed with much of the above data and added some of his own. He distinguished between "completion" implicitures (similar to saturation), and "expansion" implicitures. Unlike Sperber and Wilson, Carston and Recanati, Bach follows Grice in holding to a narrow, strict construal of what is said, one in which the words, their order and grammatical construction must be respected.[20]

> 'You won't die.' [from that]
> 'Steel isn't strong enough.' [for/to do that]
> 'There is beer [to drink] in the fridge.'

Levinson (1995, 2000), adapting Grice's category of (GCIs), proposed that communication is governed by a small number of shared "Default Heuristics" that allow a speaker to compress, and the hearer to correspondingly expand, a message in the face of articulatory restrictions, "a significant bottleneck" in the human vocal–auditory channel:[21]

> 'Some [not all] of the students failed the exam.' (Q-Heuristic)
> 'He opened the door.' [in the normal way] (I-Heuristic)
> 'Ann turned the key and [thereby intentionally] started the engine.'
> (I-Heuristic)
> 'He turned the handle and pushed open the door.' [did not open the door
> in the normal way] (M-Heuristic)

We will later return in more detail to Levinson's distinctions and to phenomena treated in terms of Q and I heuristics.

Looking across the spectrum of impliciture examples, we find numerous controversies regarding these contents. Are they semantic or pragmatic? Are they really not a part of what is said, nor a part of what is implicated? Are they linguistically represented or not? Are they subject to compositional mechanisms? Is the information recovered during sentence comprehension or after sentence comprehension? And what are the mechanisms that provide this information during comprehension? These questions have been difficult to convincingly resolve using only the methods of intuition and argument. The experimental methodology of psycholinguistics, to which we now turn, provides complementary observations that suggest answers to some of these questions and in particular, indicates significant processing differences among impliciture phenomena

---

20. See Bird (1997) and Vicente (2002) for further discussion of Bach.

21. See Bezuidenhout (2002) for further discussion of Levinson.

4. Experimental pragmatics: studies of impliciture phenomena

We review two classes of experimental work on understood elements of content. These have lessons for which modes of experimental enquiry are likely to be informative and some preliminary conclusions about the language processing systems that account for implicitures. Our discussion divides semi-historically into two parts. In the first part, we look at experimental tests of subjects' *categorization* of utterance contents as a part of what is "said" vs implicatures and implicitures. Can distinctions developed in pragmatic theory be elicited from naive language users in categorization tasks? This is a species of "psychological reality" question that used a mixture of metalinguistic judgments and intuitions about sentence and speaker meaning. The outcomes are not compelling with regard to such judgments as vehicles for investigating and clarifying impliciture phenomena. These methods do not seem to hold the potential for advances over pure pragmatic approaches --though the sentence types in focus formed the foundation for the studies we discuss in the second part of our review. In that second part, we discuss a different class of experiments centered on *mechanisms* for the recovery of implicatures and implicitures during language comprehension tasks. These raise essential questions about pragmatic processing that parallel longstanding concerns in the psycholinguistic study of sentence comprehension. The available experimental outcomes argue for significant processing differences between two subclasses of implicitures. These differences suggest multifaceted links between pragmatic processing and basic sentence processing.

Categorization: what is said vs what is implicated
Grice (1975/1989) famously distinguished what is said from what is implicated, within "the total signification of an utterance". Subsequent work in (pure) pragmatics has foundered somewhat on competing criteria and intuitions for drawing this distinction.[22] Recanati (1989) introduced his controversial "Availability" principle which, in its most recent incarnation, takes the form of the following constraint on what is said:[23]

Availability: What is said must be intuitively accessible to the conversational participants (unless something goes wrong and they do not count as 'normal interpreters'). (2004: 20).

---

22. There is no evidence for the claim that, for Grice, what is implicated is distinctive for the maxims of conversation.

23. He also puts it as the 'Availability Principle': "'what is said' must be analyzed in conformity to the intuitions shared by those who fully understand the utterance --typically the speaker and the hearer, in a normal conversational setting." (2004, 14)

Although this is only a necessary condition, it is tempting to strengthen it to a sufficient condition as well. Doing so suggests that if 'normal' interpreters think something is said, it *is* said. Going further down this path, one might suppose that we could discover what is said by surveying what normal interpreters think is said when presented with various utterances. And, if what is said is controversial, then perhaps such results might adjudicate the disputes. Bach (1994) early on questioned this idea, noting that normal speakers might conflate extraneous pragmatic information with intrinsic semantic information. Relying on normal interpreters to identify what is said would have to be a circumspect affair that would involve giving them not only controversial cases, but structurally similar cases that are not controversial, as well as contexts in which the implicit material is canceled.[24]

The first experimental study of the categorization by ordinary speakers of what is "said" vs what is "implicated" was Gibbs and Moise (1997). Their experiments were examined and repeated in later work by Nicolle and Clark (1999) and again, by Bezuidenhout and Cutting (2002). The three sets of experiments are thus closely matched and afford interesting comparisons that test the idea immanent in the availability principle. The Gibbs and Moise (1997) experiments were designed to determine:

> if people distinguished what speakers say, or what is said, from what speakers implicate, and to see if people viewed speakers' said meanings [what speakers said] as being determined by enriched pragmatic knowledge (i.e. pragmatic information beyond that needed to determine lexical disambiguation and reference assignment).

They used five categories of sentences in their tests; all relate to various of the impliciture phenomena we earlier reviewed. Their first two experiments manipulated the instructions to subjects for categorizing interpretations of examples of each category illustrated below. No context was provided. Subjects made a forced choice between minimal vs "expanded" or "enriched" interpretation, as indicated; the enriched versions correspond to impliciture.

> Cardinal sentences
> *Jane has three children.*
> a. *Minimal*: Jane has at least three children, but may have more.
> b. *Enriched*: Jane has exactly three children (no more, no less).

---

24. Recanati (2004: 15–16) endorses Bach's reservations. However, Recanati suggests there might be other, more indirect, methods for getting at what is said --for example, showing subjects pictures of situations and asking them whether q target utterance is true or false relative to that situation. Given that Recanati (ibid, 14) "take[s] the conversational participant's intuitions concerning what is said to be revealed by their views concerning the utterance's truth-conditions", this might, he thinks, give us the sought after information.

Possession sentences
Robert broke a finger last night.
a. *Minimal*: Robert broke someone's finger last night[25]
b. *Enriched*: Robert broke his own finger last night

Scalar sentences
Everyone went to Paris.
a. *Minimal*: Every single person in the entire world went to Paris
b. *Enriched*: Every singe person in some group went to Paris

Time–distance sentences
It will take us some time to get there.
a. *Minimal*: The time between our departure and arrival is unspecified
b. *Enriched*: It will take us a fairly long time to reach our destination

Temporal relation sentences
The old king died of a heart attack and a republic was declared.
a. *Minimal*: The old king died of a heart attack and republic was declared. (Order of events is unspecified.)
b. *Enriched*: The old king died of a heart attack and then a republic was declared

The outcome was that the enriched interpretation was strongly preferred (84%). Minimal interpretation was not favored in any condition. Experiment 2 attempted a more stringent test. G&M changed the instructions to briefly tutor subjects in the minimal-expanded distinction and then repeated experiment I. The results were similar: the more explicit instructions had little effect. For our purposes, the striking outcome is that subjects felt free to add substantial amounts of distinct conceptual material in the paraphrase and claim that it was 'what was said'. The instructions seemed open to very broad interpretation.

Experiment 3 manipulated context. Test sentences were preceded by a story biasing for an implicature. Subjects made a forced choice between the E-interpretation and a contextually appropriate implicature:

Bill wanted to date his co-worker Jane. But Bill really didn't know much about her. Being a bit shy, he first talked to another person, Fred. Fred knew Jane fairly well. Bill wondered if Jane was single. Fred replied: 'Jane has three children.'
a. *Implicature*: Jane is married
b. *Enriched*: Jane has exactly three children

---

25. Gibbs and Moise give: 'Robert broke a finger, either his own or someone else's'. But that is not plausibly the "minimal" interpretation.

Even in such contexts, subjects continued to favor the enriched interpretation (86%) over the implicature. This suggests a strong bias for impliciture that we will see other evidence for later.

Experiment 4 changed the context manipulation to favor the *minimal interpretations* (these were *non-preferred* interpretations in experiments 1 and 2. For example:

> A boy scout troop was doing its civic service by cleaning up the park in the middle of town. The park was a mess and the scouts needed many rakes and shovels to do the job. One scout noted that there weren't enough rakes for everyone and said that two more were needed. The scout master told him to go to the hardware store and ask for Ralph. The master said to the scout: 'Ralph has two rakes'
> a. *Enriched*: Ralph has exactly two rakes
> b. *Minimal*: Ralph has at least two rakes.

Subject preferences now reversed: the contextually supported minimal interpretations were strongly preferred (90%). So, suitable context did defeat the impliciture.

These outcomes showed that an "enriched" interpretation was preferred when test sentences (related to Grice's GCIs) were presented without context. The preference was not affected by instruction or training towards the minimal interpretation, and, surprisingly, it was preferred even in contexts geared to PCIs. But, it could be overridden in favor of minimal interpretations in suitable contexts. So instruction of the sort used by G&M did not affect judgments, but context did, and powerfully. This is an important thread that runs through the experiments we discuss here.

Nicolle and Clark (1999) reviewed and criticized aspects of G&M's experiments 1 and 2, (mostly regarding stimulus materials). They then presented three experiments of their own. The first experiment is of particular interest to us. It was based on G&M experiment 3. In N&C's experiment 1, subjects were given a story context, with a target sentence at the end and two paraphrase choices:

> An informal five-a-side football match had been arranged for Saturday morning at 11:30. That morning was warm and sunny, and over twenty people showed up. 'Can we play two five-a-side matches at the same time?' asked Steve. John answered, 'Billy's got two footballs.'
> a. *Enriched*: Billy has exactly two footballs and no more than two
> b. *Implicature*: There are enough footballs to play two matches

Subjects were tested in three instruction conditions: They were instructed to:

- Condition 1: "select the paraphrase that best reflected what each sentence said" (346).[26]
- Condition 2: "select the paraphrase that best reflected what the speaker's words meant" (in case Subjects had a different use of 'what is said') (346).
- Condition 3: "select the paraphrase that best reflected what the speaker wanted to communicate." (346)

The outcome was similar to G&M's. There was no effect of instruction. Subjects seemed indifferent to the variations, as if 'saying', 'meaning', and 'communicating' were virtually interchangeable. But, another result differed from G&M's in an interesting way. This was the effect of contextually driven preferences. N&C's contexts yielded a preference for *the implicature* rather than the enriched interpretation. Context design in the two studies produced different preference ranking. Whatever account may be offered for this, it is abundantly clear that contextual constraint is highly labile, and that fact must be systematically addressed in any experimentation. The work next discussed does so.

Bezuidenhout and Cutting (2002) presented a modified replication of the N&C experiments. Sentences represented the five categories from G&M's original study, with one added type: 'perfectives' (e.g., "I've had breakfast" — see section B). B&C ran a norming test (experiment 1) to establish a range of subject responses to the target sentences. Each sentence was preceded by a context, as in the example:

> Jane is going to New York. She needs a place to stay. She has two friends in New York, Brian and Paul. She does not know who to stay with. Another friend, Martha, knows that Jane is allergic to animals. When Jane asks Martha for advice Martha says: 'Brian has three cats.'

Subjects generated short lists of things a speaker might have been trying to communicate (re the context situations). From the lists, B&C derived a set of forced choice alternatives that distilled the most frequent notions in the data set. Then, they tested effects of instruction on distinguishing among the alternatives. They tested the same three instructional conditions as N&C did. The five response categories appear below. Instructional variation had no impact. The results differed only in minor ways across the conditions. Values averaged across the three conditions were:

- Minimal: Brain has at least three cats 6.3%
- Explicature: Brian has exactly three cats 23.55%

---

26. Note that sentences don't normally "say" anything, people do --this goes for G&M too. In so far as S's share this view, their responses might not be indicative of much that is theoretically interesting.

Chapter 3. The syntactic verge: Experimental pragmatics   **69**

- Strong implicature: Jane should stay with Paul 38.43%
- Weak implicature: Brian likes cats 9.17%
- Implicated premise: Brian's cats will cause Jane to have an allergic reaction 22.56%

The finding of no effect of instruction matched previous results. But, the outcome was even more complex — there was not even a strong dominant response. Clearly, the instructions were not understood in a uniform way. Responses were spread fairly evenly across the three most frequent response types. As a group, the subjects did not distinguish what was said, communicated or what the words meant. For example, subjects given 'Brain has three cats' in the above story context, did not reliably identify 'Jane should stay with Paul' as distinct re what was said, communicated or as the meaning of the sentence. Notice that this sentence shares not a single word-concept with the original. Similarly, for 'Brian's cats will cause Jane to have an allergic reaction' — and this sentence shares only a single word-concept ('Brian') with the original. The instructions seem roughly equivalent for very different responses.

How did subjects evaluate the test sentence 'Brian has three cats.'? Several interpretive options were viable, as demonstrated by the fact that the test scenarios displayed a robust division of preferences. But, keep in mind: subjects introspected about their understanding of the test sentences and the contexts. Thus, factors beyond those derivable directly from the target materials were in play (e.g., strategic decision and subject's understanding of the task). Moreover, their choices might well have been made at the point where the procedure called for a response, and **not** at the stage of initial comprehension. Presuppositions and pragmatic possibilities were explicitly presented in the option set, and choice among them driven by a subject's judgment of what the experimenter wanted or needed to hear. One needs an earlier window into the process if initial comprehension is the target.

In summary, the three experiments yielded similar results: naive subjects are insensitive to distinctions regarding what is said, what words mean, and what is communicated. The ordinary use of 'say' seems so flexible as to be virtually useless in theorizing. 'Availability' tested in this way is not a promising diagnostic. But, this indifference to instructions did not carry over to contextual influences. All three papers reported success in steering subjects to minimal or enriched interpretations by manipulating the context. That is our next focus. In particular, the objective is to determine whether there is, in fact, a uniformity of mental processes associated with pragmatic interpretation in context. Some models of processing deny this, treating every interpretation as "unique" because of interaction with context. Others postulate some commonalities across interpretive responses that accommodate context.

Mechanisms and processes: what is said vs what is implicated

We begin with continued attention to Bezuidenhout and Cutting (2002). They turned their efforts to processing issues in the final two experiments of that report (experiments 3 and 4). Recall that although minimal interpretations were clearly not favored in preference data for *any* of the experiments we reviewed, they were readily elicited by suitable context. B&C posed this general question re contextually driven interpretations: Is there a necessary stage in pragmatic processing at which a minimal proposition is recovered? This question requires measures sensitive to the time course of the mental processes that lead to a preference. B&C identified three processing models from the literature for test.

- *Literal-First Serial Model (LFS)*: Intended as a Gricean model; the minimal proposition must be recovered (including reference fixing and disambiguation) before pragmatic processing.
- *Ranked Parallel Model (RP)*: This was meant to represent the views of Gibbs and of Levinson. Minimal and enriched interpretations are constructed in parallel, but ranked by "accessibility". The enriched version(s) are ranked over the minimal one(s).
- *Local Pragmatic Processing Model (LPP)*: This invokes Relevance Theory (though it is compatible with other positions as well). Pragmatic processes are continuous from the beginning of the utterance. Full contextual interaction occurs as the utterance unfolds.

B&C's experiment 3 evaluated new materials to represent the six categories in their experiment 2. Test sentences were paired with two kinds of stories. One biased towards an enriched interpretation, and the other towards a minimal interpretation. Subjects made a forced choice between minimal and enriched paraphrases that followed the paragraphs. The results showed effective contextual bias (~86% contextual compliance). These materials were used to test processing issues in experiment 4.

Experiment 4 used the 24 best context/sentence pairs from experiment 3. Subjects controlled presentation of the materials by a button press to advance line by line through the paragraph. The last sentence of the sequence was the test sentence. Then a mask of X's appeared, followed by a sentence in capital letters. Subjects had to judge whether the capitalized sentence was or was not a word for word match to the just preceding test sentence. For example (implicature italicized):

> [Enriched context]
> Roger was directing a musical. For one scene he needed extras to play
> a group of onlookers watching a street fight. But the stage would already
> be pretty crowded with the principal actors in this scene. He figured that

Chapter 3. The syntactic verge: Experimental pragmatics **71**

in order to prevent the scene from looking too chaotic, *he needed six people.*
Mask: XXXXXXXXXXXXXXXXXXXXXXXX
Target: He Needed at Least Six People

[Minimal context]
Roger was trying to arrange a rafting trip for his scout troupe during the summer. Many of his scouts were on family vacations. He asked the rafting company how many committed participants he would need to be able to secure reservations for the trip. They told him that he needed six people.
Mask: XXXXXXXXXXXXXXXXXXXXXXXX
Target: He Needed at Least Six People

For experimental items, the capitalized sentence expressed the (Gricean) minimal proposition; it did NOT physically match the last sentence in the story. Thus the appropriate response for the matching task was always 'No' on experimental items. (Fillers with 'Yes' responses were included on non-experimental items). The two measurements were reading time on the last sentence of the paragraph and the matching task decision times. The entire task as seen from the participants perspective had the virtue of emphasizing attention to the interpretation of the impliciture.

No significant context effect for match-mismatch judgment times was found and we set that measure aside in our discussion.[27] However, reading times for the impliciture did show context effects: The time to read the final sentence (italicized in the example above) in the minimal vs enriched contexts is a measure of processing time for the impliciture sentences. *LFS* predicts longer reading times for target sentences in enriched contexts because it assumes that the minimal proposition must first be constructed, then rejected. *RP* predicts the opposite because it assumes enriched interpretations are more "accessible". So, no conflict arises in enriched contexts, but in minimal contexts the minimal interpretation must compete with and override the enriched interpretation. LPP models predict no difference since context is assumed to be decisive and hence no interference should arise. The B&C results showed longer final sentence reading times in minimal contexts compared to enriched contexts. That pattern disconfirmed LFS and LPP predictions. The RP Model account of the slower reading times in minimal contexts

---

27. B&C tentatively interpreted this as evidence against the LPP model since enriched context times should have been faster than minimal on their task analysis. However, we regard the match/mismatch results as inconclusive. Predictions of no difference are difficult a priori, and lacking some other validating outcome for the measure, a null result is not persuasive.

is that both minimal and enriched interpretations are always computed. Thus, for contexts that demand a minimal interpretation, the (preferred) enriched interpretation must be overridden. In our terminology, the impliciture must be defeated. We will return to this and other models that give priority to enriched interpretation after considering some other experimental findings that promote a rather different picture. A paramount feature of this additional work is its focus on one subclass of the impliciture materials.

Bezuidenhout and Morris (2004) narrowed attention to just one of the types in the B&C study. These were "scalar implicatures" (e.g., the cardinals and scalars in B&C's stimuli given earlier). However, the scalar terms in this case were, in fact, not those in B&C. Instead, the implicature [Some X VP] $\Rightarrow$ [not all X VP] was tested using a new method: eye movements during reading.

B&M evaluated two models designed to account for the processing of scalars:

- *(DM) Default Model:* The use of a weak expression from an entailment scale gives rise to a default GCI. It implicates the denial of that same sentence with any stronger expression from the same scale substituted for the weaker one. (This is Levinson's Q heuristic.)
- *(UM) Underspecification Model:* Such expressions are semantically underspecified, and must be enriched in the specific context, and this arises from local pragmatic processes.

These are not processing models in the same sense as the B&C proposals. Additional assumptions are needed for predictions about processing stages, time, resources, and errors. The models differ mainly in the semantic representations assumed to induce scalar GCIs. B&M used an eye movement measure during reading of test materials. Fixation patterns and gaze durations during reading were assumed to be sensitive to "the process of generating inferences". We return to this. Subjects were given sentences such as example (13) (original numbering).

(13) a. Some books had colour pictures. In fact all of them did, which is why the teachers liked them.
b. The books had colour pictures. In fact all of them did, which is why the teachers liked them.

The GCI is canceled upon encounter with the phrase 'of them did'. That explicitly contradicts 'not all N'. Their predictions of processing differences for the models include:

- Increased time on 'them were/did' DM: Yes UM: No
- Regressions/rereading of 'Some N' DM: Yes UM: No
- Increased time on 'all' DM: No UM: Yes

Chapter 3. The syntactic verge: Experimental pragmatics   73

1. DM predicts the GCI: 'Not all N' should be triggered automatically by 'Some N', but not by 'The N'. Cancellation of the implicature should therefore increase processing time in the 'them did' region for the 'Some N' conditions compared to the 'The N' condition.[28]

2. DM would also suggest indications of reanalysis, such as increased processing time that spills over onto the following region of the sentence, or regressions to the initial determiner phrase.

3. UM assumes that readers in the 'Some N' condition do not immediately commit to the *some but not all* reading. They engage in incremental processing utilizing whatever information is available at any given moment. The word 'all' was assumed to bias towards the *some and possibly all* interpretation. B&M assumed that this would lead to increased processing time due to assimilation of information relevant to specification of an underspecified item. The specification process is assumed to use resources to integrate new information and hence has a processing cost.

Several results for target regions in the sentences are relevant. Readers did spend significantly more initial processing time (as measured by gaze duration) on the word 'all' following 'Some N' than following 'The N'. This fits UM assumptions. Further, although DM suggests increased processing effort following cancellation in the 'of them did' region, there was no evidence of this. Conditions did not differ for time spent in the end of sentence region or rereading the initial 'Det N' region. This is consistent with the UM assumption that the specification is made incrementally as relevant information accrues, and there is no need for reanalysis. From these and other features of the experiment, B&M concluded that overall, UM best fitted the results.

Indeed, this study represents significant real-time processing questions, and the measure used can support quite detailed time dependent claims. But, the eye movement and fixation patterns that are possible in such circumstances are complex and interact with presumptive information processing in several ways. These factors raise significant problems for the conclusion that the data invalidate DM and support UM. Both theoretical assumptions and experimental methods are at issue.

First, the analysis of 'reprocessing loads' versus 'integration loads' in processing is problematic. Reprocessing accounts provide reasonably clear grounds for claims about changed levels of processing difficulty, but the notion of 'integration load' is much vaguer. This is acute for the theoretical perspective that B&M describe in which there is continuous incremental integration of contextual information into

---

28. B&M do not say why 'the' works differently.

the interpretation. The theory is in need of sharper specification of what constitutes an 'integration discontinuity' or some metric for systematic variation that is not ad hoc. Relevance theory lacks such a metric. Why, in particular, is the integration of new information prominent at the occurrence of the quantifier 'all' rather than at the phrasal integration of 'all of them'? Why not at the verb 'did'? Many parsing theories postulate integrative 'wrap up' processes triggered by end of sentence/clause. It is unclear how to address or discount such from the perspective B&M associated with UM.

More telling, however, are difficulties with the stimuli and the eye movement patterns. The assumption that the default heuristic must await the remainder of the 'of them did' phrase has two difficulties. One a possible ellipsis analysis and the other is potential parafoveal information. Intuitively, an ellipsis analysis of the sentences at the occurrence of 'all' is defensible as a reflex of the hedge phrases that introduced the quantifier phrase. So: 'Some books had colored pictures. In fact, all --which is why the teachers like them'. The prosodic contour for 'all' would be different from the target one for B&M's sentence, but in a reading task, the elliptical expression is quite acceptable. From this perspective, both UM and DM predict an analysis peak at the quantifier. In addition, there is the matter of parafoveal effects. There is good reason to suppose that fixations in the latter portion of the hedge phrase region just prior to 'all' would pick up information about the 'all' phrase, and similarly so for those fixations landing on the quantifier itself. That information includes word identity and interpretative constraint (Murray, 2000). The combination of an elliptical analysis of the expression, plus the availability of parafoveal information, compromises the contrast of the theories. B&M's study, while suggestive, does not provide strong grounds for decision.

Breheny, Katsos, and Williams (2006) examined GCI and also focused on scalar implicatures as their vehicle of investigation. They compared two pragmatic views of how speaker meaning is achieved. One was the 'default' view (Levinson, 2000), and hence corresponds to DM in the B&C work. The other they described as the 'context driven view' (Sperber and Wilson 1986). The context driven view assigns GCI no special status and holds that they are drawn only where called for by the specific context and is in this respect similar in spirit to the UM view pursued by B&M.

On the assumption (noted of B&M earlier) that more inference demands more processing time, the context driven view predicts more processing in contexts for which an implicature must be made. The canceling ('lower bound' in their terms) context is a free ride on this view –no implicature is made. By contrast, they note that the default view of scalars must call for more processing in the canceling context since the default will be made and must be overridden. BK&W cite the B&C experiments as a case of the latter outcome since it showed longer response times

Chapter 3. The syntactic verge: Experimental pragmatics **75**

for the minimal reading (canceling implicatures) and hence does not fit the predictions they sketched for the context driven models. Commenting on the B&C work, BK&W observe that "nearly half the materials" used by B&C were not "unequivocably implicature triggers," (p. 13). In particular, they question whether the use of cardinals involves an implicature. They also critiqued the quantified NP ('everyone came to the party') case and reject it as suitable for test of GCI. BK&W then report two experiments designed to address issues of processing for scalars.

The first was described as a 'replication' of B&C's experiment, but using materials that avoid the problems they identified in their critique. They choose a case they deemed a relevant implicature: the [A or B] construction. The semantics is [A or B and possibly both], and the implicature is the exclusive disjunctive [A or B and not both]. They used a self paced reading task for discourses like the following:

– Enabling context: John was taking a university course and working at the same time. For the exams he had to study from short and comprehensive sources. Depending on the course he decided to read the class notes or the summary
– Cancelling context: John heard the textbook for Geophysics was very advanced. Nobody understood it properly. He heard that if he wanted to pass the course he should read the class notes or the summary.

The subjects who participated in the experiment were "native speakers of Greek studying at Cambridge." Materials were presented in Greek (see experiment 2 below for reasons associated with the choice of test population). They compared reading times for contexts that biased for the implicature and a context that cancelled it.

Results showed longer reading times for the enabling context cases –i.e., those that required the [A or B] implicature. In B&C terms, these would be the enriched instances rather than the minimal. So, results for [A or B] (which was not tested by B&C it should be remembered) were the reverse of B&C's outcome. This reinforces the BK&W's position on the analysis of scalars and their processing. We will return later to issues of the differences between the B&C outcomes and those of BKW.

With regard to the 'some X' construction, BK&W stress the importance of testing in a neutral context in order to evaluate the default view. Default assumptions say that the implicature will be computed in a neutral environment because it is triggered by the scalar term. On a single process account (which assumes the implicature must be triggered by context), the scalar will not yield an implicature. Here BK&W raise an important issue regarding neutral contexts. This is the influence of topic–non-topic differences. They argued that topic effects in English preclude a neutral test of the 'some X' construction in isolated sentences (presented 'out of the blue' in their terms). Such presentation triggers contrastive assumptions and leads to the implicature. Hence they argue, 'context free' presentation for this kind of case isn't really context free in the relevant sense.

BK&W's second experiment was an elegant test of the 'some X' construction that was designed to avoid the topicalization issues and to test processing of scalar implicitures in a neutral context. To deal with the topic confound, they tested Greek language stimuli with native Greek speakers. In Greek, reordering the elements of the construction avoids the topic effect. To control for order effects per se they used a design with explicit triggers ('only') as a control, e.g.:

a. Some of the consultants met with the director. The rest did not manage to attend.
b. Only some of the consultants met with the director. The rest did not manage to attend.
c. The director met with some of the consultants. The rest did not manage to attend.
d. The director met with only some of the consultants. The rest did not manage to attend.

Versions a and c had the implicit trigger (the scalar); versions b and d had explicit triggers ('only'). The 'some x' phrase was sentence initial or sentence final, and thus a/b are topic versions, while c/d are non-topic versions. All versions of the test sequence were followed by a forcing phrase (e.g., 'the rest').

Relevant comparisons were between the explicit and implicit cases. Reading times for the forcing phrase ('the rest') showed an interaction: reading time for the non-topic implicit condition was longer than the reading time for the corresponding explicit condition; no difference between explicit and implicit triggers was observed for the topic position. This indicates that the implicature was made in topic position for both explicit and implicit triggers. But, in non-topic position, it was apparently not made 'on-line' –i.e. during the processing of the 'some of the X' phrase. It was made when the forcing phrase was encountered. On these grounds, the scalar implicature is context driven and not a default move –it is not driven by sentence form. (Note: the BK&W analysis applies to the B&M results modulo the comments on method we raised for the B&M reading measures. The experimental presentation in B&M makes the scalar move salient, and its cancellation would lead to the observed pattern.)

Recent work by Huang & Snedeker (2006) provides another look at the processing of scalars and adds important evidence for the time course of processing associated with making the scalar inference. In this study, another measure of processing time was employed: timing and control of gaze direction for the referents of stimulus sentences. Subjects were seated before a display board that had pictures to which test sentences referred. Their gaze direction was video recorded and measured to establish where in the display space it was pointed and at what point in time vis a vis the heard sentence. There is a tight coupling of gaze and language processes. (This is sometimes called the 'visual world paradigm; see Eberhard et al. 1995 for discussion of this class of measurements for sentence processing.)

The test sentences were locally ambiguous (vis a vis the reference space). So, listeners might hear variants as indicated in the example below:

> Point to the girl with [two, three, all, some] of the socks.

Display pictures included a boy with two socks, a girl with two socks and a girl with three soccer balls. For quantifiers 'two', 'three' and 'all', decision was determinate at the quantifier. If semantic interpretation of quantifiers were immediate, there would be no need to await the phonetic disambiguation re socks and soccer balls. And, if the impliciture from 'some x' to 'not all x' were made immediately upon encounter with the quantifier (as postulated in the default model discussed for B&M), the picture of the girl with two socks would also be a uniquely determinate target (she had 'some but not all' of the socks). The soccer ball picture was ruled out because that girl had all the soccer balls. However, if the scalar impliciture were not made in the 'some' condition (either underspecified or semantically interpreted as 'some X and possibly all'), the instruction was disambiguated only at the phonetic divergence of 'socks' and 'soccer'.

The results showed a clear difference between quantifier conditions. Gaze converged on the appropriate targets within 400 milliseconds after quantifier onset for 'two', 'three', and 'all' conditions; the 'some' condition was delayed until about 800 milliseconds after onset. Note that this is still well before the phonetic disambiguation point. This pattern shows that the scalar inference was indeed made, but significantly later than the lexical semantic interpretation of the quantifiers. The pragmatic process was rapid and contextually appropriate but followed basic sentence interpretation.

Two points need emphasis re the BK&W and H&S studies. The H&S results do not challenge the context driven SI claim that BK&W draw from their own data. The H&S experimental context was obviously one in which the option for the scalar inference was salient. But, the H&S evidence does challenge the local pragmatic processing idea as sketched in B&C. That model treats impliciture phenomena as not distinguished from the first stage sentence interpretation process. H&S results do not fit that assumption.

We now turn to a broader question: What should be made of the different outcomes re BK&W and B&C? The [A or B] test and the [some X] cases are experiments with different types of materials that produce different patterns from those observed in B&C. BK&W comment on the cardinals and quantifier cases and set those aside as not satisfactory on their analysis re GCI. What then, should be the status of the perfective, possession, time distance and temporal relation cases in B&C? So far as we can tell, none of these produced a result like the one BK&W got for the scalars they tested. Indeed, it appears that all of the six types in B&C's work should be treated in a different way than the scalars as characterized by BK&W. It is here that we find it useful to draw attention to the distinction between two types of default inferences: the Q and I heuristics as discussed in Levinson (1995, 2000). The scalars are treated by Levinson in terms of the Q heuristic, whereas most of the types in B&C, we would argue, are more appropriately treated in terms of the I-heuristic. Thus, while both are species of defaults, they differ in important respects.

Levinson sees the Q-Heuristic as requiring appeal to the notion of a "contrast set" of alternative expressions differing in informativeness (modified Q-Heuristic): "For the relevant salient alternatives, what isn't said is not the case" (2000, 36). Examples of such contrast sets of expressions would include the scalars we have just been discussing.

Levinson (2000) proposed the I-Heuristic to deal with UEC examples we discussed earlier, and we consider that it applies to most of the examples like those in the B&C experiment.[29] Levinson's says of the I-Heuristic: "What is expressed simply is stereotypically exemplified" (2000: 37). If a remark is unqualified and uses undistinctive vocabulary, it refers to the stereotypical features of a situation. That stereotypic information need not be explicitly linguistically encoded.[30]

If, as we suppose, the difference in the BK&W results and those in B&C resides in different mechanisms of processing associated with the two types of phenomena, further evidence bearing on the issue is needed. Garrett & Harnish (2007) is relevant. We reported an experiment that focused on impliciture types similar to those of B&C and bears directly on the issue of the potential contrast of these types with the processing profile typical of the scalar experiments. In addition, our experimental probe invoked a mechanism derived from Bach's proposals as contrast to the default account. Thus, we compared two mechanisms for providing understood elements of content: Bach's application of "standardization" to implicitures and the default mechanism of Levinson's I-Heuristic.

---

29. We set aside the 'cardinals' in the B&C materials. BK&W argue that these are not comparable to scalars. However, Levinson does treat these in terms of the Q-Heuristic, and so we leave that matter open.

30. Levinson splits the I-heuristic into two principles: "Speaker's maxim ... say as little as necessary; that is, produce the minimal linguistic information sufficient to achieve your communicational ends (bearing Q in mind) ... Recipient's corollary amplify the informational content of the speaker's utterance, by finding the most specific interpretation, up to what you judge to be the speaker's m-intended point ..." (2000, 114).

Bach (1994) used the term 'impliciture' to cover many of the cases of UEC we discussed earlier. These he construes as instances of not being explicit in what one says. Standardization provides access to the implicit content. By his assumption, that content could have been made explicit by adding words to the sentence. The experimental targets we used, shortly to be discussed, have this property. Standardization was first proposed in Bach and Harnish (1979, chapter 9) as the relation that certain sentence forms have to indirect illocutionary acts. These are uses that, though not a part of the sentence's literal and direct illocutionary potential, are nevertheless associated with the sentence form and do not have to be figured out de novo as non-standardized forms typically are.[31] Principal examples of standardized indirection are 'Can/could/would you VP?' (compare to: semantically similar forms 'Do you have the ability to VP?'). Standardization plausibly applies to nonliterality as well, such as familiar proverbs, metaphors and other figures of speech. To these cases, Bach would like to add some impliciture phenomena.

The I-Heuristic and standardization proposals may be applied to similar cases, and can raise distinguishable expectations about the processing of implicitures. They are, as they stand, not complete for that purpose. Indeed, they were not offered as processing solutions, but they can form the foundation of plausible processing schemas. Our working assumptions for Bach's standardization ideas and Levinson's I-heuristic are as follows.

Standardization: we have no decisive criterion for when a form is standardized.[32] We relied on generalizations from examples in the literature coupled with empirical assessment of preferences for interpretation. More, acutely, we cannot give an a priori account of the interaction of context and standardization. Suitable context may override (and/or suppress) the standardized interpretation: viz., it is present, but not contextually operative (like an irrelevant meaning). Or, a standardized interpretation may be suspended (and/or disabled) –not computed. Briefly: standardized (vs non-standardized) interpretation could be: (i) the most salient, (ii) less salient, (iii) overridden by context, or (iv) suspended by context. In the our experiment, we applied these working assumptions:

A1: Standardized interpretations are like meanings in that they "attach" to the type of form being uttered, and are retained in canceling contexts.

---

31. Searle (1975) associated "conventions of usage", which are not "conventions of meaning" with these forms. See also Morgan (1978) and Geis (1995, chapter 5). On the Bach and Harnish (1979, chapter 9) view, standardization contrasts with conventionalization.

32. Bach (1989, 81) does propose a "test" for standardized nonliterality. The idea is that the standardized interpretation is asymmetrically dependent on the nonstandardized interpretation. It also appears that 'standardized' as used in the test is roughly equivalent to 'common' --which was not a part of the technical notion in Bach and Harnish.

A2: Standardized interpretations are more salient, preferred etc.

A3: Standardized interpretations must be overridden by context when the (compositional) linguistic interpretation is favored.

The I-Heuristic: implementation of this as a processing formula poses other questions. We have no criterion for being a 'simple' form and no criterion for the stereotypical information associated with a form. Again, we relied on generalization from literature examples and selected cases in which stereotypic and standardized information seemed to intersect. A key point concerns the relation of the I-Heuristic to background information: the default in the I-heuristic is to a set of stereotypic beliefs. Levinson remarks: "such a heuristic is extremely powerful --it allows an interpretation to bring all sorts of background knowledge about a domain to bear on a rich interpretation of a minimal description." (2000, 33) Clearly, this raises the most difficult of problems regarding the relation of general knowledge to linguistic knowledge and context. We comment on this in discussion. For purposes of our experiment, we assumed that information appealed to by the I-heuristic is part of general beliefs ("knowledge"), and that in the communication situation some of this information is either assumed or made mutual by the speaker.[33] Assumptions A4 and A5 summarize this.

A4: Stereotypical information that heuristics allude to is a part of general background information we bring to most talk-exchanges. This is either (i) modified by contextual information, (ii) or modifies it.[34]

A5: Utterance interpretation takes place with ready access to such information. Important triggers for such information include specific lexical items and the evolving topic of discourse.

The Garrett and Harnish (2007) experiments with implicitures tested assumptions A1–A5 in two steps. The first was a context free materials validation and filtering step, and the second was a contextual constraint test. A set of 42 impliciture sentences was constructed: 14 each for three of the types discussed in section B: 'locative' ('It's raining.'), 'perfective' ('I've had breakfast.') and 'possession' ('I broke a finger.') We first tested whether these sentences actually had the expected behav-

---

33. See Bach and Harnish (1979, chapter 1) for the notion and role of "mutual beliefs" in communication, and see Wilks and Bien (1983) for the idea of making a piece of information "mutual" as the need arises. Taylor (2001) also sees such background information as playing a decisive role, though he does not relate it to Levinson's heuristic, whereas Brennan (2003) does.

34. There might be a psychologically relevant distinction here between what Putnam (1975) calls stereotypical information about things or events (think also of frames and scripts), and what Searle (1978) calls the 'Background' — information we would rarely think to report, but is clearly at work during utterance interpretation. For now we will ignore this.

Chapter 3. The syntactic verge: Experimental pragmatics   **81**

ioral effect. Subjects were presented with auditory versions (digital records presented by computer), followed by a visually presented question probing the presumed impliciture, e.g.:

Somebody said: 'It's raining'	WHERE?	HERE	THERE
Somebody said: 'I broke a finger.'	WHOSE?	MINE	SOMEONE'S
Somebody said: 'I've had breakfast'	WHEN?	TODAY	ONCE

Subjects answered the probe question by hitting a key to indicate a choice of one of the two indicated answers. The impliciture sentences were randomly mixed into a background set of other sentences of generally similar structure that lacked an impliciture (e.g.: Somebody said: 'It's my birthday,' Somebody said: 'I've won at poker,' Somebody said: 'She waved a flag.').

If an impliciture is computed, the choice and speed of choosing a compatible response should be fast and systematically biased as compared to non-impliciture sentences. The results confirmed the special status of the implicitures. Probe choices were in fact uniformly for the impliciture word following impliciture sentences (90% or more); the non-implicitures padding sentences were not similarly systematic. And, as might be expected, from such a choice bias result, response times to select an answer were also substantially and significantly faster following impliciture sentences than following non-implicitures. That pattern validated the stimulus construction effort and set the scene for the main experiment. The best eight examples (re bias and RT) of each of the three types were selected and used to test processing times required for contextual modification of the implicitures. Experiment 2 used these materials, but they were visually presented using a self-paced reading paradigm to test for the effects of context. Enabling contexts (these supported the impliciture) were contrasted with canceling contexts (these defeated the impliciture and called for a nonstandardized meaning).[35]

- Enabling context: Al is busy in the kitchen helping his wife by chopping the salad veggies. This is not his usual practice and he is feeling quite pleased with himself for volunteering. But, he's not really paying close attention as he is also watching a baseball game on TV. He gets a little too careless with his knife and lets out a sudden yelp. 'Ouch! I cut a finger!' [his own]
- Canceling context: Mabel is a new manicurist. She is nervous on her first job and her very first client is a fussy old man who had been coming to the shop for years. Mabel was in tears as she explained to her boss why the man shortly left in

---

35. Grice (1975) noted when he introduced the notion of 'canceling' an implicature that this could take place in two ways: (i) explicitly, by adding a disclaimer ('but I don't mean to imply that such and such'), or (ii) contextually, by having the utterance occur in a context where the implication would not naturally arise.

a huff. 'Oh', she wept, 'I worked carefully, but he moved his hand all of a sudden. You heard him say 'Ouch'? Well, I cut a finger'. [his/not hers]

Note that care was taken to insure that each context uniquely and strongly selected one of the two question probes. Off-line tests showed 95% or greater compliance with context.

On standardization assumptions A1–A3, we should observe priming for the related probes even in canceling contexts, since the standardized interpretation attaches to the form of words. On default heuristic assumptions A4-A5, we should observe priming for related probes only in enabling contexts, since stereotypical information is a part of background information and is only activated by the utterance in the context.

Reading time measures provided one kind of processing test. For the context passages leading up to the target sentence, reading times for enabling and canceling contexts give a rough index of the complexity of the contextual information. The average reading times for the two contexts were similar and did not differ statistically for enabling and cancelling contexts, suggesting comparable context complexity. Reading time for the target sentences was compared following each context type. A difference would be expected if reading time reflects integration time, and if the impliciture is available and interferes with integration. This is the pattern seen in the B&C study. In our study, there was some indication that it took longer to read the target sentence following the canceling contexts but the difference was not statistically significant.

The question answering task provided a second measure of context effects. Accuracy for contextually driven responses was very high for all sentence types, and was equally so for both canceling and supporting contexts. For question answering response times, the standardization and default accounts predict different outcomes. If context suppresses the impliciture, other things being equal, the two context types should not differ systematically. But, if the impliciture is invariably computed, this sets the stage for response competition and times for the canceling context should be longer than those for the enabling context. Results did reveal a substantial and statistically reliable difference between the contexts, with the enabling context being faster. This was true for all three of the types tested. However, though the question answering task indicated an interfering process was present, it leaves open the question of how close to the initial sentence processing that interfering process was engaged.

The upshot of the tests was that for the sorts of implicitures tested, the standardization hypothesis was supported over the default heuristic hypothesis as we framed it. It is important to bear in mind that the assumptions A4 and A5 with which we implemented the I-Heuristic may be the proper focus of the discomfir-

mation. Several things remain to be determined, including when precisely the impliciture is computed and how this pattern of results may generalize to different
instances of impliciture phenomena. And, where this pattern holds up, we need
to examine whether and how a default heuristic approach other than the one we
chose might be construed so as conform to the experimental outcomes.

5. Some conclusions

Overall, the studies of pragmatic processing reviewed here certainly pose problems for any version of "Gricean" ideas asserting that what is strictly said (or the
minimal proposition associated with the utterance in the context) is processed
first, before any "implicatures" are processed. That much seems secure. However,
the positive picture is less clear. We need to draw some distinctions among the
types of materials examined in the various experiments.

Setting aside the 'literal first' class of models, B&C's (2002) sketch of processing compared what they characterized as a default ('ranked parallel') style model with a contextually driven model ('local pragmatic processing'). Their reading
time measure showed easier processing of test sentences in contexts calling for the
enriched interpretation of the sentences as compared to contexts calling for minimal interpretation. These were sentences representing the six test cases derived
from the G&M and the N&C studies. The parallel processing model with preference ranking was deemed a better fit to this data than the local pragmatic processing model. Enriched interpretation was the preferred ('more salient'? more accessible'?) interpretation even in contexts favoring the minimal. It is perhaps well to
keep in mind that a default interpretation of this pattern is not required (although
B&C did link the RP model to Levinson as well as Gibbs). Models that accord
a stable preference for enriched interpretation, and hence for the impliciture in
these cases, will suffice.

The investigations of scalars presented another vantage point on impliciture
phenomena. B&M's (2004) experiment focused on one type (scalar implicitures)
and used an eye-movement reading measure to provide evidence against a default
style model of the sort proposed by Levinson. They argued in favor of an alternative model based on underspecification combined with contextually triggered
elaboration (which they associated with relevance theory). If generalized to the
other impliciture types, that perspective would rule out a preference for standardized interpretations in a context that favored a competing analysis, whether minimal or enriched in some way that goes beyond standardization. For a relevance
theory based account, there is actually no difference between a minimal context
and an enriched context. Both should be the direct determinant of the interpretive

outcome and, other things being equal, should be attained with equal facility. Both the B&C results and our own militate against that view. The results of experiment thus support the view that contextual penetration of sentence interpretation should be distinguished from the interpretation that relies on sentence form — viz. the one achieved for standardized sentences when they are presented without overt context. So, we resist the generalization of the relevance model and its approach to the larger class of implicitures. But, the case for something like an underspecification approach to some members of the class, in particular, the scalars remains.

The work by BK&W indicates something more about the scalar implicitures. Default inferences were not made based solely on sentence form. The experimental demonstration that in a neutral context, the scalar implicature was not drawn is persuasive. In the topic condition that 'enabled' the implicit triggers, sentences with implicit and explicit impliciture triggers were processed similarly –they showed no hint of a difference. But, in the non-topic configuration that 'disabled' the implicit triggers, the scalar implicature was not drawn until the downstream position of the forcing phrase. This presses up against the intuitively powerful feelings that an English speaker has when confronted with context free examples of the 'some X' construction. BK&W's analysis of this in light of the confound with topic effects is salutary, and it illustrates once again, and powerfully, the need to combine the intuitive data base with the experimental data base in order to find our way through the brambles of linguistic, pragmatic, and psycholinguistic theory.

These issues are very helpfully illuminated by the study of H&S, which also focused on scalars and used a measurement technique that allowed a close look at the time course of the elaboration of sentence interpretation. The technique used was one that measures comprehension by gaze timing and direction for reference objects in free visual fields, and it showed unambiguous quantifier sentences were immediately interpreted whereas scalar implicatures with 'some', while indubitably on-line, were not immediate. They took extra time to develop. Here we see evidence that suggests the earlier assignment of interpretation based on the meanings of the lexical content of the sentence as compared to the elaboration of that interpretation by implicature — in this case, the rapid application of the scalar implicature.

To conclude, we may begin to explore ideas about what distinguishes processing proposals based on standardization as compared to that we formulated for the I-heuristic and what it may suggest about relations between Q and I phenomena. For the impliciture cases treated by standardization, we may hope to sidestep some of the problems that arise in recruiting on-line background knowledge to the interpretive task. That problem is acute. The "concentric circles" model[36] gives one

---

36. See Akmajian et al. (1995: 370). Clark and Marshall (1981) discuss a model with at least five different "circles" of information beyond knowledge of language.

Chapter 3. The syntactic verge: Experimental pragmatics   **85**

working characterization of the problems this intersects. In this formulation, language forms the innermost circle,[37] contextual information forms the middle circle, and general background knowledge forms the third, outer circle, perhaps with information classed into kinds relevant for inferring that the speaker means one kind of thing rather than another (see Harnish 1983: 341). Each of these "circles" raises problems. For instance both Chomsky (1986, 2000) and Davidson (1986) have questioned the everyday idea of a common language and its role in communication, but for different reasons. The second circle poses multiple problems of how contextual constraints are identified and recruited to the interpretive task. The third "circle" is the most pertinent to our contrast of standardization and the I-Heuristic. It raises the problem of the internal organization of general knowledge. Even if restricted to information relevant to the communicative force of the utterance, we can expect that "virtually any belief can play a role in the contextual determination (by the hearer) of the actual force of the utterance … we can expect that the system of beliefs … necessary to support communication will turn out to be almost as rich as our mental life in general" (Harnish 1983: 341). If such general knowledge is to be allocated to "central systems", then if Fodor (1983, 2001) is right, there will likely be resistance to understanding such a structure by computational cognitive science. How is the relevant information to be accessed in a timely fashion? This seems to be nothing short of the "frame problem" applied to language understanding.[38] We do not have an answer to the specific problem, let alone the general one.[39]

For the case of implicitures, standardization offers a partial solution. It turns the processing operations into something very close to those that assign meaning to the utterance based on its form. It remains to be seen what more general formulation of a standardization account can be given. Indeed, there is some temptation to observe that the core of the I-heuristic idea has affinities with standardization, given its emphasis on stereotypic information and the notion of "a simple form". Standardization is driven by sentence form, and as we noted earlier, there is room to maneuver regarding the extent to which this is schematized. In formulating the experimental materials for the Garrett & Harnish experiment, we extended the examples from Bach and others by 'modeling' our constructive efforts on examples in the literature. It's a fair question –but one we will not try to answer — to ask what links those new exemplars to the original examples that inspired them.

---

37. See Bach and Harnish (1979: 7), the 'Linguistic Presumption'.

38. Recanati (2004, chapter 2) suggests that all utterance interpretation involves filling out "schemata", which like frames and scripts, have so far resisted theoretical precision regarding individuation and operation.

39. See Clark and Marshall (1981) for a provocative sketch, which applies to more than just definite reference.

Finally, we may ask what processing import we may associate with the differences in I and Q phenomena. The latter seems to rely on rapid contextual interaction with the literal interpretation assigned to sentences. The experimental evidence suggests that the logical form of scalars is initially computed and altered pragmatically only when contextually required. The former, by contrast seem to be interpreted at the outset by some version of standardization. Non-standarized interpretation is assigned only at cost. What explains this difference? We think the answer lies in the same issues we have just been discussing regarding standardization. It lies in the limited range of interpretive options that are associated with Q phenomena as compared with the potentially unbounded appeal to background knowledge characteristic of I phenomena. The computational solutions differ for the two cases. Q phenomena adjustments are rapid. But, barring some special treatment, I phenomena adjustments are slow. Standarization is a response to that exigency, but it comes at a cost.

Available I-Phenomena experiments (viz., studies of impliciture processing) are limited, but the evidence suggests a substantial slowdown in processing is associated with the cancellation of an impliciture. That evidence, however, does not permit strong locality claims. The measures used are not tied to specific loci in the test sentences with sufficient precision to decisively adjudicate between models, though the B&C evidence does suggest effects during reading of the implicitures. Future research will be necessary to test the robustness of the results and to tie processing more immediately to the relevant content elements in implicitures. But, Q-Phenomena claims have a more developed foundation for evaluation. The first question (locality) has some answers in terms of several experiments that used experimental measures common in psycholinguistic studies of lexical and syntactic processing (e.g., self-paced reading, eye-movements in reading, free field gaze measurements for spoken language comprehension, and electrophysiological measures). The measures permit relevant processing comparisons and provide a foundation for more detailed claims. Summary statements are always a bit chancy, but looking across different experiments, the evidence seems best fit to the view that although there is a rapid deployment of the scalar inference, basic sentence processing precedes the application of the interpretation associated with the scalar. Further, available evidence indicates there is a cost associated with the application of the scalar, though the precise nature of this remains to be established. In these regards, scalar processing may contrast with that for the types of implicitures in the B&C and G&H work, though that possibility remains to be experimentally evaluated. Such details of the cost accounting associated with the processing of different instances of impliciture would add dimension to the evaluation of context driven, default and standardization accounts of these cases and eventually to an empirically driven basis for location in the larger space of UEC phenomena.

References

Akmajian, A., R. Demers, A. Farmer & Harnish, R. 1995. *Linguistics*. Cambridge MA: The MIT Press.

Akmajian, A. & Heny, F. 1975. *An Introduction to the Principles of Transformational Syntax*. Cambridge MA: The MIT Press.

Bach, K. 1989. *Thought and Reference*. Oxford: OUP.

Bach, K. 1994. Conversational impliciture. *Mind and Language* 9:124–62.

Bach, K. 1994. Semantic slack. In *Foundations of Speech Act Theory*, S. Tsohatzidis (ed.). London: Routledge.

Bach, K. 2000. Quantification, qualification and context. *Mind and Language* 15:262–84.

Bach, K. 2001. Speaking loosely: Sentence nonliterality. *Midwest Studies in Philosophy* 25: 249–63.

Bach, K. & Harnish, R. 1979. *Linguistic Communication and Speech Acts*. Cambridge MA: The MIT Press.

Bezuidenhout, A. 2002. Generalized conversational implicatures and default pragmatic inferences. In *Meaning and Truth*, J. Campbell et al (eds). New York NY: Seven Bridges.

Bezuidenhout, A. & Cutting, J. 2002. Literal meaning, minimal propositions and pragmatic processing. *Journal of Pragmatics* 34:433–56.

Bezuidenhout, A. & Morris, R. 2004. Implicature, relevance and default pragmatic inference. In *Experimental Pragmatics*, I. Noveck & D. Sperber (eds). New York NY: Palgrave Macmillan.

Bird , G. 1997. Explicature, impliciture, explicature. *Linguistische Berichte* 8 : 72–91.

Borg, E. 2004. *Minimal Semantics*, Oxford: OUP.

Brennan, J. 2003. Encyclopedic knowledge and default pragmatic inference. Ms, University of Arizona.

Breheny, R., Katsos, N. & Williams, J. 2006. Are generalized implicatures generated by default? An on-line investigation into the role of context in generating pragmatic inferences. *Cognition* 100:343–463.

Cappelen, H. & Lepore, E. 2005. *Insensitive Semantics*. Malden MA: Blackwell.

Carston, R. 1988. Implicature, explicature, and truth-theoretic semantics. In *Mental Representations*, R. Kempson (ed.). Cambridge: CUP.

Carston, R. 2002. *Thoughts and Utterances*. Malden MA: Blackwell.

Chomsky, N. 1986. *Knowledge of Language*. New York NY: Praeger.

Chomsky, N. 2000. *New Horizons in the Study of Language and Mind*. Cambridge: CUP.

Clark, H. 1996. Communities, commonalities and communication. In *Rethinking Linguistic Relativity*, J. Gumperz & S. Levinson (eds). Cambridge: CUP.

Clark, H. & Marshall, C. 1981. Definite knowledge and mutual knowledge. In *Elements of Discourse Understanding*, A. Joshi (ed.). Cambridge: CUP.

Davidson, D. 1986. A nice derangement of epitaphs. In *Truth and Interpretation*, E. Lepore (ed.). Malden MA: Blackwell.

Dowty, D. 1991. Thematic proto-roles and argument selection. *Language* 67(3): 547–619.

Eberhard, K. M., Spivey-Knowlton, M. J., Sedivy, J. C. & Tanenhaus, M. K. 1995. Eye movements as a window into real-time spoken language comprehension in natural contexts. *Journal of Psycholinguistic Research* 24:409–36.

Elugardo, R. & Stainton, R. (eds). 2005. *Ellipsis and Nonsentential Speech*. Dordrecht: Kluwer.

Fodor, J. 1983. *The Modularity of Mind*. Cambridge MA: The MIT Press.

Fodor, J. 2001. *The Mind Doesn't Work that Way*. Cambridge MA: The MIT Press.

Garrett, M. & Harnish, R. 2007. Experimental pragmatics: Testing for impliciture. In *Pragmatics and Cognition* 16(1): 65–90. (Special Issue on Pragmatic Interfaces).

Geis, M. 1995. *Speech Acts and Conversational Interaction*. Cambridge: CUP.

Gibbs, R. & Moise, J. 1997. Pragmatics in understanding what is said. *Cognition* 62: 51–74.

Grice, H. P. 1975. Logic and conversation. Reprinted in Grice 1989, op cit.

Grice, H. P. 1989. *Studies in the Way of Words*. Cambridge MA: Harvard University Press.

Haegeman, L. 1991. *Introduction to Government & Binding Theory*. Malden MA: Blackwell.

Harnish, R. 1976. Logical form and implicature. In *An Integrated Theory of Linguistic Ability*, T. Bever (ed.). New York NY: T. Crowell.

Harnish, R. 1983. Pragmatic derivations. *Synthese* 54: 325–73.

Huang, Y. & Snedecker, J. 2006. Online interpretation of scalar quantifiers: Insight into the semantic–pragmatic interface. http://www.cogsci.rpi.edu/CSJarchive/Proceedings/2006/docs/p351.pdf

Jackendoff, R. 1987. The status of thematic relations in linguistic theory. *Linguistic Inquiry* 18(3): 369–411.

Katz, J. & Postal, P. 1964. *An Integrated Theory of Linguistic Descriptions*. Cambridge MA: The MIT Press.

Levinson, S. 1995. Three levels of meaning. In *Grammar and Meaning*, F. Palmer (ed.). Cambridge: CUP.

Levinson, S. 2000. *Presumptive Meanings*. Cambridge MA: The MIT Press.

Morgan, J. 1978. Two types of convention in indirect speech acts. In *Syntax and Semantics* 9, P. Cole (ed.), New York NY: Academic Press.

Murray, W. 2000. Sentence processing: Issues and measures. *Reading as a Perceptual Process*, A. Kennedy et al (ed.). Oxford: Elsevier.

S. Nicolle & Clark, B. 1999. Experimental pragmatics and what is said. *Cognition* 69: 337–54.

Perry, J. 1986. Thought without representation. In *Proceedings of the Aristotelian Society* 60, reprinted in *The Problem of the Essential Indexical*. Oxford: OUP.

Putnam, H. 1975. The meaning of 'eeaning'. In *Language, Mind and Knowledge*, K. Gunderson (ed.). Minneapolis MN: University of Minnesota Press.

Recanati, F. 1989. The pragmatics of what is said. *Mind and Language* 4: 295–329.

Recanati, F. 1993. *Direct Reference*. Oxford: Blackwell.

Recanati, F. 2002. Unarticulated constituents. *Linguistics and Philosophy* 25: 299–345.

Recanati, F. 2004. *Literal Meaning*. Cambridge: CUP.

Sag, L. & Hankamer, J. 1977. Syntactically and pragmatically controlled anaphora. In *Studies in Language Variation*, R. Fasold & R. Shuy (eds). Washington DC: Georgetown University Press.

Searle, J. 1978. Literal meaning, *Erkenntnis*. Reprinted in Searle, J. 1979, *Expression and Meaning*. Cambridge: CUP.

Searle, J. 1975. Indirect speech acts. In *Syntax and Semantics* 3, P. Cole & J. Morgan (eds). New York NY: Academic Press.

Sells, P. 1985. *Lectures on Contemporary Syntactic Theories*. Stanford CA: CLS.

Sperber, D. & Wilson, D. 1986. *Relevance*. Cambridge MA: Harvard University Press.

Stainton, R. 1995. Non-sentential assertions and semantic ellipsis. *Linguistics and Philosophy* 18: 281–96.

Stainton, R. 1997. Utterance meaning and syntactic ellipsis. *Pragmatics and Cognition* 5(1): 51–78.

Stanley, J. 2000. Context and logical form. *Linguistics and Philosophy* 23:391–434.

Stanley, J. & Z. Szabo. 2000. On quantifier domain restriction *Mind and Language* 15:219–61.

Taylor, K. 2001. Sex, breakfast and descriptus interuptus. *Synthese* 128:45–61.

Tyler, L. & Marslen-Wilson, W. 1977. The on-line effects of semantic context on syntactic processing. *Journal of Verbal Learning and Verbal Behavior* 16:683–92.

Vicente, B. 2002. What pragmatics can tell us about (literal) meaning. *Journal of Pragmatics* 34: 403–21.

Wilks, Y. & Bien, J. 1983. Beliefs, points of view, and multiple environments. *Cognitive Science* 7:95–119.

Williams, E. 1977. Discourse and logical form. *Linguistic Inquiry* 8:101–39.

CHAPTER 4

Current challenges to
the Lexicalist Hypothesis

An overview and a critique

Frederick J. Newmeyer
University of Washington, University of British Columbia,
and Simon Fraser University

In this chapter, arguments against several variants of the modern syntax-based analyses of deverbal nominalizations are presented, and the classic lexicalist approach deriving from Chomsky's 1970 *Remarks on nominalization* is defended. The modern approaches of Alexiadou (2001), Fu, Roeper and Borer (2001), Harley and Noyer (1998), which revive in various forms the sentential Generative Semantics analyses of event nominals, are each considered and rejected in turn. In such approaches, argument-structure nominals contain some amount of verbal structure as a proper subpart. Yet, all such nominals exhibit surface syntactic patterns that resemble exactly those of nonderived nominals. The absence of verb-phrase syntax within nominalizations is a fundamental generalization about such nominals, and is very problematic for analyses which propose such substructure.

1. Introduction

In deciding on a topic for a Festschrift chapter to honor Terry Langendoen, I felt it appropriate to choose some issue that has spanned his more than 45 years in the field of linguistics.[1] One that immediately sprung to mind was the question of the 'abstractness' of syntactic structure. The problem of the degree of remove of underlying levels of structure from surface levels and the permitted operations deriving the latter from the former is as alive now as it was in 1961, the first year of Terry's graduate studies at MIT. Furthermore, Terry himself has, over the years, contributed to the solution of the problem. Among other work, one thinks of his conclusion that facts about the *can't seem to* construction in English lead to fairly abstract syntactic representations and his recent exploration of the 'merge' operations within the Minimalist Program (Langendoen 1970 and Langendoen 2003 respectively).

---

1 A version of this paper was presented at the Word-Formation Theories Workshop, Presov, Slovakia, in June 2005. I am indebted to Hagit Borer, Heidi Harley, Ray Jackendoff, and Peter Svenonius for their helpful comments on an earlier draft.

The question of 'abstractness' is also one that has formed a constant thread throughout my own work. No publication was more instrumental to my own development as a linguist than Chomsky's paper 'Remarks on Nominalization' (Chomsky 1970). I was trained at the University of Illinois as a generative semanticist, but had the opportunity to spend my last year as a student at MIT, where the 'Remarks' paper was all the rage. While my experience at MIT did not deter me from generative semantics, at least not for a while, it did provide me with a more open mind about how to do things than most generative semanticists had at that time. Also, the first published debate in which I took part was over the question of what we can conclude about abstractness from English nominalizations (Newmeyer 1970; Wasow and Roeper 1972). I took the generative semantic position that nominalizations are all deverbal, while Wasow and Roeper defended the lexicalist approach in Chomsky's 'Remarks' paper. Now close to 40 years later the roles are completely reversed. In the present chapter I defend the Chomsky of the 1970s against the attempt by Roeper and others to revive a version of the generative semantic analysis!

The chapter is organized as follows. Section 2 outlines the lexicalist hypothesis and its motivation, followed by Section 3, which presents the four principal current approaches to nominals that are incompatible with the hypothesis. Section 4 argues that these non-lexicalist approaches are inadequate. Section 5 is a brief conclusion.

2. Chomsky's lexicalist hypothesis

Before 1970, all generative grammarians assumed that all nominalizations were both deverbal and desentential. Such an analysis was taken for granted in Lees (1960), and defended and given a generative semantic spin in Lakoff (1965/1970). Things began to change with Chomsky's 'Remarks' paper, circulated in 1967 and published in 1970. In that paper, Chomsky put forward the 'lexicalist hypothesis', in essence the hypothesis that derivational (as opposed to inflectional) processes of word-formation are not performed in the transformational component. More specifically, he argued that an important class of surface nouns enters the transformational derivation as nouns. The data involved three types of nominalizations in English. The first, gerundive nominals (or simply 'gerunds'), are illustrated in (1):

(1) a.   John's riding his bicycle rapidly (surprised me).
     b.   Mary's not being eager to please (was unexpected).
     c.   Sue's having solved the problem (made life easy for us).

Second, he pointed to derived nominals, as in (2):

(2) a. John's decision to leave (surprised me).
 b. Mary's eagerness to please (was unexpected).
 c. Sue's help (was much appreciated).

And, third, he illustrated an intermediate class, exemplified in (3), all of whose members have the suffix *-ing* like gerundive nominals, but which share many properties with derived nominals:

(3) a. John's refusing of the offer
 b. John's proving of the theorem
 c. the growing of tomatoes

In the remainder of this chapter, following Harley and Noyer (1998), I refer to the third type as 'mixed nominals'.

Chomsky had no problem with the idea that gerundive nominals are deverbal with an inflectional suffix, given that they exhibit most of the hallmarks of full sentences. As can seen in (1), they allow aspect, negation, and adverbs. In the remainder of this chapter I have nothing to say about gerundive nominals, since their deverbal nature is too uncontroversial to devote time to discussing.[2]

Under the lexicalist hypothesis, derived nominals (henceforth 'DNs') and mixed nominals are simply listed as nouns in the lexicon and generalizations between them and their morphologically related verbs are captured by lexical redundancy rules (Jackendoff 1975) or inheritance hierarchies (Sag, Wasow, and Bender 2003). In other words, (4a) and (4b) are attributed essentially the same underlying syntactic structure, something like (5) (or its obvious counterpart, given binary branching):

(4) a. Mary's three boring books about tennis
 b. Mary's three unexpected refusals of the offer

---

2. There is a debate, however, on whether they are also desentential, with Zucchi (1993), Harley and Noyer (1998), and Alexiadou (2001) taking the position that they are not. Zucchi points to the absence of sentences with genitive subjects (cf. ia–c) and Alexiadou claims that (iib) show that gerundive nominals do not involve 'high' functional projections:

(i) a. The committee rejected John.
 b. The committee's rejecting John.
 c. *The committee's rejected John.
(ii) a. *John's probably being a spy
 b. *John's fortunately knowing the answer

But to account for the possessive marker in (i) it suffices to assume that all subjects of DPs are genitive (Jackendoff 1977). Phrases (iia–b) seem perfectly well-formed to me.

(5)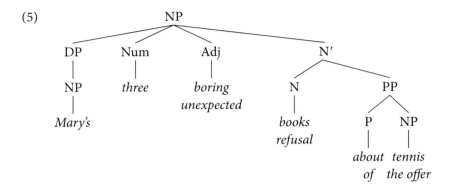

Chomsky gave three arguments in support of the lexicalist hypothesis. The first I call the 'Idiosyncrasy Argument'. It was well accepted at the time that a transformational rule should capture a regular productive relationship. But, as Chomsky noted, the relationship between DNs and their corresponding verbs is highly irregular. For one thing, not every DN has a corresponding verb:

(6) motion, but *mote; usher, but *ush; tuition, but *tuit; etc.

In those cases in which no verb corresponding to a DN exists, a transformational account, Chomsky noted, would have to invent an abstract verb whose only function would be to undergo the nominalization transformation. Furthermore, the meaning relation between verbs and adjectives and their morphologically corresponding DNs is an idiosyncratic one:

(7) a. profess ('declare openly')–professor ('university teacher')–profession ('career')
   b. ignore ('pay no attention to')–ignorance ('lack of knowledge')–ignoramus ('very stupid person')
   c. person ('human individual')–personal ('private')–personable ('friendly')–personality ('character')–personalize ('tailor to the individual')–impersonate ('pass oneself off as')
   d. social ('pertaining to society'; 'interactive with others')–socialist ('follower of a particular political doctrine')–socialite ('member of high society')

Chomsky argued that a lexicalist treatment of DNs allows their irregularity to be captured in a natural manner. Concretely, he suggested that the verb *refuse* and the noun *refusal* share a neutral lexical entry that lists those features common to both. This neutral entry incorporates a N branch and a V branch, each terminating in a representation that specifies the properties distinct to the nominal manifestation and the verbal manifestation (see 8):[3]

At deep structure, the verb *refuse* is inserted into a VP frame and the noun *refusal* into a DP frame.[4]

(8)

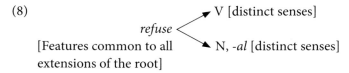

I call Chomsky's second argument for the lexicalist hypothesis the 'Internal Structure Argument'. Its point of departure is the fact that the structures in which DNs occur resemble noun phrases in every way. They can contain determiners, prenominal adjectives, and prepositional phrase complements (as in 9a), but not adverbs, negation, aspect, nor tense (9b–d):

(9) a. the stupid refusal of the offer
 b. *the refusal stupidly of the offer
 c. *the not refusal of the offer
 d. *the have refusal of the offer

Such facts follow automatically if DNs are nouns in the lexicon and are inserted as such into the initial syntactic representation. That is, a lexicalist treatment predicts them to have the same distribution as ordinary nouns. A transformational analysis, on the other hand, would be forced to posit ad hoc conditions on the nominalizing process to ensure that the underlying sentences end up looking like surface noun phrases.

Chomsky's third argument, the 'Frozen Structure Argument', was more complex. The problem in need of explanation is that DNs occur in DPs corresponding to base structures, but not to transformationally derived structures. Consider the contrast between the (b) phrases and the (a) phrases in (10–16):

(10) a. Harry was certain to win the prize.
 b. *Harry's certainty to win the prize (no Raising within DP)

---

[3]. There is no directionality inherent in the representation in (8). Since the publication of Chomsky (1970), however, most lexicalist accounts have assumed that for many nominals, either the N entry is more lexically basic than the V entry, or vice-versa. For a recent defense of this idea using zero-derivation nominals (conversions) as data, see Kiparsky (1997) and Don (2004).

[4]. Anachronistically, but for the sake of consistency, from hereon I refer to the node label 'DP', rather than 'NP', even for work that preceded the DP hypothesis.

(11) a. Mary gave Peter the book.
      b. *Mary's gift of Peter of the book (no Dative Movement within DP)

(12) a. There appeared to be no hope.
      b. *there's appearance to be no hope (no There-Insertion within DP)

(13) a. I believed Bill to be a fool.
      b. *my belief of Bill to be a fool (no Raising-to-Object within DP)

(14) a. John interested the children with his stories.
      b. *John's interest of the children with his stories (no Psych-Movement within DP)

(15) a. Lee is easy to please.
      b. *Lee's easiness to please (no Tough-Movement within DP)

(16) a. Mary looked the information up.
      b. *Mary's looking of the information up (no Particle Movement within DP)

Chomsky argued that the data in (10–16) follow automatically from the treatment of DNs as deep structure nouns. If one assumes that the domain of movement is confined to verbal projections, but not to purely nominal ones, then the ungrammatical (b) phrases are simply underivable.

Unfortunately, the rule of Passive appeared to be a glaring counterexample to the claim that transformations do not apply in the DP domain. One's first thought might be that Passive applies internally to DP, since (17b) is unexpectedly grammatical:

(17) a. John was rejected by the committee.
      b. John's rejection by the committee (Passive seems to apply within DP)

To account for (17b), Chomsky — rather inconsistently — hypothesized that Passive *does* apply in a DP domain.

3. Recent updates of the generative semantic analysis

In this section I present the four most comprehensive non-lexicalist approaches to English nominalizations that have been put forward in recent years: Borer (2003); Alexiadou (2001); Roeper (2005); and Harley (in press).[5] All are developed within

---

5. I discuss Borer (2003) before Alexiadou (2001) because the essentials of the former work had been presented at least a decade earlier (see Borer 1993). See also Marantz (1997) for an earlier, but quite sketchy, parallel treatment.

the general rubric of the Minimalist Program (MP), which, given its employment of cascades of functional projections, provides a congenial way of deriving surface nouns from a deeper structure with a lower verbal projection. However, the question of whether a transformational treatment of nominals is literally entailed by the set of assumptions guiding work in the MP will not be considered here.

A distinction first proposed, I believe, in Grimshaw (1990) is central to most non-lexicalist approaches. Grimshaw divided derived nominals into two classes, which she called 'complex event nominals' and 'result nominals'. These were later respectively relabeled 'Argument-Structure Nominals (AS-Nominals)' and 'Referential Nominals (R-Nominals)' in Borer (2003) and 'process nominals' and 'result nominals' in Alexiadou (2001). In the remainder of this chapter I adopt Borer's terminology. (18) and (19) illustrate each class:

(18) AS-nominals
    a. the instructor's (intentional) examination of the student
    b. the frequent collection of mushrooms (by students)
    c. the monitoring of wild flowers to document their disappearance
    d. the destruction of Rome in a day

(19) R-nominals
    a. the instructor's examination/exam
    b. John's collections
    c. these frequent destructions

The two classes are said to be distinguished in the following way (the table is a summary of Borer (2003:45); see also Alexiadou (2001:10–12):

(20)

AS-Nominals	*R-Nominals*
θ-assigners, Obligatory arguments	Non-θ-assigners, No obligatory arguments
Event reading	No event reading
Agent-oriented modifiers	No agent-oriented modifiers
Subjects are arguments	Subjects are possessives
by-phrases are arguments	*by*-phrases are non-arguments
Implicit argument control	No implicit argument control
Aspectual modifiers	No aspectual modifiers
frequent, constant etc. possible without plural	*frequent, constant*, etc. possible only with plural nouns
Mass nouns	Count nouns

Let us now turn to a few concrete non-lexicalist proposals.

3.1 Borer (2003)

Borer proposes a radically computational theory, with a diminished role for the lexicon and lexical operations.[6] In particular, in this 'exo-skeletal' approach, she 'attempt[s] to reduce as many as possible of the formal properties traditionally attributed to lexical listing to formal computational systems, be they syntax or morphology. [In this approach] the structure, rather than the listed item, determines not only grammatical properties, but also the ultimate fine-grained meaning of the lexical items themselves ...' (Borer 2003:33).

Borer argues that the properties of AS-Nominals and R-Nominals as summarized above lead to markedly different derivations for each. AS-Nominals are syntactically derived by nominalizing a VP in the syntax, while R-nominals are derived pre-syntactically and inserted into the syntactic derivation directly as Ns. In particular, she posits that AS-Nominals contain an internal VP and full event structure, as illustrated in the following representation (Borer 2003:51):

(21) a. Kim's destruction of the vase

b. $[_{NP}$ -tion$_{NOM}$ $[_{EP}$ Kim $[_{ASPQ}$ the vase $[_{VP}$ destroy$]]]]$

In other words, for AS-Nominals, each morphological element heads its own categorial projection, itself dominated by the appropriate functional projection. Successive head movements merge the root with affixes to create the appropriate complex lexical item. R-Nominals, on the other hand, project only nominalizing functional structure (DP, NumP, etc.), not verbalizing functional structure (TP, ASP$_Q$, etc.), and have no internal argument structure.

Borer recognizes that attributing argument structure to AS-Nominals qua nouns (along the lines of (8) above) would also account for many of their distinct characteristics. However, she argues that one (putative) property of AS-nominals does not follow from a purely lexicalist approach and therefore, in her view, decides in favor of their deverbality. She writes:

> Only nouns which are derived from verbs (or, as we shall see, from adjectives) by means of overt affixation can be AS-Nominals, while nouns which do not have a verbal or an adjectival source never are. Viewed from that perspective, one is certainly tempted to view argument structure as well as event interpretation as deriving from the source verb or adjective, rather than from the noun itself.   (Borer 2003:47)

To illustrate with an example adapted from Grimshaw, *examination* can have both an AS-Nominal reading and an R-Nominal reading (22a–b), but affixless *exam* has only the R-Nominal reading (23a–b):

---

6. Borer's general approach is presented in detail in Borer (2005a, b). A more comprehensive treatment of nominalizations is promised to be developed in Borer (to appear).

(22) a. the professor's examination of the students (took two hours)
 b. the students' examinations (were handed out by the professor)

(23) a. *the professor's exam(s) of the students (took two hours)
 b. the students' exams (were handed out by the professor)

Borer goes on to claim, following Grimshaw, that zero-derivation nominals can be R-Nominals, but not to AS-Nominals, pointing to the following examples in support of this claim:

(24) a. *the/John's drive of the car
 b. *the/Mary's walk of the dog
 c. *the/Kim's break of the vase
 d. *the air force's murder of innocent civilians (Borer's grammaticality assignment)

Again, she argues that such facts follow naturally from her framework if we assume that what appears as a Ø-morpheme is in actuality a category-neutral stem, unmarked for being either a noun or a verb. The absence of an overt nominalizing morpheme, then, will prevent the merger of the stem with a higher N-forming affix, predicting the impossibility of (24a–d). Borer concludes that 'it is hard to see how a theory which attributes role assignment to lexical entries can likewise capture these facts' (Borer 2003: 56).

3.2 Alexiadou (2001)

Alexiadou (2001), in its broad outline, has features that are quite parallel to those of Borer (2003). Like Borer, Alexiadou posits a complex structure for AS-Nominals (which she calls 'Process Nominals') to account for their aspectual properties and a much simpler structure for R-Nominals (which she calls 'Result Nominals'), which are inserted directly under nominal projections. (26) illustrates her proposed structure for (25):

(25) the destruction of the city

Alexiadou goes well beyond Borer, however, in the number and types of functional layers that she posits. Drawing on crosslinguistic evidence to a greater extent than Borer, Alexiadou suggests that nominals can vary with respect to the presence or absence of CP, of AspectP, of vP, of NumP, and of other projections as well.

(26)

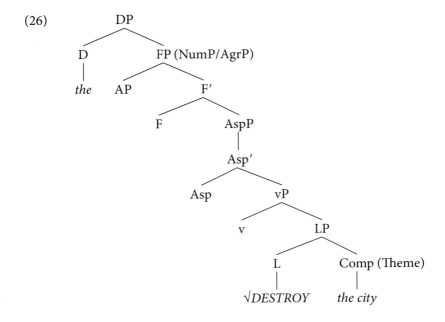

3.3 Roeper (2005)

Roeper (2005) follows Borer (2003) and Alexiadou (2001) in its essentials. As his trees representing the words *destruction* and *mowing* indicate, DNs and mixed nominals have an internal V node:

(27) a.   b.

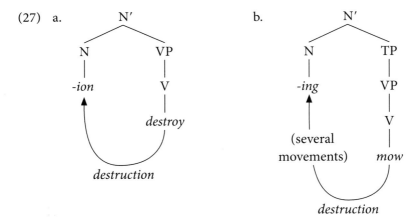

And for Roeper as well, projections have semantic relevance and particular types of nominals are associated with particular projections (e. g. for event nominals, N' immediately dominates VP; for bare result nominals like *help* and *advice*, N' immediately dominates a bare V stem; and so on.).

3.4 Harley (in press)

Harley in press differs from the three aforementioned works by proposing a transformational treatment of all derived nominals, not just AS-Nominals. Its assumption of the framework of Distributed Morphology (DM) entails that all morphemes occupy terminal nodes of a hierarchical structure built by normal syntactic processes. Hence a Borer-type approach where pre-syntactic word formation produces a syntactically atomic N^0 which has the interpretation of a result nominal 'is not possible within DM; to adopt the notion that words can be built either pre- or post-syntactically would make most of the framework's strongest predictions and claims vacuous' (Harley in press, ms. p. 25). Harley proposes to derive the distinct properties of R-Nominals (their being count nouns, their lack of objects, etc.) by a process of semantic coercion.

4. A critique of current non-lexicalist accounts of nominalizations

I argue in this section that the current non-lexicalist analyses do not capture the three properties of nominalizations pointed out by Chomsky — at least not without additional assumptions that are not discussed explicitly in these works. The following subsections take Chomsky's arguments one-by-one and measure the work of Borer, Alexiadou, Roeper, and Harley against them.

4.1 The Idiosyncrasy Argument

As noted above, Borer and Alexiadou postulate that AS-Nominals are derived from successive head movements in the syntax. What is not clear from their presentations is whether (pre-syntactic) word-formation rules (WFR's) *also* derive this class of nominals. If they do, then there is an obvious redundancy, since the same generalization would need to be stated in both the morphology and in the syntax. If they do not, then morphologically identical words would need to be derived by two types of rules. The word *examination*, for example, would be derived by a WFR in its R-Nominal manifestation and by head movement in its AS-Nominal manifestation, thereby missing an obvious generalization.

If any affix could attach to any root or to any other affix, then the non-lexicalist successive head-movement approach to nominalization would find remarkable support. But of course that is not the case. As discussed in Fabb (1988), certain non-occurring nominalizations are excluded by general principles of English word formation (the suffix -*ment* does not attach to any already-suffixed word: *replacement*, but not **classifiment*), while others, like **refusion (of the offer)*, seem in principle possible, but accidentally non-occurring. The question is how Borer and Alexiadou would handle the latter cases. For R-Nominals there would presumably be no problem, since a separate word formation component is posited to handle restrictions governing roots and affixes. But what about AS-Nominals? Again, it is not clear to me what Borer's and Alexiadou's stance on this issue is. If a pre-syntactic WFR blocks *refuse* from attaching to *-tion*, then we have an even clearer example of duplication of process between the lexicon and the syntax. On the other hand, constraining head movement not to merge some α with some β seems little more than a cumbersome way of building the entire machinery of subcategorization into the computational system.

There is also the question of how the approaches under discussion might handle nominalizations whose stems are not actually occurring verbs. Such nominals can be either of the R-type (28a) or the AS-type (28b):

(28) a. conniption, but *connip
     b. disapprobation, but *disapprobe, *disapprobate

Example (28a) presumably poses no problems for treatments in which R-Nominals are handled by WFR's. However, one wonders how it would be analyzed by Harley, for whom only syntactic processes are available for word formation. Would there be an abstract root *connip-, marked to obligatorily undergo fusion with the suffix *-tion*, along the lines of Lakoff (1965/1970)? Such an approach would seem to imply that *connip should have an independent meaning, which it surely does not. (28b) creates problems for any treatment of AS-Nominals that does not allow for them to be derived by WFR's as well as by head movement in the syntax (which might or might not be Borer's and Alexiadou's position — see above). If the AS-Nominal *disapprobation* is underlain by (29), it is not obvious where and how its meaning would be represented.

(29)
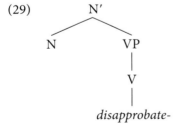

(29) also leads to a false prediction about the occurrence of the pro-form *do so*. Roeper takes the grammaticality — in my mind the dubious grammaticality — of (30a) as an argument for a VP node under *destruction*. But surely he would agree that (30b) is impossible. (29) predicts that (30b) should be fine.

Chapter 4. Current challenges to the Lexicalist Hypothesis **103**

(30) a. John's destruction of the city and Bill's doing so too
b. *John's disapprobation of the new methods and Bill's doing so too

Borer's primary empirical argument for AS-Nominals being deverbal or deadjectival, namely the idea that such nominals always contain affixes attached to verbal or adjectival stems, appears to be faulty. Many suffixless nouns behave like AS-Nominals, in that they manifest the full argument structure and event reading that she attributes to such nominals. The following are examples:[7]

(31) a. Mary's metamorphosis of the house (made it unrecognizable)
b. the IRS's scrutiny of dubious looking tax forms
c. my lab assistant's culture of new forms of bacteria
d. the anathema by the church of those taking part in satanic rituals
e. America's moratorium on helping to support UNESCO
f. Iraq's frequent changeover of its currency (has left its people confused)
g. the constant mischief by the boy
h. Quisling's ongoing treason (was the shame of Norway)
i. the frequent recourse to long discredited methods
j. my impulse to be daring
k. Yahoo's homicide of AltaVista and AllTheWeb
l. Pope's and Swift's persiflage of the Grub Street hacks

Analogously, Borer seems to have explained non-existent 'facts' in her account of why we should not expect to find AS-Nominals with Ø-morphology. To begin, (25d) above seems perfectly well-formed to me and to the half-dozen native speakers of English whom I consulted. Literally dozens of zero-derivation nouns allow full argument structure, among which are the following:[8]

(32) a. my constant change of mentors from 1992–1997
b. the frequent release of the prisoners by the governor
c. the frequent use of sharp tools by underage children
d. an officer's too frequent discharge of a firearm (could lead to disciplinary action)
e. the ancient Greeks' practice of infanticide
f. my constant need for approval
g. the student's conscious endeavor to improve her grades

---

7. (31k–l) were the result of a Google search.

8. Borer herself cites (32a–c), noting that 'all generalizations concerning WF [have] counterexamples' (Borer 2003:53).

h. the constant abuse of prisoners by their guards
i. Smith's consent to accept the nomination
j. Mary's resolve to be more assertive
k. access to the mainframe by qualified users (will be permitted)
l. France's test of nuclear weapons in the South Pacific

In other words, the formal realization of AS-Nominals shows little morphological productivity. However, I suspect that is indeed the case that the majority — perhaps the large majority — of AS-Nominals are morphologically complex. The question is whether this fact belongs to the domain of I-language. I doubt that it does. Consider an analogous phenomenon. It was first pointed out, I believe, in Storm (1977) that the great majority of English verbs that occur in the double object construction are monomorphemic. But this circumstance is pure historical accident, and reveals nothing about the competence of native English speakers. The construction existed in Old English, where most verbs allowing indirect objects happened to be monomorphemic. In later periods, a number of indirect object-taking verbs were borrowed from French and Latin (both of which lack the double object construction), and most of which happened to be bimorphemic. Since the process allowing double objects had ceased to be fully productive, double objects as a consequence continued to be found primarily with monomorphemic verbs. But there is no reason to think that this fact ever came to be 'registered' in the grammar of English. While I do not know the history of AS-Nominals, I suspect that their characteristic morphological complexity is a product of historical accident as well.

The question is whether there are *any* purely syntactic properties that distinguish the two types of nominals. Two of the criteria for distinguishing them that are listed in (20) above appear to be spurious. For example, there are numerous cases of Arg-S-Nominals that do not have obligatory arguments (Williams 1985: 301; Law 1997: 43):

(33) a. Dr. Krankheit's operation (on Billy) took three hours.
      b. John submitted himself to her scrutiny.
      c. Human rights in third world countries are subject to constant repression.
      d. The poor are susceptible to constant repression by the rich.
      e. A very strong will for survival helped the villagers sustain such heavy bombardment.
      f. Political dissidents in the ex-USSR were under constant surveillance by the KGB.
      g. The sea water was sent to the plant for desalination.
      h. The analysis needs further refinement.

i. The UN officials appeared to be in constant negotiation.

j. Constant exposure to the sun is harmful to the skin.

And contrary to the position taken by Grimshaw and Borer, there are numerous examples of Arg-S-Nominals that are count nouns:

(34) a. Mary's constant refusals of the committee's offer

        b. Paul and Frank's many discussions of modern jazz

        c. your interpretations of the new rules

        d. the apostle Peter's three denials of Jesus

        e. the custom officials' inspections of suspicious baggage

        f. (I can't take anymore) rejections of my submissions by the journal *Linguistics Illustrated*

        g. Sam's constant attentions toward Susan (were not welcomed)

        h. Coca Cola's twelve interruptions of the Super Bowl game

        i. Mary's incessant arguments against the theory of Goofy Grammar

In all three approaches under discussion one is left wondering what formal mechanisms specify the particular levels of functional structure that occur with each nominal type — a prerequisite to determining whether their non-lexicalist treatment represents an improvement over the lexicalist. So consider, for example, Alexiadou's account of eventive *-er* nominals, such as those in (35):

(35) a. the defenders of human rights

        b. a devourer of fresh fruit

Alexiadou concludes that such nominals lack AspectP, allow NumP, and include a v with agentivity features (as opposed to v in process nominals such as *destruction*, whose v lacks agentivity features). But where is this information recorded for, say, the nominal in (35a)? After all, the lexical category is simply the category-less root √DEFEND (see 26 above), so it is hard to see how it could be recorded there. What determines, then, which functional projections can accompany this root when it surfaces as an *-er* nominal? I do not see how such a specification can be made without the equivalent of a lexicon and lexical rules, whose scope would necessarily be partially duplicated in the postulated syntactic derivation. What makes such an approach even more awkward is the fact that not all *-er* nominals have an eventive interpretation. There are occupation, instrumental, and object nominals with this morphology as well:

(36) a. Mary is a farmer.

        b. I bought a new toaster.

        c. Your new bracelet is a keeper.

Clearly, what one would like to incorporate into the grammar of English is a specification along the lines of (37):

(37) [$_N$ V-*er*]

Either such a specification is unformulable in the approaches under discussion or it partially duplicates part of the syntactic derivation.

The peculiar features of mixed nominals also challenge a transformation-based account. As Chomsky noted: '... there is an artificiality to the construction that makes it quite resistant to systematic investigation' (Chomsky 1970:214). For example, passives forms are impossible:

(38) a. *the lawn's mowing by Mary
       b. *the offer's refusing by John

Roeper, whose one explicit tree that outlines derivational steps is of a mixed nominal (see (27b)), handles this ungrammaticality by hypothesizing that -*ing* is purely transitive, but this stipulation does not *follow* from anything intrinsic to his approach. Even so, that stipulation would appear to make the wrong prediction about unaccusatives, since (39) is fine:

(39) Mary's arriving on time surprised us.

Assuming that *arrive* is an unaccusative verb and that *Mary* originates in object position, (39) should be underivable, given Roeper's assumptions.

Part of Roeper's program is to try to find a unique meaning — and therefore a unique projection — for each affix. I do not think that he has been successful. For example, he argues that the -*tion* suffix refers to the notion of EVENT. Sometimes that is the case, but more often than not, it is not. In fact, I would estimate that at most 10% of -*tion* nominalizations refer exclusively to events. Some non-event examples are listed below:

(40) abbreviation, absorption, acceleration, addiction, addition, adoration, agglutination, ambition, annotation, augmentation, bijection, causation, citation, coalition, compensation, conception, confederation, contention, corruption, decoration, desperation, devotion, direction, duration, emotion, exception, faction, fiction, generalization, hesitation, imagination, indiscretion, inflation, isolation, jurisdiction, limitation, malnutrition, misconception, navigation, nutrition, obligation, option, overproduction, perfection, petition, preposition, qualification, recollection, reflection, relation, salvation, separation, sophistication, suggestion, toleration, utilization, ventilation

Roeper refers to 'semantic drift' to explain the existence of items like (40), but underestimates the extent of it (if drift is what really happened), and does not discuss any formal mechanism for handling the drifted items.

One could make the same point about bare nominals, which Roeper says encode results. Again, I would say that well under half of them do. Some non-result bare nominals are listed below:

(41) advice, cry, drink, hate, help, look, love, nap, run, shoot, shout, sleep, step, talk, trap, try, walk

Roeper defends his assigning different suffixes to different projections by noting that 'we expect a node to capture a semantic difference' (Roeper 2005: 15). That is probably correct. However, in reality Roeper (and to a lesser extent Borer and Alexiadou) go a lot farther than that. The position that they defend is the idea that each semantic difference should be captured by a different node, an idea that generative semantics attempted and failed to execute (see Newmeyer (1986) for discussion). By appealing to meaning as a justification for conflating the morphology and the syntax, Borer, Alexiadou, Roeper, and Harley are led to privilege the latter at the expense of the former. The linchpin of generative grammar for 50 years, and that which distinguishes it from all other approaches to language, is the autonomy of syntax, namely, the idea that formal generalizations do not map smoothly onto semantic ones. I do not feel that the current non-lexicalist attempt to subvert autonomy has been successful.

4.2. The Internal-Structure Argument

Consider three types of DP: those whose nominal heads are monomorphemic and unnominalized (42a), those whose heads are R-Nominals (42b), and those whose heads are AS-Nominals (42c):

(42) a. Mary's boring book by Williams about tennis
      b. The gallery's precious portrait by Rembrandt of Saskia
      c. The Huns' brutal destruction of Rome in one day

For Borer, Alexiadou, and Harley, (42b) and (42c) have markedly different derivations, while for Roeper, the derivations of all three phrase types differ considerably. Yet the surface structures of these three phrases are essentially identical. The question is how this near identity follows from any of the four approaches in a natural way. That is, we need something explicit that tells us what the structure of a DP is and why the structures of (42a–c) are so similar. But we are not told what that device is.

Alexiadou's strategy, for example, is to tease out subtle aspectual differences among the different classes of nominalizations and to thereby conclude that different classes of nominals take different functional projections. But such a conclusion follows only if the formal realization of aspect is in sync with the particular aspectual interpretation. That is almost never the case, however. Consider for example the telic/atelic distinction. Alexiadou appeals to this distinction (2001: ch. 2) to motivate particular functional structures. But the *formal* realization of the distinction, as noted by Jackendoff (1997), can be manifested in quite a number of different ways: by the choice of verb (43a), the choice of preposition (43b), the choice of adverbial (43c), and the choice of determiner in the subject (43d), the object (43e), or the prepositional object (43f):

(43) a. John destroyed the cart (in/*for an hour)   (telic)
          John pushed the cart (for/*in an hour)   (atelic)
      b. John ran to the station (in/*for an hour)   (telic)
          John ran toward the station (for/*in an hour)   (atelic)
      c. The light flashed once (in/*for an hour)   (telic)
          The light flashed constantly (for/*in an hour)   (atelic)
      d. Four people died (in/*for two days)   (telic)
          People died (for/*in two days)   (atelic)
      e. John ate lots of peanuts (in/*for an hour)   (telic)
          John ate peanuts (for/*in an hour)   (atelic)
      f. John crashed into three walls (in/*for an hour)   (telic)
          John crashed into walls (for/*in an hour)   (atelic)

Since all of these formal devices can be used to express other semantic distinctions having nothing to do with aspect, there is no justification for drawing conclusions about the *syntactic* structure of nominals (or any other constituent type) on the basis of whether they permit telic or atelic readings.

Fu, Roeper, and Borer (2001) attempt to motivate an internal VP for *-tion* nominalizations by giving examples of where they occur with *do so* (presumptively a VP anaphor) and adverbs (the question marks are those assigned in Roeper (2005):

(44) John's destruction of the city and Bill's doing so too

(45) a. While the removal of evidence *purposefully* (is a crime), the removal of
          evidence *unintentionally* (is not).
      b. ?His explanation of the problem *thoroughly* to the tenants (did not
          prevent a riot).
      c. ?Protection of children *completely* from bad influence (is unrealistic).
      d. His resignation so *suddenly* gave rise to wild speculation.

Chapter 4. Current challenges to the Lexicalist Hypothesis **109**

I would be inclined to attribute phrases like (44) to performance error or to a recency effect. But if (44) argues for a VP node with event nominalizations, then the equal acceptability (or lack of it) of (46) should argue for a VP node with *bare* nominalizations:

(46) America's attack on Iraq was even less justified than the latter's doing so to Kuwait.

Yet, these are just the nominalizations for which the three of the four approaches posit that there is no VP node. I find (45a–c) so marginal that it is surely inadvisable to appeal to their grammaticality to prop up a theoretical proposal. In any event, they seem no better or no worse than (47a–c), where Roeper and Borer would argue that there is no internal VP node.[9] (45d) is most likely an example of a *so*-phrase modifying a Noun, analogously to (47d):

(47) a. I must deplore the recourse all too frequently to underhanded tactics.
     b. The use — I must say somewhat frighteningly — of mercury to cure gastric ulcers has been condemned by the AMA.
     c. Could we arrange for the prisoners' release more gradually than has been the practice?
     d. With a heart so pure he will never go astray.

Alexiadou (2001: 15), on the other hand, unlike Roeper, recognizes that adverbs do not occur within AS-Nominals in English, an unexpected fact, given her position that they embed a VP. However, in defense of an internal VP for English AS-Nominals she points to data from Hebrew and Greek that show that in those languages adverbials do occur with such nominals. I do not know why that fact should be relevant to the analysis of English nominals, particularly given that Alexiadou is willing elsewhere to posit crosslinguistic differences in functional projections.

Turning to mixed nominals, in virtually every respect they have the same internal structure as DNs. For example, they forbid internal aspect and negation and they demand a preposition after the head:

(48) a. *the having mowed of the lawn
     b. *the not mowing of the lawn
     c. *the mowing the lawn

Roeper has no means for explaining the ungrammaticality of (48a–c), since the suffix is generated as the sister of TP (see 27b) and TP's contain negation, aspect, and bare objects.

---

9. Ackema and Neeleman (2004: 21) find that '[t]he native speakers [they] have consulted … reject [45b and other similar examples] as clearly ungrammatical'.

In summary, the non-lexicalist accounts under review have no mechanism that explains why 'ordinary' nouns, derived nominals, and mixed nominals have the same internal structure. On the other hand, this fact follows automatically from the lexicalist treatment, in which all three enter the transformational derivation as N heads within DP.

4.3 The Frozen-Structure Argument and the problem of passive nominals

The following subsections argue that the principal minimalist account of the lack of displacement within DP is not successful (§4.3.1), nor is the attempt in Harley and Noyer (1998) to provide a minimalist account of why displaced particles do not occur within DP (§4.3.2). Section 4.3.3 argues that there is no passivization within DP, thereby supporting the strong generalization that DP is never the domain for movement.

4.3.1. *On the minimalist approach to frozen structure in nominals*

Alexiadou (2001: 59–61) provides a minimalist account of some of the data involved in the Frozen Structure Argument for the lexicalist hypothesis. Her key assumption is that Tense is absent from nominals. Since the Extended Projection Principle (EPP) feature is associated with T, the absence of this feature in nominals has the consequence that 'arguments of nouns do not exhibit obligatory movement to a designated functional position in order to satisfy the requirements of this projection the way subjects move to Spec,TP or to $T^{0\prime}$ (p. 61). It follows therefore that there will be no expletives or raising in nominal constructions:[10]

(49) a. *there's arrival of a man
    b. *Mary's appearance to have left

Along the same lines, ECM constructions (50) are predicted to be impossible in nominalizations:

(50) *my belief of Mickey to be a genius

Alexiadou writes that 'the structure proposed her permits a natural implementation of [the analysis in de Wit (1997)]. ... In other words, no tense chain can be formed, as the higher clause lacks tense, in fact it lacks any tense specification' (p. 61).

---

10. Ray Jackendoff (p. c.) has pointed out the (possibly unexpected) grammaticality of (i):

(i) John's likelihood of winning

I would be inclined to regard *John's* as a true possessive in this case (cf. *John has a 75% likelihood of winning*).

Alexiadou's account can be criticized at several different levels. First, and most seriously, there does not seem to be a robust correlation between the possibility of movement within DP projections and the presence of Tense. So (verbal) gerunds freely allow movement (51a), but prohibit the presence of Tense (51b):

(51) a. Mary's being likely to enter the race
      b. *Mary's was being likely to enter the race

Consider also the failure of DNs to occur within *easy-to-please* and double object constructions (52a–b):

(52) a. *Lee's easiness to please
      b. *Mary's gift of Peter of the book

I do not see how the impossibility of either can be tied to the absence of Tense in nominals. Nevertheless, (49–52) all follow from the blanket interdiction of any DP which does not dominate verbal projections as a domain for movement.[11]

Second, it is by no means obvious, given Alexiadou's overall framework of assumptions, that it is justified to conclude that Tense *is* absent from nominals. Alexiadou herself gives the example of (53), where the temporal interval of the referents of DP being fugitives does not coincide with the interval of their being in jail and she cites the arguments in Enç 1987 for the necessity for DPs to be given a temporal reading independently of that of the clause in which they appear:

(53) Every fugitive is now in jail.

Elsewhere in her book, Alexiadou concludes the existence of covert levels of syntactic functional structure on the basis of interpretation, so why not here as well?

Third, as Alexiadou herself notes, a number of languages seem to have overt tense in DP, including Halkomelem (Burton 1997), Potawatomi (Hockett 1958), St'at'imcets (Demirdache 1996) and Somali (Lecarme 1996). Since Alexiadou readily posits levels of functional structure for English on the basis of its overt

---

11. Williams (1982) has argued that Predication (i) and Obligatory Control also fail to apply within simple DPs (the possibility of (iib) and (iic) alongside (iia) shows that Nonobligatory Control is involved in the three cases):

(i)   *John's$_i$ arrival dead$_i$
(ii) a. John's attempt PRO to leave
      b. any attempt by John to leave
          (parallel to: *It was attempted by John to leave.)
      c. any attempt to leave
          (parallel to *It was attempted to leave.)

Interestingly, within the MP, both non-verbal predication and control have been treated as deriving from movement (see Carnie 1995 and Hornstein 1999, respectively).

manifestation in other languages, what would prevent the conclusion that English DP contains Tense?

In sum, I do not feel that Alexiadou has provided an adequate minimalist account of the frozen structure phenomena.

4.3.2. *On Harley and Noyer on particle shift in mixed nominals*
Recall that one of Chomsky's arguments for the lexicalist hypothesis was the apparent inability of Particle Movement to apply internally to mixed nominals, as illustrated by (16a–b), repeated here as (54a–b):

(54) a. Mary looked the information up.
     b. *Mary's looking of the information up

Harley and Noyer (1998) propose an explanation of the contrast between (54a) and (54b) that employs the mechanisms of both the MP and the framework of Distributed Morphology 'without recourse to a pre-syntactic component (Lexicon)' (p. 143) — an analysis which 'refutes one of the classical arguments for the lexicalist hypothesis' (p. 144). Unlike Roeper (see above §3.3), they assume that mixed nominals are just √P under D, with no vP or FP available in the structure. Hence, as illustrated below, the object cannot move to a higher functional projection and therefore has to remain in situ:

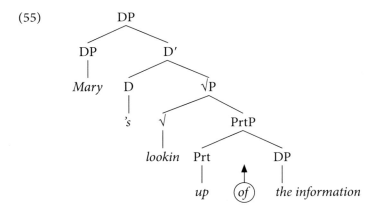

(55)

Harley and Noyer's account of the impossibility of phrase types like (54b) is fine as far as it goes, but as pointed out to me by Thomas Wasow (p. c), one *never* finds particles in English following PP:

(56) a. The river ate away the canyon wall.
     b. The river ate the canyon wall away.
     c. The river ate away at the canyon wall.
     d. *The river ate at the canyon wall away.

Chapter 4. Current challenges to the Lexicalist Hypothesis   **113**

In Harley and Noyer's theory, PPs like *at the canyon wall* do not need to check accusative case and hence will not undergo Case-driven movement. However, there are other (non-Case-related) mechanisms in English grammar which, all other things being equal, license free ordering of PPs (I assume that particles are intransitive PPs, à la Emonds 1972). For example, without a constraint blocking sequences of PP-intransitive PP, (56d) would be generated by the same mechanism that licenses both orders in (57):

(57) a. Mary looked all over the city for Bill.
     b. Mary looked for Bill all over the city.

One might suggest then that the ungrammaticality of (56d) is explained by prosodic conditions (the PP being too 'heavy' for the particle to move to the right over it) or by a condition preventing focus-driven movement from postposing particles. I am skeptical that either would work. For one thing, (58a) has essentially the same prosodic contours as (56d), yet is fine. And for another thing, there is no general prohibition against particles being in focus (58b):

(58) a. The river ate all the canyon wall away.
     b. Shall we let him IN or keep him OUT?

Note also that there is a blanket prohibition against DN's with particles (either adjacent to the verb or in postposed position):

(59) a. I'll try out the new software./I'll try the new software out.
     b. *my trial out of the new software/*my trial of the new software out

(60) a. He lived down his failure./He lived his failure down.
     b. *his life down of this failure/*his life of his failure down

(61) a. Mary gave away her money./Mary gave her money away.
     b. *Mary's gift away of her money/*Mary's gift of her money away

I do not see how that prohibition can be captured in their account, given both the availability of the necessary functional structure and the absence of a lexicon.

Furthermore, zero-derived nominals allow particles adjacent to the verb, but not separated from it, again a possibly unformulable generalization for Harley and Noyer:

(62) a. the blast off of the rocket
     b. *the blast of the rocket off

(63) a. the pay off from our investments
     b. *the pay from our investments off

All of the above examples point to 'particle shift', at least as far as it applies (or does not apply) to nominals, being the sort of lexical process incompatible with current transformational accounts of this phenomenon.[12]

4.3.3. *Passive nominals do not involve movement*

Ideally, we would expect a blanket prohibition against movement internal to DP, but the problematic case again is Passive, represented by examples like (64a), conceivably derived from (64b):

(64) a.   John's rejection by the committee
      b.   the rejection of John by the committee

In fact, I think that a strong case can be made against movement of *John* from nominal object position to nominal subject position. First of all, the movement would have to be endowed with a strange structural restriction, namely failing to apply if the noun has a determiner:

(65)   *the/that John's rejection by the committee

Another structural restriction that would need to be placed on movement is its blocking if the noun is followed by a preposition, as (66a–b) illustrate (Emonds 1976):

(66) a.   The strike was briefly referred to in the newspaper.
      b.   *I saw the strike's brief reference to in the newspaper.

Furthermore, as pointed out in Williams (1982), the possessive DP in nominals can have virtually any interpretation whatever:

---

12. One might question as well whether *verb*-particle idioms are derived by movement (whether leftward or rightward). As noted in Fraser (1976), there are numerous cases where the particle must be adjacent to the verb (i–ii) and equally numerous cases where adjacency is forbidden (iii–iv):

(i)   a.   It's time to close up shop.
       b.   *It's time to close shop up.
(ii)   a.   She's just blowing off steam.
       b.   *She's just blowing steam off.
(iii) a.   *I'm going to take off Friday. (In the 'miss work' sense of *take off*)
       b.   I'm going to take Friday off.
(iv)   a.   *Stop bossing about your little brother!
       b.   Stop bossing your little brother about!

That sort of irregularity is the hallmark of a lexical process. For more support for a lexical account, as well as discussion of its relevance to the autonomy of syntax, see Jackendoff (2002).

Chapter 4. Current challenges to the Lexicalist Hypothesis **115**

(67) a. your cat = 'the cat you stepped on'
      b. your destruction of Rome = 'your account of the destruction of Rome'

Williams notes that a preposing analysis does little in the way of accounting for the thematic status of the possessive subject.[13]

But most seriously, possessive subjects of nominals have all of the thematic restrictions that are characteristic of a lexical process, rather than a movement process. On the one hand, time DPs are allowed in subject position, but not manner DPs:

(68) a. Last week's discussion about Chicago
      b. *That way's refusal (shocked us all)

Anderson (1983) notes that movement is impossible if the object is not affected (69a) or if the nominalization is suffixless (69b):

(69) a. *Algebra's knowledge by high school students
      b. *Mary's love, *Cuba's attack

And as pointed out in Rothstein (1983) and Alexiadou (1991), if in passive nominals the thematic genitive were an underlying object, we would, contrary to fact, expect movement with resultative phrases:

(70) a. the collapse of the building apart
      b. *the building's collapse apart

(71) a. the arrival of John nude
      b. *John's arrival nude

All of the above facts lead me to the conclusion that DP-internal movements should be excluded entirely.

5. Conclusion

To conclude, I have long believed that Chomsky was on the right track in his 1970 paper 'Remarks on Nominalization'. In short, nothing in the current minimalist attempts to overthrow the lexicalist hypothesis have led me away from the idea that

---

13. Higginbotham (1983) and Grimshaw (1990) also conclude from similar facts that movement of DP within DP is not involved. For the former, the impossibility of movement is incompatible with the idea that all arguments of N are optional and for the latter, movement would result in a theta-criterion violation.

Chomsky was indeed on the right track. As Borer herself notes, 'most researchers who have attempted to construct a model explicitly reducing ... word formation to [phrasal] syntax have concluded that the task is impossible and quite possibly an undesirable one' (Borer 1998: 157). Desirable or not, I hope that this chapter has explained why the task is impossible.

References

Ackema, P. & Neeleman, A. 2004. *Beyond Morphology: Interface Conditions on Word Formation*. Oxford: OUP.

Alexiadou, A. 2001. *Functional Structure in Nominals: Nominalization and Ergativity* [Linguistik Aktuell 42]. Amsterdam: John Benjamins.

Anderson, M. 1983. Prenominal genitive NPs. *Linguistic Review* 3: 1–24.

Borer, H. 1993. Parallel morphology. Ms, University of Massachusetts.

Borer, H. 1998. Morphology and syntax. *The handbook of morphology*, ed. by Andrew Spencer and Arnold M. Zwicky, 151–90. Oxford: Basil Blackwell.

Borer, H.. 2003. Exo-skeletal vs. endo-skeletal explanations: Syntactic projections and the lexicon. In *The Nature of Explanation in Linguistic Theory*, J. Moore & Maria Polinsky, 31–67. Stanford CA: CSLI.

Borer, H. 2005a. *Structuring Sense, Vol. II: The Normal Course of Events*. Oxford: OUP.

Borer, H. 2005b. *Structuring Sense, Vol. I: In Name Only*. Oxford: OUP.

Borer, H. To appear. *Structuring Sense. Vol. III: Taking Form*. Oxford: OUP.

Burton, S. C. 1997. Past tense on nouns as death, destruction, and loss. *Proceedings of NELS* 27: 65–78.

Carnie, A. 1995. Non-verbal Predication and Head Movement. PhD Dissertation, MIT.

Chomsky, N. 1970. Remarks on nominalization. *Readings in English Transformational Grammar*, R. Jacobs & P. Rosenbaum, 184–221. Waltham MA: Ginn.

de Wit, P. 1997. Genitive Case and Genitive Constructions. PhD Dissertation, University of Utrecht.

Demirdache, H. 1996. The Chief of the United States: Sentences in St'at'imcets (Lillooet Salish): A cross-linguistic asymmetry in the temporal interpretation of noun phrases and its implications. *International Conference on Salishan and Neighboring Languages* 31: 71–100.

Don, J. 2004. Categories in the lexicon. *Linguistics* 42: 931–56.

Emonds, J. E. 1972. Evidence that indirect object movement is a structure-preserving rule. *Foundations of Language* 8: 546–61.

Emonds, J. E. 1976. *A Transformational Approach to English Syntax*. New York NY: Academic Press.

Enç, M. 1987. Anchoring conditions for tense. *Linguistic Inquiry* 18: 633–57.

Fabb, N. 1988. English suffixation is constrained only by selectional restrictions. *Natural Language and Linguistic Theory* 6: 527–39.

Fraser, B. 1976. *The Verb-particle Combination in English*. New York NY: Academic Press.

Fu, J., Roeper, T. & Borer, H. 2001. The VP within nominalizations: Evidence from adverbs and the VP anaphor *do so*. *Natural Language and Linguistic Theory* 19: 549–82.

Grimshaw, J. 1990. *Argument Structure*. Cambridge MA: MIT Press.

Harley, H. In press. The morphology of nominalizations and the syntax of *v*P. In *Quantification, Definiteness and Nominalization*, M. Rathert & A. Giannadikou (eds). Oxford: OUP.

Harley, H. & Noyer, R. 1998. Mixed nominalizations: Short verb movement and object shift in English. *North East Linguistic Society* 28: 143–58.

Higginbotham, J. 1983. Logical form, binding, and nominals. *Linguistic Inquiry* 14: 395–420.

Hockett, C. F. 1958. *A Course in Modern Linguistics*. New York NY: Macmillan.

Hornstein, N. 1999. Movement and control. *Linguistic Inquiry* 30: 69–96.

Jackendoff, R. 2002. English particle constructions, the lexicon, and the autonomy of syntax. In *Verb-particle Explorations*, N. Dehé, R. Jackendoff, A. McIntyre & S. Urban, 67–94. Berlin: Mouton de Gruyter.

Jackendoff, R. 1975. Morphological and semantic regularities in the lexicon. *Language* 51: 639–71.

Jackendoff, R.. 1977. *X-bar Syntax: A Study of Phrase Structure*. Cambridge MA: MIT Press.

Jackendoff, R. 1997. *The Architecture of the Language Faculty*. Cambridge MA: MIT Press.

Kiparsky, P. 1997. Remarks on denominal verbs. In *Complex predicates*, A. Alsina, J. W. Bresnan & P. Sells, 473–99. Stanford CA: CSLI.

Lakoff, G.. 1965/1970. *Irregularity in Syntax*. New York NY: Holt, Rinehart, and Winston.

Langendoen, D. T. 1970. The 'can't seem to' construction. *Linguistic Inquiry* 1: 25–36.

Langendoen, D. T. 2003. Merge. In *Formal Approaches to Function in Grammar: In Honor of Eloise Jelenek*, A. Carnie, H. Harley & M. A. Willie, 307–18. Amsterdam: John Benjamins.

Law, P. 1997. On some syntactic properties of word-structure and modular grammars. In *Projections and Interface Conditions: Essays on Modularity*, A.-M. Di Sciullo, 28–51. Oxford: OUP.

Lecarme, J. 1996. Tense in the nominal system: The Somali DP. *Studies in Afroasiatic Syntax*, J. Lecarme, J. Lowenstamm & U. Shlonsky, 159–78. Amsterdam: HAG.

Lees, R. B. 1960. *The Grammar of English Nominalizations*. The Hague: Mouton.

Marantz, A. P. 1997. No escape from syntax: Don't try morphological analysis in the privacy of your own lexicon. *University of Pennsylvania Working Papers in Linguistics* 4: 201–25.

Newmeyer, F. J. 1970. The derivation of the English action nominalization. *Chicago Linguistic Society* 6: 408–19.

Newmeyer, F. J. 1986. *Linguistic Theory in America*: 2nd edn. New York NY: Academic Press.

Roeper, T. 2005. Chomsky's remarks and the transformationalist hypothesis. In *Handbook of English Word-formation*, R. Lieber & P. Stekauer, 1–22. Dordrecht: Kluwer.

Rothstein, S. 1983. The Syntactic Forms of Predication. PhD Dissertation, MIT.

Sag, I. A., Wasow, T. & Bender, E. M. 2003. *Syntactic Theory: A Formal Introduction*, 2nd edn. [CSLI Lecture Notes, Vol. 152]. Stanford CA: CSLI.

Storm, P. 1977. Predicting the applicability of dative movement. In *CLS Book of Squibs*, S. E. Fox, W. A. Beach & S. Philosoph, 101–02. Chicago IL: Chicago Linguistic Society.

Wasow, T. & Roeper, T. 1972. On the subject of gerunds. *Foundations of Language* 8: 44–61.

Williams, E. 1982. The NP cycle. *Linguistic Inquiry* 13: 277–95.

Williams, E. 1985. PRO and subject of NP. *Natural Language and Linguistic Theory* 3: 297–315.

Zucchi, A. 1993. *The Language of Propositions and Events*. Dordrecht: Kluwer.

PART 2

Psycholinguistics

CHAPTER 5

On the homogeneity of syntax

How similar do coordinates and subordinates look to the comprehension system?

Wayne Cowart and Tatiana Agupova
University of Southern Maine

> Our goal here is to explore an unusual approach to the long-standing problem of
> coordination in natural language — the problem of accommodating subordinate
> and coordinate structures within a consistent and empirically sound syntax. In what
> follows we'll offer a brief overview of the problem and identify a central assumption
> about the syntax of coordinates (the Homogeneity Thesis) that seems to be very
> widely shared by investigators working on coordination regardless of their theoretical
> orientation. We will then review some recent experimental results that seem to clash
> with certain implications of the Homogeneity Thesis. Though the evidence reviewed
> here is far from definitive, we argue that serious consideration of alternatives to the
> Homogeneity Thesis is in order.

1. Kinds of recursion

At a descriptive level, it might be said that sentences exhibit two rather differ-ent kinds of recursion. In embedding or subordinating recursion each successive elaboration of a constituent is nested inside of that constituent and lies at the end-point of a unique path up toward the topmost node of the phrase marker that or-ganizes the entire structure. Nested prepositional phrases exemplify the general pattern, though the phenomenon is evident in many different kinds of construc-tion (see (1)).

Crucially, there seems to be no finite grammatical bound on the number of times recursive elaborations of this kind can be applied inside a given containing structure.

A second form of recursion, coordination, is also extremely common, acces-sible, and natural. Again taking a strictly descriptive perspective, this form of re-cursion seems to differ from subordinating recursion in that it allows for so-called 'flat' structures, ones where two or more constituents seem to share equally a syn-tactic role (e.g., clause subject or object) that is assigned to a single constituent in subordinate structures, as in (2).

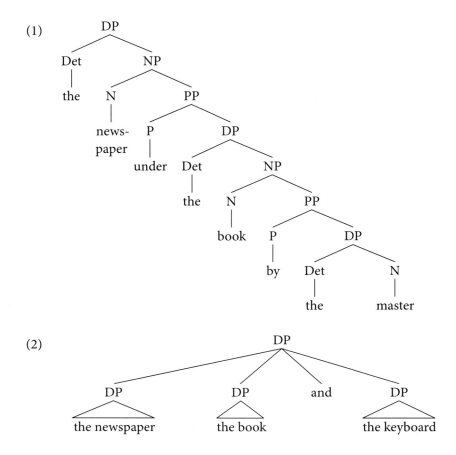

Here each of the coordinated DPs, as well as the structure as a whole, typically has the same functional role in the containing sentence. Almost every kind of sentential substructure can be the basis of a coordinate structure: [*Some or all*] *children in affected villages are ill*; *The* [*book and newspaper*] *fell*; *The book* [*fell on and shattered*] *the glass*; *Jill put the car* [*in the garage and out of sight*].

It appears that here as well there is no grammatical finite bound on the number of times this mechanism can apply to yield another conjunct in a structure like (2). See Huddleston & Pullum (2002: ch. 15) for a descriptive overview of coordination in English and Payne (1985) for a cross-linguistic survey.

There is a notable lack of consensus as to how a model of natural language syntax might correctly describe both kinds of recursive structure. The earliest generative approaches to coordination (e.g., Chomsky 1955) assumed that the structures were flat or symmetrical (in the sense that (2) allows several constituents of the same kind to stand at the same rank in the larger structure). Several models currently under investigation maintain this assumption. Dalrymple & Nikolae-va (2006), Dalrymple & Kaplan (2000) and Peterson (2004) offer treatments of coordinate phenomena within the framework of Lexical-Functional Grammar (Bresnan 2001). Generalized Phrase Structure Grammar (Gazdar, Klein, Pullum, & Sag 1985) and Head-Driven Phrase Structure Grammar (Pollard & Sag 1994) provide the framework for a variety of ongoing investigations, while Bayer (1996), Steedman (2000) and others apply varieties of categorial grammar. These samples merely suggest the range of alternatives allowing for symmetrical coordinate structures.

Another quite different approach has emerged within the Minimalist framework (Chomsky 1995). Here a rigidly asymmetrical, hierarchical model of phrase structure is under investigation, one that is generally taken to rule out any flat or symmetrical syntactic model of coordinates. Collins (1988), Munn (1993), and Progovac (1998a, 1998b), among others, have offered various ways of treating coordinates hierarchically. Recent contributions in a similar spirit include Citko (2005), Cormack & Smith (2005) and Zhang (2006). Borsley (2005) surveys some of these models and offers a critical analysis.

2. The Homogeneity Thesis

Despite the variety of proposals on the structure of coordinates, the notion that coordinates must somehow fall under the same general regime of syntactic principles as apply to non-coordinates is widely assumed.

This is not surprising given the fact that coordinates seem to be so intimately and smoothly integrated with the subordinating structures that are otherwise so central and characteristic a feature of natural language syntax. As noted, whole sentences and almost every kind of constituent can be coordinated, and coordinate structures generally participate in displacement, case, agreement and other syntactic phenomena that appear in non-coordinates, though often in rather eccentric ways. For coordinates not to fall within the purview of some general model of syntax would amount to declaring them in some sense 'ungrammatical'. Chametzky registers a note of dismay many would share. Referring to coordinates, among others, he says: "It cannot be the case that such thoroughly unexceptional sentences ... have no well-formed base PM..." (2000:47).

Linguistic investigations guided by this baseline intuition have generally applied relatively conventional methods and considered the question somewhat narrowly as a problem in syntactic theory or the syntax-semantics interface. The main task we undertake here is to consider whether close experimental examination of the intuitions of naive native speakers can uncover relevant phenomena (perhaps ones that are more or less inaccessible to conventional methods). The results we describe do seem to us relevant to the issue and to raise questions about the Homogeneity Thesis.

2.1. Research strategy

It should perhaps be emphasized that we are not attempting to directly address questions about how coordinates are structured syntactically. That is, we are not primarily attempting to determine whether coordinates have flat or hierarchical syntactic structure. Because on any model there are many differences between subordinate and coordinate structures and further issues in processing, it is difficult to devise a behavioral test that might bear directly and at least somewhat unequivocally on this question. Our goal instead is to assess the character of the cognitive processes that are engaged. The approach draws on a well-established line of investigation dealing with agreement relations where grammatically illicit effects are known to operate over the right edge of a complex NP. By examining judgments in parallel cases with subordinates and coordinates, we test whether superficially similar agreement relations in the two targeted construction types engage similar cognitive processes. In short, we ask not whether different syntactic configurations are being built in subordinate and coordinate forms, but whether the same kind of cognitive project is under way.

3. Processing agreement: Are coordinates handled like subordinates?

The experimental work we review here owes much to Bock and her colleagues (e.g., Bock 2004; Bock & Miller 1991; Eberhard, Cutting, & Bock 2005), who have closely examined language production processes that implement agreement-marking on a verb. This work has demonstrated, among other things, that when a 'local noun' other than the relevant head noun immediately precedes a main verb, the local noun can sometimes induce erroneous agreement with itself. This is called an 'attraction effect'. For example, participants cued with *The key to the cabinets...* will sometimes continue this sentence with *are* instead of *is*, apparently because the plurality of *cabinets* somehow interferes with making the canonical link to the singular head *key*.

While there is ample evidence that hierarchical representations play a central role in this phenomenon, even when the error occurs (e.g., Franck, Lassi, Frauenfelder, & Rizzi 2006; Franck, Vigliocco, & Nicol 2002; Vigliocco & Nicol 1998), there is no dispute that linear order becomes relevant at some point, since the speaker must ultimately organize and produce the utterance as a linear string of elements.

Chapter 5. On the homogeneity of syntax **125**

What has been disputed is just how the hierarchical and linear aspects of the structure are addressed in the production process (see, for example, Haskell & MacDonald 2005). Whatever the syntactic structure of coordinates the well-established appearance of attraction effects with subordinates suggests that attraction-like effects could arise with coordinates as well, and there is some evidence that they do (Haskell & MacDonald 2005). The various proposals that ascribe hierarchical structure to coordinates suggest that they too could induce attraction effects somewhat like the attraction effects to which subordinate structures give rise. This could be either because they are hierarchically similar to subordinates or because their linear layout can be superficially very similar to subordinates in which attraction effects are known to arise.

Thus there were several goals for the work we describe here. One was to determine whether effects analogous to those demonstrated in production tasks can be detected in judgments of acceptability for relevant subordinate and coordinate examples. Another goal was to determine whether any attraction-like effects pattern similarly here to those found in prior work. Further, and most importantly for our concerns here, we hoped to determine whether any attraction-like effects also arise with coordinate structures, and whether any such effects with coordinates suggest the engagement of cognitive processes similar to those in subordinate structures. More particularly we were concerned to know whether readers seemed to weight the morphological and semantic content of our examples, together with their linear layout and/or hierarchical structure, differently in coordinate and subordinate forms. We take the Homogeneity Thesis to imply that these parameters should have about equal weight in determining judgments in coordinate and subordinate forms.

The materials and design of the study are summarized in Table 1.[1] Superficially, the coordinate and subordinate forms exhibit the same structure. An initial NP based on a count noun is either explicitly or implicitly marked for number. This is

Table 1. Experiment design with an example item

Factor	NP_1	Linker	NP_2	Grammaticality
Levels	Singular	Subordinate	Same	Grammatical
	Plural	Coordinate	Different	Ungrammatical
Example	*A book*	*on*	*A newspaper*	*is/are*
	Some books	*and*	*Some newspapers*	

---

1. Details of materials, procedure, and results appear in Cowart & Agupova (2007). All of the contrasts we discuss here are statistically significant at the .05 level or beyond in both by-subjects and by-sentences tests and pairwise comparisons are addressed only where the relevant interaction is reliable. Note that in this table the levels of the NP_2 factor are defined relative to NP_1, that is, 'Same' indicates that the plurality of NP_2 is the same as that of NP_1. With this coding the

joined to a second NP of the same general type either by a preposition or by a conjunction. The immediately following verb shows number agreement. In the subordinate cases agreement is canonically controlled by the number of the initial NP, while in the coordinate cases the coordinate structure as a whole standardly functions as the agreement controller.

We asked participants to rate the sentences on a scale in a paper and pencil procedure conducted in classroom settings.

Expectations: In the subordinate cases grammatical principles predict that agreement is controlled entirely by the plurality of the head NP (NP_1), but the psycholinguistic literature on attraction effects suggests that whether the plurality of the local noun is the same as or different from that of the head could affect the perceived acceptability of the structure, presumably by altering the grammaticality effect (the judged difference between the grammatical and ungrammatical cases). That is, any failure or breakdown in processing the hierarchical structure of the material preceding the verb could increase the likelihood that the second NP will be erroneously taken as the agreement controller, which could make ungrammatical agreement with the second NP seem more acceptable than it might otherwise be and make grammatical agreement less acceptable. A strong preference for well-formed cases implies successful construction of the appropriate hierarchical structure and primary reliance on that structure to determine agreement. In so far as attraction-like effects show up in the subordinate structures, this implies errors in analyzing or representing the hierarchical structure of the subordinate. As we'll see, there are such effects and our first concern in addressing them is to discover what features of the subordinate cases exert the greatest influence on those effects. We then look to see whether more or less the same properties of our coordinate cases shape judgments with those items. That is, we hope in the subordinates to detect something of a signature, a characteristic pattern of reliance upon particular properties of the judged structure. We then look at the coordinates to determine whether the processing system seems to rely on the same set of properties in judging the acceptability of these coordinates.

3.1. Findings: subordinate cases

The first observation to make is that there was clear evidence of attraction-like effects in participants' judgments of the subordinate cases (see Table 2). When the

---

NP_2 factor distinguishes cases where the second NP tends to reinforce or conflict with whatever number value is instantiated on NP_1. Similarly, the fourth factor, Grammaticality, cannot be specified in terms of the form of the verb (singular/plural) because attraction effects are defined in relation to grammaticality, not verb number per se. Thus, Subordinate examples are Grammatical if the verb agrees with NP_1. Coordinate examples are Grammatical if the verb is plural.

Table 2. Judged acceptability for subordinate cases with singular heads

Grammatical		
The book on the newspaper	is	.64
The book on some newspapers	is	.45
Ungrammatical		
The book on the newspaper	are	.19
The book on some newspapers	are	.38

number of the local noun was different than that of the head, this diminished acceptability if the verb agreed normally, and increased it where the verb failed to agree. Thus, it appears that the presence of a local noun carrying different number than the head can disrupt or interfere with the recognition that canonical agreement is present, or make noncanonical agreement more acceptable than it would otherwise be.

The cases in Table 2 all have singular heads. Similar effects appeared with the parallel cases where the head NP was plural (Table 3), but only where the sentences showed ungrammatical agreement. In these ungrammatical cases the attraction-like effect ran in the same direction and was of similar magnitude as in the examples with singular heads shown in Table 2. But there was clearly no attraction-like effect in the grammatical cases with a plural head; a singular local noun in the presence of a plural head did not reduce the perceived acceptability of the grammatical plural verb. On the face of it, this may raise questions about the origin or generality of the attraction-like effects we've observed with other subordinate cases.

There is, however, a respect in which these cases are distinct from the other subordinates. The difference can be specified in terms of a notion of markedness, one where overtly coded features (e.g., the regular plural on English nouns) count as marked. By this standard regular English singular verbs are marked, a characterization we will also apply to the subset of our cases where the main verb was *be*, considering *is* marked and *are* unmarked. Using this way of discriminating among our cases distinguishes among the the first and second pair of cases in Table 3. The second grammatical sentence is the only subordinate case where neither the local

Table 3. Judged acceptability for subordinate cases with plural heads

Grammatical		
Some books on some newspapers	are	.33
Some books on the newspaper	are	.34
Ungrammatical		
Some books on some newspapers	is	−0.9
Some books on the newspaper	is	.13

noun nor the verb appeared in a marked form. In *Some books on the newspaper are* ... the local noun is unmarked because it is singular and the verb is unmarked because it is plural. Exploiting these observations we can provide at least a descriptive account for the lack of attraction-like effects in these cases; attraction effects arise only where either the alternative (ungrammatical) agreement controller or the target verb is a marked form.

Perhaps a more perspicuous account would suggest that two properties can make the local noun an effective competing controller for the agreement relation. Either the local noun, where it contrasts in number with the head, can be marked, or the presented verb form can be ungrammatical. The one case where an attraction effect arose with an unmarked local noun was of the form (NPpl–NPsing–Vsing) where the verb is both marked and ungrammatical. Though the merits of these accounts of the non-appearance of the attraction effect in the grammatical cases in Table 3 can only be decided by further investigation, the analysis offered above suggests that this case might be evidence that the attraction effects we observed with subordinates are sometimes dependent upon a rather narrowly morphological property — whether the local noun carries an overt marking.

This analysis also brings the findings discussed here into alignment with an interesting feature of the results from production studies on attraction. Singular local nouns relative to plurals induce attraction effects much less reliably, cf. Bock & Miller (1991), and much subsequent work. On the analysis described above, the results here seem to be consistent with this finding despite the fact that there is an attraction-like effect associated with the singular NP_2 in the ungrammatical cases in Table 3. That effect is now attributed to the presence of the marked verb, not the unmarked local noun.

These findings suggest that readers are recognizing the number properties of the two NPs and the agreement feature on the verb as we'd expect, but that the local nouns can become competitors for the role of agreement controller. These data don't, however, indicate what kind of error readers are making. It could be that the linear proximity of the local noun and the verb in these cases makes the local noun a competitor regardless of its hierarchical position in the subject NP, i.e., that the linear representation of the sentence somehow comes to override the hierarchical representation to some degree. Alternatively, it could be that the fact of contrasting number features on the local noun and the head induces occasional errors in the processes by which the controller is identified within the hierarchical structure of the sentence, see Franck et al. (2002, 2006); Haskell & MacDonald (2005) for discussion of the analogous issue in production studies. On this account the linear proximity of the local noun and verb does not drive the observed effects.

Recent work in our lab suggests that it is the hierarchical relation, not linear proximity, that is operative here. An experiment similar in design and procedure

Table 4. Judged acceptability for three-NP subordinate structures in relation to variations in number on the third NP

Various portraits of a (few) former president(s) with **some foreign ambassadors**	is	.26
Various portraits of a (few) former president(s) with **a foreign ambassador**	is	.30

to the main experiment under discussion was done to compare any attraction-like effects that might be attributed to the second and third NPs in three-NP structures of the kind illustrated by Table 4.[1] The findings show that there were no reliable attraction-like effects connected with number variations on the third NP.

There were, however, reliable attraction-like effects deriving from the second NP, as illustrated in Table 5. From this pattern we conclude that it is not the linear proximity of the local nouns to the verb in the main experiment that drives the effects observed there. Rather, it seems that the presence of an NP embedded to the right of the head, differing from the head in number, induces some confusion into the process of identifying the appropriate controller. But only the NP hierarchically closest to the head is effective in becoming the alternative controller. These effects suggest that in the main experiment it is the hierarchical position of the second NP that determines its ability to become an alternative controller, not its linear proximity to the verb.

Table 5. Judged acceptability for three-NP subordinate structures in relation to variations in number on the second NP

Various portraits of **a few former presidents** with some foreign ambassadors	is	.18
Various portraits of **a former president** with some foreign ambassadors	is	.37

Taken together, these findings suggest that our readers gave great weight to the form of the subordinate cases in determining agreement, taking into account the morphological number of the local nouns and verbs, the markedness of these forms, and hierarchical structure.

3.2. Findings: coordinate cases

The results for the coordinate cases were quite different. As the examples in Table 6 suggest, there were no reliable attraction effects in the grammatical coordinate conditions whether the first conjunct was singular or plural. This of course is just what canonical grammatical agreement would predict, but the subordinate results just described suggest that canonical grammaticality is not in itself incompatible with the appearance of attraction effects. Hence, the lack of those effects

---

1. The experiment, executed by Winnie Paulino, used only subordinate structures.

Table 6. Judged acceptability for grammatical coordinate cases

Grammatical		
The book and the newspaper	are	.74
The book on some newspapers	are	.69

with the grammatical coordinates, despite their robust appearance with grammatical and ungrammatical subordinate examples may suggest that substantially different considerations are in play with coordinates.

Further investigation will be required, however. The lack of attraction effects with grammatical coordinates may not say much about how coordinates are processed. The analysis suggested above, indicating that attraction effects with our judgment task are triggered by ungrammatical verb forms or by marked local nouns also indicates that there would be no attraction effects with grammatical coordinates under any account of the structure of coordinates. All the cases here are grammatical, so that consideration should not drive any search for an alternative controller. The only local noun that might be seen as a competing controller is singular and thus unmarked, so it should not be an effective trigger for an attraction effect on the model we suggested above.

More interesting effects appeared with the ungrammatical coordinate cases, as seen in Table 7. Whatever view of the structure of these cases the processor might assume, this seems to have played no role in these effects. A hierarchical analysis of coordinates would distinguish between the positions of the plural NPs in the two middle cases in Table 7, as would any process sensitive to the linear layout of the sentences. Nevertheless, the two middle cases, each incorporating one singular and one plural NP, were judged worse than the first case, better than the fourth case, but indistinguishable from each other.

Morphological distinctions also seem to contribute nothing to these effects. If something like a hierarchically-defined agreement mechanism is in play here, presumably the processor would be seeking some agreement controller that would sanction the singular verb occurring in each of these cases. A suitable alternative controller is available in the middle cases in Table 7, though differently situated in each. Adding a second alternative controller, as in the first case, should be irrel-

Table 7. Judged acceptability for ungrammatical coordinate cases

Ungrammatical		
The book and the newspaper	is	.47
The book and some newspapers	is	.23
Some books and the newspaper	is	**.23**
Some books and some newspapers	is	.09

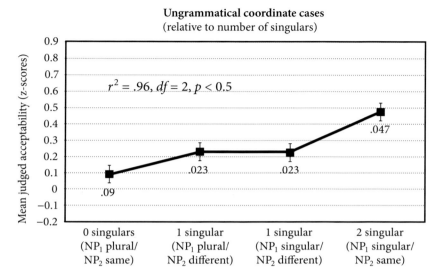

Figure 1. Differences in judged acceptability for the ungrammatical coordinate cases as a function of the number of singular NPs in the structure

evant, though this case is associated with a marked increase in acceptability. The markedness distinction discussed above also seems irrelevant to these effects. On the model suggested earlier, the ungrammatical verb in these cases would trigger the search for an alternative controller regardless of the markedness of the local noun. Further, the local nouns differ in markedness in the middle two cases in Table 7, but yield the same acceptability.

What does seem to account for the differences observed with the ungrammatical coordinate cases is obvious, but surprising in relation to typical models of agreement. The fourth coordinate in Table 7 contains no conceptually singular NP, the middle two cases each contain one, and the first case contains two. It appears that the observed increases in acceptability track the number of singular NPs in the structure. Indeed, as shown in Figure 1, this feature of the materials accounts for almost all the variance in acceptability across these four cases.

3.3. Overview

The results we've reviewed above are not what we'd expect if the Homogeneity Thesis is true. Despite the fact that we presented full sentences, not fragments, and used a judgment task, the subordinate cases produced attraction-like effects that seem to be intelligibly related to those found in the production literature. As expected, those effects seem to be sensitive to the hierarchical structure of the materials and details of their morphological properties down to the level of discriminating among marked and unmarked forms. By contrast, the processor seems to approach the coordinate cases we tested quite differently. Though at least the superficial layout of the grammatical coordinate cases is comparable to the subordinate cases, there was no evidence of attraction-like effects with grammatical coordinates. The ungrammatical coordinates produced what appear to be attraction effects (in the sense that variations in the content of the coordinate structure did affect judged acceptability). But those effects show no evidence that the processor is attending to any syntactic differences in the internal organization of the coordinates or to the aspects of their morphological form that seem relevant to the subordinates. Rather, the processor seems to adopt a conceptual approach to the coordinates, modulating the acceptability of the ungrammatical singular verb according to the sheer number of singular NPs in the structure.

4. Alternatives to the Homogeneity Thesis

There are at least three ways that the Homogeneity Thesis might be preserved in the face of results of the kind described above. It could be that even though the syntax of coordinates flows smoothly from the same framework of principles as organizes subordinate structures, there is some syntax-internal reason why the same syntactic agreement mechanisms that apply elsewhere cannot operate with coordinates. Another possibility is that while ordinary syntactic agreement principles apply with coordinates, they present some specific processing difficulty that does not arise with subordinates. Finally, the lexical-semantic differences between the conjunction *and* and prepositions could induce substantial differences in processing even if coordinates and subordinates derive from a single coherent syntactic framework. Differences along any of these lines could drive the processing system to adopt different approaches to agreement in coordinates and subordinates.

Clearly, the present results do not allow for definitive conclusions. The findings are based on only a few forms from a single language. But the forms used are commonplace and the subordinate results align rather well, in our judgment, with relevant findings from the production literature on attraction effects. Thus, it seems reasonable to suppose that, if the Homogeneity Thesis is true, the coordinate cases should have reflected a mode of processing more similar to that that appeared with subordinates. Instead, none of the factors that seem to dominate results in the subordinate forms (morphological number, markedness, and structure — whether hierarchical or linear) seemed to account for the findings with coordinates, especially the ungrammatical cases.

Thus, the observations we have reviewed here suggest that the comprehension system is treating agreement relations in the coordinates we tested quite differently than those in the corresponding subordinates. In so far as the relevant comprehension processes can be differentiated by the kinds of information they attend to, and the way they integrate that information, it seems that a very different kind of process handled agreement in the coordinates. While agreement in the subordinate cases was sensitive to hierarchical structure and morphology, agreement in the coordinates seemed to be blind to these factors in the grammatical cases and to respond to a kind of aggregated measure of 'singularity' in the ungrammatical coordinates.

In our view, further work is in order. Results of this kind suggest that some part of the numerous well-established oddities of coordinate structures could derive from the fact that, at least in part, the language comprehension system regards them as a different kind of object than a non-coordinate sentence, applying to them cognitive resources of a quite different character.

References

Bayer, S. 1996. The coordination of unlike categories. *Language 72*(3): 579–616.
Bock, K., (ed.). 2004. *Psycholinguistically Speaking: Some Matters of Meaning, Marking, and Morphing.* New York NY: Elsevier Science.
Bock, K. & Miller, C. A. 1991. Broken agreement. *Cognitive Psychology* 23:45–93.
Borsley, R..D. 2005. Against ConjP. *Lingua 115*(4): 461–82.
Bresnan, J. 2001. *Lexical-functional Syntax.* Malden MA: Blackwell.
Chametzky, R. A. 2000. *Phrase Structure: From GB to Minimalism.* Malden MA: Blackwell.
Chomsky, N. 1955. *The Logical Structure of Linguistic Theory.* Ms, Cambridge MA.
Chomsky, N. 1995. *The Minimalist Program.* Cambridge MA: The MIT Press.
Citko, B. 2005. On the nature of merge: External merge, internal merge, and parallel merge. *Linguistic Inquiry 36*(4): 475–96.
Collins, C. 1988. *Part II. Alternative Analyses of Conjunction.* Ms, MIT.
Cormack, A. & Smith, N. 2005. What is coordination? *Lingua 115*(4): 395–418.
Cowart, W. & Agupova, T. 2007. *Mental representations of coordinates: Evidence from English coordinate subjects.* Ms, Portland ME.
Dalrymple, M. & Kaplan, R. M. 2000. Feature indeterminacy and feature resolution. *Language 76*(4): 759–98.
Dalrymple, M. & Nikolaeva, I. 2006. Syntax of natural and accidental coordination: Evidence from agreement. *Language 82*(4): 824–49.
Eberhard, K. M., Cutting, J. C. & Bock, K. 2005. Making syntax of sense: Number agreement in sentence production. *Psychological Review 112*(3): 531–59.
Franck, J., Lassi, G., Frauenfelder, U. H. & Rizzi, L. 2006. Agreement and movement: A syntactic analysis of attraction. *Cognition 101*(1): 173–216.
Franck, J., Vigliocco, G. & Nicol, J. 2002. Subject-verb agreement errors in French and English: The role of syntactic hierarchy. *Language and Cognitive Processes 17*(4): 371–404.

Gazdar, G. Klein, E., Pullum, G. K. & Sag, I. A. 1985. *Generalized Phrase Structure Grammar*. Oxford: B. Blackwell.

Haskell, T. R. & MacDonald, M. C. 2005. Constituent structure and linear order in language production: Evidence from subject-verb agreement. *Journal of Experimental Psychology: Learning, Memory, and Cognition 31*(5): 891–904.

Huddleston, R. D. & Pullum, G. K. (eds). 2002. *The Cambridge Grammar of the English Language*. Cambridge: CUP.

Munn, A. 1993. *Topics in the Syntax and Semantics of Coordinate Structures*. PhD Dissertation, Unviersity of Maryland.

Payne, J. R. 1985. Complex phrases and complex sentences. In *Language Typology and Syntactic Description*, Vol II, T. Shopen (ed.), 3–41. Cambridge: CUP.

Peterson, P. G. 2004. Coordination: Consequences of a lexical-functional account. *Natural Language & Linguistic Theory 22*(3): 643–79.

Pollard, C. J. & Sag, I. 1994. *Head-driven Phrase Structure Grammar*. Chicago IL: University of Chicago Press.

Progovac, L. 1998a. Structure for coordination: Part I. *Glot International 3*: 3–6.

Progovac, L. 1998b. Structure for coordination: Part II. *Glot International 3*: 3–9.

Steedman, M. 2000. *The Syntactic Process*. Cambridge MA: The MIT Press.

Vigliocco, G., & Nicol, J. 1998. Separating hierarchical relations and word order in language production: Is proximity concord syntactic or linear? *Cognition 68*(1): B13-B29.

Zhang, N. 2006. On the configuration issue of coordination. *Language and Linguistics 7*(1): 175–223.

CHAPTER 6

The effect of case marking on subject–verb agreement errors in English*

Janet Nicol and Inés Antón-Méndez
University of Arizona/UiL OTS, University of Utrecht

It is commonly assumed that the occurrence and distribution of processing errors offer a "window" into the architecture of cognitive processors. In recent years, psycholinguists have drawn inferences about syntactic encoding processes in language production by examining the distribution and rate of subject–verb agreement (SVA) errors in different contexts. To date, dozens of studies have used a sentence repetition-completion paradigm to elicit SVA errors. In this task, participants hear a sentence fragment (or "preamble"), repeat it, and provide a well-formed completion. These experiments have shown that when a singular head is modified by a phrase containing a plural NP (e.g. *The bill for the accountants...*), a significant number of SVA errors may occur. Several experiments have shown that, in English, the phonological form of words within a subject NP plays virtually no role in the rate of error occurrence. Yet recent data from our lab suggests that overt morphophonological case information does matter: speakers are more likely to produce the error *The bill for the accountants were outrageous* than *The bill for them were outrageous*. In this paper, we will present the results of this case-marking study and discuss the implications for models of language production.

1. Introduction

It is widely held that the occurrence and distribution of processing errors offer a "window" into the architecture of cognitive processing systems. In language research, this general approach has been seen in the elicitation of comprehension errors, most notably "garden-path" errors, in which a perceiver misanalyzes an input sentence. In language production, corpora of spontaneously produced 'slips of the tongue' have been amassed, and errors have been induced in the laboratory via creative construction of materials and sometimes special task demands. In both comprehension and production research, processing errors have been taken to reflect the organization and workings of the processors; many in the field have concluded that language is processed in stages and each stage is privy to only certain kinds of information.

---

* We thank Roland Pfau for helpful comments on a previous draft of this manuscript.

The focus of this chapter is on the encoding of sentences during language production, and whether a process such as the implementation of subject–verb agreement may be affected by morphophonological information. It will be shown that this is indeed the case: overt case morphology reduces the incidence of agreement errors by making more salient the true agreement relation.

The organization of the chapter is as follows: First, we will review some of the research in which subject–verb agreement errors have been induced experimentally and provide a characterization of them in terms of a particular model of language production. Then we will present data from our agreement experiment in English. Finally, we will discuss implications of this line of research for models of language production.

2. Error induction in the laboratory

In 1991, Bock and Miller reported the results of several experiments that they had conducted in which they elicited subject–verb agreement (SVA) errors. They elicited errors by creating sentence beginnings ("preambles") containing two NPs that mismatched in number (e.g. *The key to the cabinets..., The keys to the cabinet...*), along with their number-matched counterparts, which served as a baseline. They had their participants listen to each preamble, repeat it, and complete the sentence. Responses were tape-recorded, transcribed, coded, and statistically analyzed. The results showed that participants did make errors in the number-mismatching conditions, with most of the errors occurring in the condition in which a singular head noun was followed by a PP containing a plural NP. This mismatch asymmetry has been interpreted as due to the markedness of the plural feature, the idea being that marked items are more likely to interfere with the agreement process (Bock and Eberhard 1993, Eberhard 1997). This asymmetry further indicates that agreement errors arise not because participants fail to remember the head NP, but rather because they (perhaps only momentarily) lose track of the number specification of the head NP.

This initial set of experiments and numerous subsequent studies have explored the question of which factors affect the agreement process—or to turn the question around, which types of information the agreement process takes into account. These studies have focused primarily on the influences of semantic information on one hand, and phonological information on the other.

Semantic effects on agreement. With respect to the effects of semantics, Bock and Miller (and Bock and Eberhard 1993, Vigliocco, Butterworth, and Semenza 1995, Vigliocco, Butterworth, and Garrett 1996a, Vigliocco, Hartsuiker, Jarema, and Kolk 1996b) explored this question by using cases in which grammat-

Chapter 6. Case-marking and subject–verb agreement errors **137**

ical number and "semantic number" diverged. Bock and Miller examined whether preambles that were "notionally plural" would induce a greater number of errors than those that were "notionally singular". Hence, they contrasted preambles like *The label on the bottles...* (where *label* is grammatically singular but in this context, suggests multiple tokens of a type) with *The key to the cabinets...* (in which grammatically singular *key* is most plausibly a single token). Their results showed that the multiple token preambles induced *no more errors* than did the single token preambles, suggesting that the agreement process does not have access to this kind of information. Another approach was to manipulate the type of nonhead noun that was used (the nonhead noun is standardly referred to as the "local noun" because it occurs just before the verb). In studies by Bock and Eberhard (1993), the local noun was either a regular noun such as *ship* or a collective term such as *fleet*. These appeared within the same preamble context (*The condition of the ship...* vs. *The condition of the fleet...*), along with their number-mismatched counterparts. The question, of course, was whether the singular 'fleet' would induce errors, given that it means multiple ships. Results showed that such grammatically singular collectives *induced no errors at all,* just like the singular regular nouns.

Subsequent research has complicated this picture: multiple token effects (more errors with multiple token preambles than single token preambles) have been reported for speakers of other languages with richer agreement systems, such as Italian (Vigliocco et al. 1995), Spanish (Vigliocco et al. 1996a, Nicol, Teller and Greth 2001, Nicol and Greth 2003), French and Dutch (Vigliocco et al. 1996b). These findings raised the intriguing possibility that certain linguistic processes might be implemented at different stages of processing in different languages. However, a multiple token effect has also been reported for English (Eberhard 1999), when preambles are used that contain nouns that are more easily imageable than those used in the original Bock and Miller study.[1] Research by Barker, Nicol and Garrett (2001) is consistent with Eberhard's. In one of their studies, they compared error rates for preambles containing semantically similar nouns (*The canoe by the sailboats...*) with those containing semantically distinct nouns (*The canoe by the cabins...*). They found significantly more errors when the nouns were semantically similar.

Overall, then, it appears that message-level (semantic) representations may directly influence the subject–verb agreement process.

This makes sense if one considers prevailing models of language production. Various models (based on Garrett 1976, Bock and Levelt 1994, and others) propose that the initial stage of production involves the conception of a message that is essentially meaning based: non-linguistic, but of a form that interfaces with

---

1. Note that cross-linguistic differences may well exist along with concreteness effects.

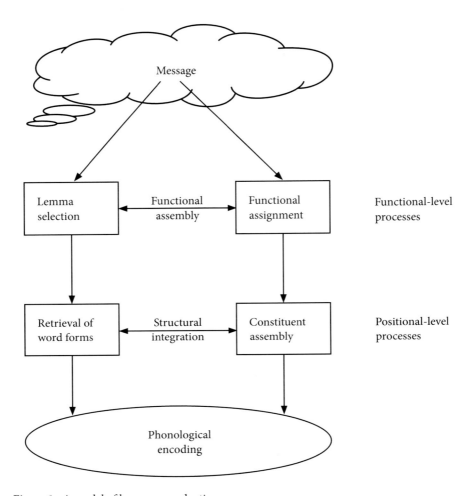

Figure 1. A model of language production

language processes. As shown in Figure 1, this message is then mapped onto abstract lexical entries referred to as 'lemmas' and onto a logical structure which captures the relationships among the concepts (e.g. 'agent of action', 'patient of action', 'modifier of agent', etc...). The latter process, which deals with syntactic properties of the lexical items, not word meanings, is sometimes called *Functional Assignment*. This overall stage of processing, including lemma selection and functional assignment, is often referred to as the *Functional Level* of processing. At the next stage, the *Positional Level*, syntactic structure is assembled and word forms ('lexemes') that are associated with the selected lemmas are retrieved, and are slotted into position within the syntactic structure. Based on speech error data, there is a distinction between how content words (including pronouns) and inflectional morphemes are stored: the former comprise the lemma and lexeme sets; the latter are encoded as features of syntactic frames. Following the Positional Level, phonological and articulatory processes come into play. Bock and colleagues (Bock, Eberhard, Cutting, Meyer, and Schriefers 2001; Eberhard, Cutting and Bock 2005; Bock, Eberhard, and Cutting 2004; Bock 2005) elaborate this model to accommodate what is known about subject–verb agreement. On their view, number information associated with concepts within the message is mapped onto elements within a functional sentence representation. This is referred to as *marking*. They argue that in English, the verb representation does not inherit number directly from the message level. Rather, in a process they call *morphing*, a verb inherits its number from the subject phrase, at the level at which constituents are assembled. These processes are shown in Figure 2 for the example sentence *the dogs chased the cat*. Both marking and morphing processes could be prone to error at different points during sentence processing. A number marking error would arise during the initial processing of the message and could be influenced by conceptual or semantic factors. If the message representation contains a multiple token as subject, such as the *label on the bottles*, and if, during the mapping process the critical notion that these are tokens of a type (i.e. that it is the same label on all those bottles) is lost, the subject of the sentence may be marked as plural even though the head is actually singular. This, in turn, will result in a plurally marked verb. A number morphing error, on the other hand, would arise during functional assembly and could be influenced by more syntactic factors. At this level, if a plural NP appears in the same phrase as a singular head NP, the verb could be mistakenly specified as plural, thereby agreeing with the local NP instead of the head NP.

3. Morphophonological effects on agreement

An important feature of the model described above is that there is a unidirectional flow of information: this is a "feed-forward" model of language production. According to this model, phonological information should play no role whatsoever in agreement processes because verb agreement is specified independently of form information. Several experiments have shown that, in English, the phonological form of words within a subject NP plays little or no role in the rate of error occurrence (Bock and Eberhard 1993, Barker 2001). Bock and Eberhard, for example, constructed stimuli in which the local noun was a pseudo-plural, such as *course* (preambles were presented visually). They found that such items caused no agreement errors at all, while a true plural like *courts* did. Both Bock and Eberhard (1993) and Haskell and MacDonald (2003) found that irregular plural local nouns like *mice* (in *the trap for the mice*) gave rise to as many errors as a regular

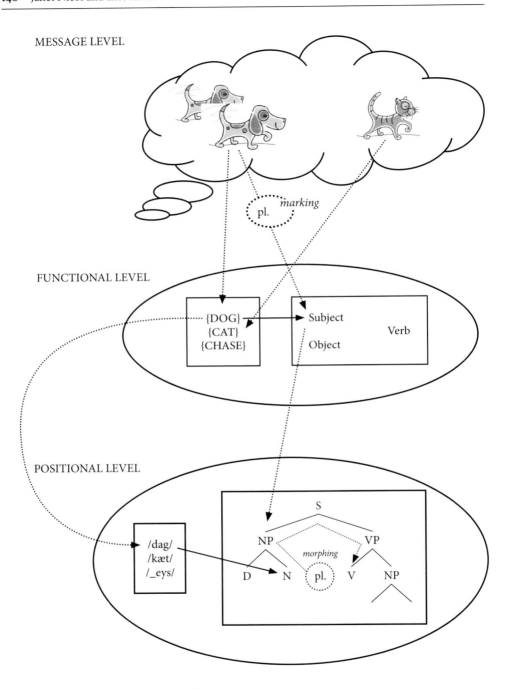

Figure 2. An example of some of the mapping processes involved in producing a sentence which conveys the proposition of dogs chasing a cat. Included here are Bock et al.'s (2001) notions of *marking* and *morphing*.

plural like *rats*, suggesting that it is not the plural morpheme *-s* that triggers errors, but rather abstract plurality. Barker (2001) took a different approach to the question of phonological effects on verb agreement. In one study, he compared preambles in which the two nouns were phonologically similar (e.g. *The student near the statues...*) with preambles containing phonologically distinct nouns (e.g. *The student near the paintings...*). In contrast to the study cited above in which semantic similarity was manipulated (Barker et al. 2001), both preamble types elicited the same number of errors.[2] Overall, it appears that the subject–verb agreement process is unaffected by phonological factors.

This failure to find robust phonological effects in English is consistent with the model presented in Figure 1. However, it is surprising in light of findings for Italian, German and Dutch of morphophonological effects on subject–verb agreement. A study in Italian was conducted by Vigliocco et al. (1995). They contrasted NPs in which both the noun and determiner were number-marked (1) and NPs in which only the determiner was number-marked (2):

(1) la scoperta/le scoperte
     'the.SG discovery/the.PL discoveries'

(2) il camion/i camion
     'the.SG truck/the.PL truck'

In the conditions of interest (those conditions in which the head noun was singular and local noun plural) they found *fewer* agreement errors when the head NP was doubly marked as singular than when the head NP contained only a marked determiner. Consistent with this is the finding by Hartsuiker, Antón-Méndez, and van Zee (2001), who elicited subject–verb agreement errors in Dutch. In this experiment, they had participants repeat a preamble consisting of a subject and object, and then say a specific verb. They contrasted the morphophonologically case-unambiguous[3] pronoun *hen* (*them*), and the case-ambiguous pronoun *ze* (*they, them*):

(3) Ed ziet dat de kapitein hen...
     'Ed sees that the captain them....'

---

2 There were actually more errors in the phonologically-dissimilar condition than in the phonologically-similar condition, though this difference was not statistically significant.

3 Here and throughout the paper, when talking about case we will be referring to morphological case as opposed to abstract case. On some theories, nouns and pronouns will carry different abstract case according to the function they play in the sentence even if they are morphologically indistinguishable from each other.

(4) Tanja zegt dat de verkoper ze…
'Tanja says that the salesman them/they….'

Participants repeated the preambles and then would have produced a verb in its singular or plural form. Note that it is possible to use such constructions in Dutch and German because verbs are clause-final in embedded clauses. Results showed more agreement errors when the local pronoun was case-ambiguous (*ze*) than when it was case-unambiguous (*hen*).

Hartsuiker, Schriefers, Bock and Kikstra (2003) studied morphophonological effects in both Dutch and German by manipulating the form of the determiner. They found that, in German, more subject–verb agreement errors were produced when the local noun determiner was morphophonologically case-ambiguous (*die*, as in (5), which could be either nominative or accusative) than when it was unambiguous (*den*, as in (6), which is dative):

(5) Die Stellungnahme gegen die Demonstrationen…
'The position against the.NOM/ACC demonstrations….'

(6) Die Stellungnahme zu den Demonstrationen…
'The position on the.DAT demonstrations….'

They also found that in both German and Dutch, more errors arose when the determiner in the *head NP* was morphophonologically number-ambiguous (e.g. (8)) than when it was unambiguous (e.g. (7)):

(7) Het plein bij de kerks
'The.SG square near the churches.'

(8) De straat bij de kerks
'The.SG/PL street near the churches.'

It is worth noting that these morphophonological effects on subject–verb agreement have been found for languages in which determiners carry information about gender, number and sometimes case, so NPs in these languages are more likely to bear this information than, for example, English.

The question we address in this paper is whether subject–verb agreement in English will show similar effects when morphophonological case marking is manipulated. To investigate this, we compared agreement errors for preambles which contained a noun (not overtly case marked in English) in the local NP position and preambles with a pronoun (overtly case marked in English) in the local NP.

4. Experiment

4.1. Method

Participants. There were 40 participants in this study. They were enrolled in an undergraduate Psychology course at the University of Arizona and received course credit for their participation.

Materials and Procedure. Thirty-two sentence quadruplets such as those in Table 1 were created. The head noun was always singular, the local noun was either singular or plural. Participants were required to produce as the local NP, either a pronoun or full noun phrase. Sentences were presented visually in the following way: Participants first saw an initial noun phrase such as "The accountant" or "The accountants", presented for approximately 1 sec in the center of the screen in yellow letters. Then an incomplete sentence was presented for 3 seconds two lines below where the noun phrase had appeared, in white letters. This preamble contained a head NP and a PP modifier, followed by a blank, followed by an adjective. The modifying phrase contained either a pronoun (as in, e.g., "The bill from him") which matched the initial NP in gender and number, or it contained "XXXX", which was intended to stand in for the initial NP (e.g., "The bill from XXXX"). Participants were instructed to repeat the entire sequence and fill in the blank. In the condition in which the string of X's appeared, participants were asked to repeat the initial NP. Possible responses are shown in Table 1.

The experimental items were counterbalanced across four presentation lists such that any given participant saw one variant of a given item, and was presented with equal numbers of items (eight) in the four conditions. In addition to the critical items, 36 fillers (most containing preambles with plural head NPs) were interspersed throughout the set of 32 experimental trials. These were preceded by

Table 1. Sample stimuli and desired responses

Participant reads	Participant says
The accountant./ The bill from him _____ reasonable.	The accountant. The bill from him was reasonable.
The accountant./ The bill from XXXX _____ reasonable.	The accountant. The bill from the accountant was reasonable.
The accountants./ The bill from them _____ reasonable.	The accountants. The bill from them was reasonable.
The accountants./ The bill from XXXX _____ reasonable.	The accountants. The bill from the accountants was reasonable.

4.2. Results

Responses were transcribed and coded according to the following scheme. There were three response categories for items in which the preamble was correctly produced: Those which contained a correctly inflected verb (*Correct Inflected*), those which contained a misinflected verb (*Agreement Error*), and those which contained an uninflected verb (*Uninflected*), such as *seemed*. Responses were coded as *Number Repetition Errors* if they contained a noun with the wrong number specification (e.g. *accountant* instead of *accountants*, in the plural noun condition). Responses were coded as *Miscellaneous Errors* if they consisted of preamble errors, multiple errors, incomplete utterances, and failures to respond.

One item was removed prior to analyses of variance (this item contained the noun *policewomen*, which was frequently misread by participants (and construed) as singular). Responses for the rest of the items were tallied; number and percentages of responses in different response categories appear in Table 2.

Agreement Errors. As is clear from Table 2, plural pronouns as local "nouns" induced substantially fewer errors than lexically specified nouns: speakers were significantly more likely to produce the error *The bill for the accountants were outrageous* (15%) than *The bill for them were outrageous* (6%) (compared to the number-matched controls, which elicited errors about 1% of the time). Analyses of variance (with participants (F1), and items (F2) as the random factor) were conducted. ANOVAs for agreement errors revealed a significant main effect of Local Noun Type (Noun vs. Pronoun): $F1(1,39) = 11.366, p = .002, F2(1,28) = 12.413, p = .001$, a significant main effect of Local Noun Number: $F1(1,39) = 29.026, p < .001, F2(1,28) = 28.873, p < .001$, and a significant interaction of the two variables: $F1(1,39) = 9.887, p = .003, F2(1,28) = 9.224, p = .005$.

Table 2. Distribution of agreement errors and other response types in the four stimulus conditions (pronoun local noun conditions are displayed in italics; proportions may not add to 100% due to rounding)

Local noun type	Local noun number	Agreement error (%)	Correct inflected (%)	Uninflected verb (%)	Number repetition errors (%)	Other errors (%)	TOTAL
Pronoun	*S*	*2 (.007)*	*284 (.917)*	*0 (.0)*	*5 (.015)*	*19 (.060)*	*310*
Pronoun	*P*	*20 (.065)*	*263 (.847)*	*1 (.002)*	*5 (.017)*	*21 (.066)*	*310*
Noun	S	4 (.013)	276 (.890)	2 (.005)	8 (.027)	20 (.065)	310
Noun	P	47 (.151)	204 (.658)	1 (.004)	35 (.112)	23 (.075)	310

Other Responses. Two other response categories show variation. The correctly inflected verb responses are a virtual mirror-image of agreement errors, which is not surprising. The other category is the Number-Repetition Error category, which shows the most errors in the plural noun condition. Note that this is also not a surprising pattern, because this is just the condition which allows the greatest opportunity for participants to make a number error. As Table 1 shows, this is one of the conditions that requires participants to "fill in" the noun based on a string of X's (recall that participants see "The accountants. The bill from XXXXX....."); the pronoun condition does not require this. Second, participants in these experiments are generally more likely to remember a plural noun as a singular one than vice versa, possibly for reasons of "markedness", as mentioned in the Introduction.

5. Discussion

This study revealed that the presence of overt case-marking of a local NP affects the incidence of subject–verb agreement errors: fewer errors arise when the local NP is not overtly case-marked. These results are consistent with the findings described above for languages such as German and Dutch (Hartsuiker et al., 2003), and Italian (Vigliocco et al. 1995).

These results are also compatible with findings reported by Nicol and Wilson (2000), who elicited subject–verb agreement errors in Russian. They used the same methodology as that used here, and their preambles contained as the local noun either a pronoun or a full noun phrase. Thus, for example, participants were presented with:

(9) Sčet ot buxgalterov...
     'Bill from accountants.DAT....'

(10) Sčet ot nix...
     'Bill from them....'

However in Russian, both types of NP are overtly case-marked. Results from this experiment showed equivalent numbers of errors in the two mismatch (singular head, plural local NP) conditions. Interestingly, a comparison of the error rates in the Russian study and the current experiment reveals that the proportions of errors in the mismatch conditions for overtly case-marked local NPs is similar: around 5%-6% for Russian, 6% for English. This is less than half the proportion of errors found in the non (overtly) case-marked (mismatch) condition in English, which is at 15% in this experiment.

Note, however, that in addition to the case-marking distinction in our materials is the difference in whether or not a plural is signaled with a plural inflection.

Our lexically-specified plural NPs (e.g. *the accountants*) are not only ambiguous for case but also regularly inflected. In contrast, the plural pronoun *them* bears a plural feature, but not a plural suffix. Could this be the source of the difference in error rate? We think this is unlikely, given the findings that irregular plurals in English, such as *mice*, and *children* give rise to as many errors as regular plurals (Bock and Eberhard 1993, Haskell and MacDonald, 2003).[4] Hence, we believe that the difference is related to the morphological case-marking.

But how does morphological case-marking interact with the production of subject–verb agreement? Hartsuiker et al. (2003) consider several options. One is that the production system is interactive in such a way that word forms can activate higher level representations, in a non-feed-forward (feedback) system. The idea here is that phonological forms could activate Functional Level case representations such as "nominative", "accusative", "dative", etc... So, for instance, in Dutch, the case-ambiguous pronoun *ze* would activate multiple case representations (possibly case "nodes") including 'nominative', but *hen* would not. Hartsuiker et al. characterize this possibility this way: "...if we assume feedback between word forms and lemma-based codes for morphosyntactic features that are compatible with them, it follows that ambiguously specified word forms will activate both incorrect and correct feature codes." Applying this idea to our study, it would have to be argued that while a pronoun like *them* activates only the nodes for non-nominative cases (i.e., accusative and dative, a distinction that may or may not be lost in English speakers' minds), the word form representations of specified NPs such as *the accountants* activates (in bottom-up fashion) nominative and non-nominative case nodes.[5] Thus, thousands of word forms would be linked to case nodes in English, even though the overt manifestation of case is limited to pronouns. Although it is true that nouns may need to be linked to abstract case according to their syntactic positions, this still seems implausible since it would be highly uneconomical. An alternative is that only the pronouns are linked to case nodes and the activation of non-nominative case nodes makes a difference for subject–verb agreement. Even if we accept this scenario, however, the feedback idea still doesn't specify *how* the activation of case information would directly affect subject–verb agreement. In addition, an approach which includes a feedback mechan-

---

4 In fact, Haskell and MacDonald (2003) found fewer errors associated with irregular (vs. regular) plural local NPs in phrases in which the head was a collective (e.g. *the family of mice* vs. *the family of rats*). However, a followup rating study showed that participants give higher 'multiple entity' ratings to the phrases with regular plurals, suggesting that there were (potentially) differences in notional plurality between the two types of phrases.

5 In fact, the NP ceases to be case ambiguous when the preposition is taken into account, but the argument here is that the noun on its own would be linked to all the case nodes it is compatible with.

Chapter 6. Case-marking and subject–verb agreement errors **147**

ism would have trouble accommodating the failures to find phonological effects of various kinds on subject–verb agreement, as discussed above. Another possibility raised by Hartsuiker et al. (2003) is that morphophonological effects "arise when morphemes are integrated with structural frames for phrases". For example, when a word is slotted into a phrase structure, its case information may be compared to the case information inherent in the phrase structure: these should match (or not mismatch). If a case-ambiguous word bears multiple features (e.g. nominative, accusative), this verification process may go awry, "forcing a spurious feature into the frame". A problem with this explanation is that, like the one described above, this account does not clearly connect case ambiguity with the subject–verb agreement process. No mechanism is offered for how these would interact.

The intuitive explanation for our finding is that the case specification of a pronoun local NP helps to keep the head NP and the local NP from getting confused. Assuming a feed-forward model of production, there are two logical points in the production process at which this could happen. One is at the point when verbs inherit their number specification from the head NP. An error arises when the plural feature associated with a non-nominative NP is transmitted to the verb. If the local noun is *overtly* case-marked as non-nominative, this erroneous transmission may be less likely, *if* the subject–verb agreement process considers both explicit and abstract case marking in identifying the NP that controls verb agreement. Another possibility is that case-marking has *no effect* on the verb number-specification process; rather it affects the ability of speakers to filter out errors. One prevalent proposal is that there is a monitoring component that assesses a to-be-uttered output and edits out errors. There is good experimental evidence in favor of such a component (e.g. Levelt 1983, 1989, Hartsuiker and Kolk, 2001), and the monitor idea is compatible with our experience as speakers that we can prevent ourselves from producing speech errors. On this analysis, agreement errors would arise equally often following both case-marked and case-ambiguous local nouns. But as the speaker is about to utter a sentence, she might notice that the verb agrees with the wrong noun. Case-marking would make it easier to notice this because the form *them* cannot be the subject of the following verb, but *the accountants* could be:

(11)   The bill from [the accountants were outrageous]
(12)   The bill from *[them were outrageous]

An important point about this explanation is that it assumes that whether or not a subject–verb agreement error is uttered depends on whether it is generated (which we believe happens at an earlier point in the production process) and then whether it is detected and corrected. We assume that some factors that have been shown to affect error rate (such as the hierarchical structure of the NP subject) affect error generation, and other factors (such as the form of the linear sequence of words) could affect detection but not generation.

Such an account is compatible with the German results of Hartsuiker et al. (2003). In their case, the local NPs with case-ambiguous determiners would be less likely than the ones with case unambiguous local NPs to be detected as having been erroneously selected as heads of the agreement:

(13) Die Stellungnahme gegen [die Demonstrationen waren kräftig]
      'The position against [the.NOM/ACC demonstrations were strong].'

(14) Die Stellungnahme zu *[den Demonstrationen waren kräftig]
      'The position on *[the.DAT demonstrations were strong].'

The same would apply to the Dutch results of Hartsuiker et al. (2001):

(15) Tanja zegt dat de verkoper [ze hadden gezien]
      'Tanja says that the salesman [them/they had.PL seen].'

(16) Ed ziet dat de kapitein *[hen hadden gezien]
      'Ed sees that the captain *[them had.PL seen].'

The results of Vigliocco et al. (1995) and the Dutch result of Hartsuiker et al. (2003) are of a slightly different nature. In these cases, what affects error rates is the non-ambiguity of the real controller of the agreement, the head noun, with respect to number. What would be happening in this case is that the clash between the features of the head NP and the verb would be made more salient by having an unambiguously singular determiner. Consider sentences (17) and (18).

(17) Het.SG plein.SG bij de kerks waren.PL groot.
      'The.SG square.SG near the churches were.PL big.'

(18) De.SG/PL straat.SG bij de kerks waren.PL groot
      'The.SG/PL street.SG near the churches were.PL big.'

In sentences such as (18) only the noun "straat" marks the clash between the head number feature and the verbal inflection, whereas in sentences such as (17) both the determiner "het" and the noun "plein" can be indicators of a mismatch. Obviously, the more clues there are pointing to an agreement error, the easier it will be for the monitor to detect it and filter it out.

Taken together, what all these cases suggest is that increasing the number of indicators for an agreement error makes it more conspicuous and, therefore, less likely to be produced. The indicators can be found either in incompatibilities of the local NPs as sources of agreement given their case, or in incompatibilities of the head NPs' overt morphological features with the verbal inflection.

In sum, our finding that overt case-marking affects the incidence of subject–verb agreement errors fits with previous findings for languages like Italian, Dutch, German and Russian. However, possibly until more is known about how case information is represented within the production system, it remains difficult to definitely characterize this effect in detail within current models of production.

References

Barker, J. E. 2001. Semantic and Phonological Competition in the Language Production System. PhD Dissertation, University of Arizona.

Barker, J., Nicol, J. & Garrett, M. 2001. Semantic factors in the production of number agreement. *Journal of Psycholinguistic Research* 30: 91–114.

Bock, K. 1995. Producing agreement. *Current Directions in Psychological Science* 4: 56–61.

Bock, J. K. & Eberhard, K. M. 1993. Meaning sound and syntax in English number agreement. *Language and Cognitive Processes* 8: 57–99.

Bock, J. K., Eberhard, K. M. & Cutting, J. C. 2004. Producing number agreement: How pronouns equal verbs. *Journal of Memory and Language* 51: 251–78.

Bock, J. K., Eberhard, K. M., Cutting, J. C., Meyer, A. S. & Schriefers, H. J. 2001. Some attractions of verb agreement. *Cognitive Psychology* 43: 83–128.

Bock, J. K. & Levelt, W. J. M. 1994. Language production: Grammatical encoding. *Handbook of Psycholinguistics*, M. A. Gernsbacher (ed.), 945–84. San Diego CA: Academic Press.

Bock, J. K. & Miller, C. A. 1991. Broken agreement. *Cognitive Psychology* 23: 35–43.

Eberhard, K. 1997. The marked effect of number on subject–verb agreement. *Journal of Memory and Language* 36: 147–64.

Eberhard, K. M. 1999. The accessibility of conceptual number to the processes of subject–verb agreement in English. *Journal of Memory and Language* 41: 560–78.

Eberhard, K. M., Cutting, J. C. & Bock, K. 2005. Making syntax of sense: Number agreement in sentence production. *Psychological Review* 112: 531–59.

Franck, J., Vigliocco, G. & Nicol, J. 2002. Subject–verb agreement errors in French and English: The role of syntactic hierarchy. *Language and Cognitive Processes* 17: 371–404.

Garrett, M. F. 1976. Syntactic processes in sentence production. In *New Approaches to Language Mechanisms,* R. Wales & E. Walker (eds), 231–56. Amsterdam: North-Holland.

Haskell, T. R. & MacDonald, M. C. 2003. Conflicting cues and competition in subject–verb agreement. *Journal of Memory and Language* 48: 760–78.

Hartsuiker, R. J., Antón-Méndez, I. & Van Zee, M. 2001. Object attraction in subject–verb agreement constructions. *Journal of Memory and Language* 45: 546–72.

Hartsuiker, R. J. & Kolk, H. H. J. 2001. Error monitoring in speech production: A computational test of the perceptual loop theory. *Cognitive Psychology* 42: 113–57.

Hartsuiker, R., Schriefers, H. J., Bock, K. & Kikstra, G. M. 2003. Morphophonological influences on the construction of subject–verb agreement. *Memory and Cognition* 31: 1316–1326.

Levelt, W. J. M. 1983. Monitoring and self-repair in speech. *Cognition* 14: 41–104.

Levelt, W. J. M. 1989. *Speaking: From Intention to Articulation.* Cambridge MA: The MIT Press.

Nicol, J. & Greth, D. 2003. Subject–verb agreement in Spanish as a second language. *Experimental Psychology* 50: 196–203.

Nicol, J., Teller, M. & Greth, D. 2001. The production of verb agreement in monolingual, bilingual, and second language speakers. In *One Mind, Two Languages: Bilingual Language Processing*, J. L. Nicol (ed.), 117–33. Malden MA: Blackwell.

Nicol, J. & Wilson, R. 2000. Agreement and case-marking in Russian: A psycholinguistic investigation of agreement errors in production. In *Proceedings from the Eighth Annual Workshop on Formal Approaches to Slavic Linguistics,* I. Sekerina (ed.), 314–27. Ann Arbor MI: Michigan Slavic Publications.

Vigliocco, G., Butterworth, B. & Semenza, C. 1995. Constructing subject-verb agreement in speech: The role of semantic and morphological factors. *Journal of Memory and Language* 34: 186–215.

Vigliocco, G, Butterworth, B. & Garrett, M. F. 1996a. Subject–verb agreement in Spanish and English: Differences in the role of conceptual constraints. *Cognition* 61: 261–98.

Vigliocco, G., Hartsuiker, R. J., Jarema, G. & Kolk, H. H. J. 1996b. How many labels on the bottles? Notional concord in Dutch and French. *Language and Cognitive Processes* 11: 407–21.

CHAPTER 7

First language acquisition of coordination

The mud-puddle study and beyond*

Barbara Lust, Suzanne Flynn, Yuchin Chien,
and Barbara Krawiec

Cornell University/MIT/California State University, San Bernardino/
Utica School District, New York

In this chapter, we provide a brief overview of a history of studies of coordination. We then report the results of one experiment concerning the acquisition of coordination in English that has not before been reported, "The Mud-Puddle" study, and set it in the context of this history and our developing quest for understanding the nature of linguistic coordination and the fundamental competence that underlies its acquisition. This experiment was conducted by an honors student at Cornell at the time (Krawiec 1980); its data have been preserved and now reanalyzed. Its results, although preliminary, bear on the nature of the syntax-semantics interface that coordinate structures involve, integrate with certain current theoretical advances, and suggest future research possibilities.

1.   Introduction

Infinity, created through recursion, is clearly one of the most fundamental properties of natural language and of the human competence for language (see Langendoen and Postal 1984; Hauser, Chomsky and Fitch 2002; Pinker and Jackendoff 2005; Fitch et al. 2005 for proposals and debates on this issue; Gentner et al. 2006;

---

* Our study of coordination in natural language began with a dissertation completed in 1974 (Lust 1974) and an early paper given at a Linguistic Society of America annual meeting (Lust 1976), both under the inspiration and mentorship of D. T. Langendoen. Since then, close to 30 years of research, conducted with generations of new students and collaborators, has built on this initial inspiration and guidance, resulting in a continual series of studies of the grammatical structure of coordination and its acquisition in language. (This course of studies extended naturally to other forms of complex sentence formation (e.g., adverbial subordinate clause adjunction and relative clause formation). Indeed, the formal 'tree grammar' distinction between CP coordination and Chomsky-adjunction has been questioned (Lust 1994). We concentrate in this chapter on the coordination component.) Since its origins in the 1970s, that series of research studies, which continues today, pursues the nature of the fundamental human competence for language by linking linguistic theory to empirical studies of language acquisition.

see Everett 2005 for a recent counter-argument). Coordination, as in the example in (1), is clearly a paramount example of recursion in natural language, occurring in some form universally (e.g., Dik 1968). It therefore provides a rich domain for investigation of the most fundamental properties of the human competence for language and its acquisition.

(1) What do you know about tweetle beetles? Well...
*When tweetle beetles fight, it's called a tweetle beetle battle, **and** when they battle in a puddle, it's a tweetle beetle puddle battle. **And** when tweetle beetles battle with paddles in a puddle, they call it a tweetle beetle puddle paddle battle. **AND**...* (Seuss 1965)

The representation of coordinate structures has long provoked linguistic theory (e.g., the collection of papers in Reibel and Schane 1969; Gleitman 1969; Smith 1969; Hankamer and Sag 1976; Sag 1976, 1980; Williams 1977a, b); and continues to do so today (e.g., Munn 1993; Kayne 1994; Johannessen 1998; Johnson 2000; see Progovac 1998a, b for a review). Although theoretical approaches to linguistic theory have shifted from construction-specific inquiries to principle-based inquiries, coordination continues to be recognized as central to the human competence for language and a challenge to theories of design of the Human Language Faculty. Recent work on language typology provokes new studies of both its universal syntax and its semantics (Zwart 2005a, b; see also Comrie 1988).

Debates continue on the location of recursion in the grammar (e.g., Langendoen and Postal 1984; Lasnik 2000; and Chomsky's 1995 renewed proposal for Generalized Transformations and the abstract operation of 'merge'). Coordinate structures continue to raise issues regarding the representation of hierarchical structure in infinitely expandable constructions (Progovac 1998a, b), as well as the constraints on the creation of new syntactic structures through coordination.

At the same time, coordination raises more specific issues. For example, debate continues regarding the exact mechanisms of relation between the semantic representation of coordinate structures at the level of logical form and the interaction between this semantic representation and a corresponding syntactic representation. Questions also persist regarding the valid representation of ellipsis in natural language (i.e., a condition, essential to coordination, as in (2), for example).[1] Here acoustic evidence grossly underdetermines the knowledge represented through null sites and the various forms of anaphora this ellipsis involves (e.g., Johnson 2000; Merchant 2001).

---

1. We use the term 'ellipsis' here in general to refer to cases where semantically intended elements are missing, and are phonetically null (represented as Ø in the examples); we are leaving aside the exact mechanism by which such representations are achieved.

Chapter 7. First language acquisition of coordination **153**

(2) a. Susan worked on her sonata yesterday and Ellen did [Ø] too.
   b. Susan worked on her sonata yesterday and [Ø] was pleased with it.

Because of the range of fundamental issues raised by coordination, it provides a rich domain for investigation of various aspects of human competence for language and its acquisition.

Remarkably, while the complexity of coordinate structures has long challenged linguists, these structures appear to provide one of the very earliest, most accessible components of language acquisition. Overt evidence for knowledge of coordination appears from the time the child begins to combine words into sentences (e.g., Lust and Mervis 1980). Henceforth, children show an early awareness of distinct grammatical properties attributable to coordinate, as opposed to non-coordinate (embedded or adjoined), structures (e.g., Nunez del Prado et al. 1993, 1994; Cohen Sherman and Lust 1993; Lust 1994, 2006), as well as early control of subtle grammatical constraints on interpretation of ellipsis involved (e.g., Foley et al. 2003).

Research studies that have been conducted over the last decades on the acquisition of coordination have made several discoveries regarding this acquisition, both in English and cross-linguistically. They have led to implications for linguistic theory, e.g., provoking a new theoretical analysis of VP ellipsis involving 'sloppy identity' (e.g., Foley et al. 2003). At the same time, they have led to new, more precise questions regarding both the acquisition and the linguistic theory of coordination.

2. Early issues in study of the first language acquisition of coordination

Early experiments in English compared children's acquisition of sentential coordinations as in (3a) to that of phrasal coordinations as in (3b). The leading issue then was: is there a relation between these forms in the development of grammar and, if so, wherein does the relation lie? Are they related through syntax? Early theories, for example, postulated a syntactic "conjunction reduction" transformation which mapped from "deep structure" (involving the expanded representation, e.g., (3a) and (4a)) to "surface structure" (involving a phrasal coordination structure, e.g., (3b) and (4b)), relating these by syntactic deletion. Or are they related through semantic representation, with or without mediation by syntax? This alternative hypothesis was always possible, since propositional coordination may be naturally viewed as the form of coordination consistent with Boolean logic, where the connective 'and' in natural language is viewed as a propositional operator (Krifka 1990).

(3) a. [*Babies* laugh] and [*babies* cry].
   b. *Babies* [laugh and cry].

(4) a. [*The daddy ate* the crackers] and [*the daddy ate* the ice-cream].
     b. *The daddy ate* [the crackers and the ice cream].

The parallel questions for language acquisition at the time were: Are these different coordination forms, sentential and phrasal, related in acquisition? Or alternatively, does the child learn them independently? Is one of these forms developmentally primitive (i.e., providing an epistemological primitive for development of the infinite set of potential coordinations which natural language allows)?[2] If so, which is primitive? Is it the phrasal form, which would appear intuitively to be more 'simple' on the surface, or the full expanded form, which would correlate both with the posited 'underlying' syntactic structure of reduced coordinations and with the semantics of coordination involving the Boolean 'and' as a propositional operator? The latter, sentential coordinations, on the surface appear to be more complex (e.g., in relative length of overt information content required for online lexical processing).

If there was a system to the child's early grammar, which related expanded and reduced forms of coordination in language development, this would begin to explain the competence for infinite recursion that the child's grammar and 'coordination' allow. Clearly, given the infinite recursive possibilities of coordination in natural language, the child cannot 'learn' each individual coordinate form separately. If phrasal forms of coordination were the epistemological primitives and the foundations of language development, this would appear to require a learning theory based on analogies that supersedes any yet available. Such analogies would have to account both for the infinite coordination possibilities, and the constraints ruling out a potentially infinite set of ungrammatical forms (e.g., ruling in (1)-(4) above as well as (5a), but ruling out (5b)).

(5) a. Mary began Ø and Sarah completed their sonata.
     b. *Mary began their sonata and Sarah completed Ø.

If sentential forms of coordination were primitive, and some form of coordination reduction or other form of grammatical device were available in the Initial State through a Language Faculty, this would explain the possibility for infinite recursive competence of coordination in syntax, as well as the underlying semantic mapping these involve. But the Language Faculty would have to specify this 'conjunction reduction' device, or some alternative to it, as well as grammatical constraints that apply to it.

---

2. By 'developmentally primitive' here we intend: *A is developmentally primitive to B, if A develops either earlier than B, or by the time that B develops.* The latter would allow the case where *A* and *B* develop together, but not the case where *B* develops in isolation before *A*.

Early studies in English, which compared children's access to these varied co-ordinate structures with experimental designs and extensive experimental con-trols (e.g., on sentence length and semantics as well as on the child's develop-mental level; cf. Lust 1974, 1976, 1977), were combined with studies of children's coordination production in natural speech (Lust and Mervis 1980) at early stag-es of acquisition and over the early course of language development.[3] Language production was experimentally elicited through a standardized Elicited Imitation (EI) task that allows testing of precise hypotheses regarding grammatical prin-ciples underlying these linguistic structures, and is an effective means of evaluat-ing grammatical competence (Lust, Flynn and Foley 1996; Lust, Flynn, Foley and Chien 1999).[4] Evidence shows that in order to imitate a sentence, children must analyze the input heard (i.e., the stimulus in the experiment) and actively decon-struct and reconstruct it, filtering the stimulus through both their semantic and syntactic knowledge. For example, in (6b), the child has accessed and maintained the syntactic structure of the stimulus sentence (a sentential coordination) while dissociating this from the semantics; in (7b), the child has accessed and main-tained the semantic representation of the stimulus sentence, while dissociating this from the syntactic structure of the stimulus sentence (converting a sentential coordination to a phrasal coordination).

(6) a. Experimenter (Slobin and Welsh 1973:492):
         The Batman got burned and the big shoe is here.
     b. Child: Echo, 2.3.3:
         Big shoe is here and big shoe is here.

---

3. These studies revealed that results were linked not only to age of the child, but also to language development level as much as it could be measured by MLU (Lust 1977). Sentences structurally similar to those in (3a) and (3b) (5–7 words, 7 syllables) were tested with children from 1.11.19 to 3.1.3 (years, months, days of age) with MLUs ranging from 1.97 to over 4.76; and those like (4a) and (4b) (7–9 words, 11 syllables) were tested with children ranging from 2.4.17 to 3.3.24 in age with MLU ranging from 3.75 to over 4.76. These studies also pinpointed the need for com-parability in scientific methodology (i.e., established 'best practices') in order to foster valid rep-lication studies in first language acquisition (e.g., Lust 1981; Ardery 1980; Hakuta et al. 1982, deVilliers et al. 1977; Lust and Mazuka 1989).

4. In contrast, tests of a child's language comprehension usually assume that the child is rep-resenting the stimulus sentence in the same way that the adult who administers it is. However, a language production task like elicited imitation often shows that the child's representation of the model sentence differs from that of the adult (e.g., Lust, Solan, Flynn, Cross and Schuetz 1986; Cohen Sherman and Lust 1993), thus calling for a different interpretation of the child's 'comprehension' data. Presumably in comprehension tasks the child is demonstrating his or her comprehension of the form of the sentence, which characterizes his or her own representation of it, not necessarily the adult's.

(7) a. Experimenter (Slobin and Welsh 1973:492):
Daddy is going to get some cookies and Daddy is going to get some juice.
   b. Child: Echo, 2.3.3:
He gonna get some cookie and juice.

Children's differential patterns of successful reproduction of the stimuli that reflect grammatical variables manipulated in an experimental design (e.g., whether a stimulus sentence is a sentential or a phrasal coordination), and children's reformulations of these stimuli (i.e., where they mismatch the adult stimulus through conversions; cf. (6b) and (7b)), offer the essential data in these studies. In an experimentally controlled EI task, statistically significant variations in the amount of children's correct reproductions that correlate with manipulated factors in the experimental design provide indications of factors at work in grammatical competence. Qualitative analyses of children's reformulations of the stimuli provide precise windows into the child's theory of language, revealing for example unmarked systems and constraints.[5] When children 'reduce' sentential coordinations like (3a) or (4a) to (3b) or (4b), or 'elaborate' coordinations like (3b) or (4b) to (3a) or (4a), they show that they can and do compute the relations between these forms. These data from EI studies thus provide useful evidence on the child's grammatical competence, allowing the researcher to make discoveries regarding the child's grammatical competence for coordination.

Over many years, experimental design and systematic data analyses, combined with the EI task, has allowed hypothesis testing regarding specific grammatical factors in the acquisition of coordination. Converging evidence is attained by systematic study of children's natural speech (e.g., Lust and Mervis 1980).

3. Early discoveries

Several discoveries resulted from these early studies:

(i) Constraint on the course of acquisition of coordination was discovered through analysis of the earliest stages of language acquisition in English. Phrasal coordination forms did not precede sentential forms in development. In fact, sentential forms of coordination developed early, were initially available, and were always available during acquisition of corresponding phrasal forms. At the earliest

---

5. Children's changes of the stimulus sentence are often viewed as 'errors' or 'deformations'. However, since it is precisely these changes that reveal the child's theory of the structure they are reconstructing, we have chosen the word 'reformulations' here.

Chapter 7. First language acquisition of coordination   **157**

periods of development, full-formed phrasal coordinations did not appear until sentential coordinations had also been achieved. Spontaneous conversions from one form to another were productive (i.e., elaboration of phrasal coordinations to sentential forms and reduction of sentential coordinations to phrasal forms). These inter-structural conversions confirmed that a structured grammatical system, one that linked different grammatical structures to each other, underlay the child's knowledge of specific coordinate structures.

(ii) Directionality significantly affected the acquisition of coordination. Directionality was represented through patterns of redundancy location or ellipsis location in sentential and phrasal coordination. In our experimental design, the directionality of possible 'reduction' of redundancy in the sentential form corresponds to the directionality of the ellipsis site in the phrasal form. Children's patterns of reduction of sentential coordinations and elaboration of phrasal coordinations were found to be similarly affected by the location of redundancy in sentential forms and the parallel location of putative ellipsis in the phrasal form. In these results, 'forward' patterns of directionality in phrasal structures (e.g., (3b) and (4b)) were more accessible to children acquiring English than 'backward' patterns like (8b) and (9b). At the same time, these children frequently reduced redundancy in a forward direction in the matched expanded sentences like (3a) or (4a), but rarely if ever did so in 'backward' patterns like (8a) and (9a).[6] This correspondence between children's operations on sentential and phrasal forms further confirmed the role of a structured grammatical system underlying the acquisition of coordination.

(8) a. [The kitties *hide*] and [the dogs *hide*].
     b. [The kitties and the dogs] *hide*.

(9) a. [The bunnies *eat grass*] and [the squirrels *eat grass*].
     b. [The bunnies and the squirrels] *eat grass*.

Subsequent studies of coordination which involved gapped coordinate sentences as in (10) (Lust, Pinhas-Langweiler and Flynn 1980) and those with VP ellipsis as in (11) (Foley, Nuñez del Prado, Barbier and Lust 2003) further confirmed structure dependence involved in the children's acquisition of English coordinate structures.

---

6. The terms 'forward' and 'backward' here were used in keeping with the 'conjunction reduction' model of the time, which assumed that a reduction operation, producing null sites, resulted in phrasal forms of coordination as in:

(i)   The kitties Ø and the dogs *hide*. (Backward = (8))
(ii) *Babies* laugh and Ø cry. (Forward = (3))

In these cases, the antecedent of the null site may either precede (e.g., (ii)) or follow (e.g., (i)) the null site, producing coordination with either forward or backward anaphora, respectively.

(10) Tommy drank chocolate milk and Mary Ø juice.
(11) Big Bird scratches his arm and Ernie does too.

These discoveries were important for several reasons. They suggested that a grammatical system was being built by the child, as opposed to item-by-item sentence construction, and suggested that a grammatical system underlies the infinite power of the child's grammar, just as it does the adult's. They suggested a new form of empirical data in the study of language acquisition (i.e., grammatical constraint *on the course of* acquisition). Finally, they suggested evidence for and the beginning of an explanation for the child's access of ellipsis, or missing elements in language.

These early discoveries also led to several new questions, and subsequent inquiries. For example, would these findings in English first language acquisition be universal; more specifically, would they generalize across language acquisition in different languages? This question was fundamental to determining the degree to which the early results were attributable to Universal Grammar (i.e., to a theory of the Language Faculty). Would these results also generalize to second language acquisition and, as in first language acquisition, would they do so universally (Flynn 1987, 1993)? These issues would further bear on the role of the Language Faculty in adult L2 acquisition (e.g., Flynn and Martohardjono 1994).

4. Cross-linguistic studies

Cross-linguistic studies became critical in order to further resolve the nature of the grammatical system at work in children's early language acquisition.

A series of cross-linguistic studies subsequently confirmed that (i) sentential coordination was primitive in early acquisition across languages, possibly universally; but (ii) that the forward 'directionality constraint' discovered in English was not. Critically, cross-linguistic studies revealed that the forward directionality effect was linked to the grammar of the language being acquired. Left-branching languages like Japanese (Lust and Wakayama 1979; Lust, Wakayama, Snyder, Bergmann 1980) and Chinese (Lust and Chien 1984) showed reverse effects from English (i.e., the putative 'backward' forms of coordination as in (8) and (9) above were found to be more accessible early in development in these languages; see also Lust, deAbrew and Sharma 1982 for comparable studies in the acquisition of Hindi and Sinhala coordination). The directionality factor thus was found to reflect the child's integration of a syntactic property of the specific grammar for their language. This suggested that a forward directionality effect in English reflected neither a universal syntactic constraint on deletion (e.g., Harries, 1973) nor a universal forward processing principle (e.g., O'Grady et al. 1986; Lust, Flynn, Chien and Clifford 1980). These results implicated parameter setting (Lust 1981; Mazuka et al. 1986). More specifically, they suggested that a fundamental syntactic dimension of language variation (whether the language was principally left- or right-branching (right- or left-headed)) was being consulted by the child and that this variation systematically constrained early periods of language acquisition, including acquisition of coordination. These cross-linguistic results thus reflected 'structure-dependence' of early periods of language acquisition in a profound and broad sense.

These studies led beyond coordination. Early study of English acquisition had shown that the directionality effect did not characterize coordinate structures uniquely, but extended to adverbial subordinate clauses with pronominal anaphora (Lust 1981), suggesting that the language-specific setting of a grammatical parameter may have wide deductive consequences for the child's acquisition of a specific language grammar. These results also suggested that the child's acquisition of coordination was subsumed under a broader grammatical theory and not construction-specific in its underlying principles.

To test this hypothesis, a wide set of cross-linguistic studies of language acquisition then expanded beyond the study of the acquisition of coordinate structures to that of adverbial subordinate clauses and relative clauses, across varied forms of anaphora both within and across languages, and theoretical work began on the precise formulation of the parameter at issue (Japanese, Sinhala, Chinese, Hindi, Arabic, as well as English; Lust in prep).

These combined results began to clarify the cognitive computational processes that underlie language acquisition in this area. In particular, they implicated an integration of various specific languages and universal grammatical components in the language acquisition process. They began to lead to a developed theory of language acquisition that acknowledged change in the child's knowledge of specific language grammars over time, while supporting continuity of certain principles and parameters of Universal Grammar. This theory of language acquisition constituted a form of what has subsequently been called 'grammatical mapping' (Lust 2006).

5. Returning to coordination: A lingering problem

At the same time, these early results left open many questions regarding the nature of coordination in grammar and in language acquisition. From the beginning, early forms of generative theory of coordination, which posited a conjunction reduction operation involving a 'deep structure'–'surface structure' relation between sentential and phrasal coordinations (i.e., between expanded coordinations and phrasal coordinations appearing to involve ellipsis by a deletion transformation), were forced to confront coordinate structures that did not allow this analysis.

From the time of the first postulation of coordination reduction, various forms of coordination (e.g., what had been termed 'symmetric predicates', cf, (12a) and (13a), 'reciprocals', cf. (14a) and (15a), or 'reflexives', cf. (16a), as well as others, cf. (17a)), challenged this syntactic proposal. They also challenged existing theories of their semantic representation as instances of 'non-Boolean 'and'' (Krifka 1990). These phrasal forms ((12)-(17)) in 'a' do not allow expanded sources, (e.g., 'b').

(12) a. John and Mary are alike.
          (= (2), Lakoff and Peters 1969:113)
      b. ≠ John is alike and Mary is alike.

(13) a. Bill and John left together.
          (= (70), Lakoff and Peters 1969:123)
      b. ≠ Bill left together and John left together.

(14) a. Sue and Mary admired each other.
      b. ≠ Sue admired each other and Mary admired each other.

(15) a. Sue and Mary disagreed.
      b. ≠ Sue disagreed and Mary disagreed.

(16) a. John and Mary prepared themselves.
      b. ≠ John prepared themselves and Mary prepared themselves.

(17) a. The red and white and yellow and green flags were put together
          (Krifka 1990:15)
      b. ≠ The red flags were put together and the white flags were put to-
          gether and the yellow flags were put together and the green flags
          were put together.

In sentences (12) through (17), the phrasal coordination forms in 'a' do not appear to be derivable from sentential coordinations like their 'b' counterparts, by deletion, or by any other simple syntactic conjunction reduction function. In each case, the 'b' expanded counterparts are either semantically anomalous, (e.g., "John is alike") or semantically variant in interpretation from the phrasal form in 'a', (e.g., in (17), a potential 'b' form would allow: The red flags were put together and the white flags were put together, and the green flags were put together). The meaning of (17b), at least in its preferred form, appears to vary from that of the (17a) form. Clearly, in sentences (12)–(17) there is no semantic equivalence between the phrasal and sentential forms. Such cases raised questions about how a general theory of coordination could accommodate both coordination forms like those exemplified in sentences (3)–(11) and those in (12)–(17). In particular, how could a syntactic account accommodate this range without conjunction reduction, or how could a generalized semantic theory account for these phenomena?

Cases like (12)–(17) also energize a question of interpretation of previous language acquisition results. If children's acquisition of coordination is constrained by syntax, would children bring the same principles to bear on structures like (12)–(17), in spite of the mismatch between semantics and syntax that these structures provide? For example, would children show that they try to access full syntactic representations of structures like (12)–(17) even though semantically these structures do not allow such? If so, this would appear to suggest a precedence of syntactic representation over semantic representation in these structures. Would sentential coordinations be developmentally primitive to these phrasal coordinations, as they are in (3)–(11) above? Alternatively, would the semantic representations required by these new structures lead the acquisition process, divorcing the acquisition of these coordinations from those exemplified in sentences (3)–(11) above, and indicating that semantic representation alone could support the representation and acquisition of these structures?

Testing children with coordinate structures like those represented in (12)–(17) can help to begin to test these hypotheses and to differentiate possible interpretations of previous acquisition research in the area of coordination.

6. The Mud-Puddle study

We report here selected results from one early preliminary experiment concerning the acquisition of coordination in English, the *Mud-Puddle* study, which began to pursue these issues experimentally. It does so by varying the semantic content of the predicates in coordinate structures as an experimental factor, varying whether the phrasal coordinations do or do not allow syntactic expansions with semantic equivalence.[7]

We briefly summarize the design, methods, and results of this experiment; we complement this chapter with an electronic form of the Mud-Puddle study's full

---

7. Previous experiments had controlled coordinate structures against semantic variation as much as possible (e.g., attempting to eliminate concepts of temporality or causality that would have interacted with the neutral coordinate form being tested). Here we explicitly vary that semantic content.

experimental design and methods, as well as results in an Experiment Bank in the Virtual Center for the study of Language Acquisition (www.clal.cornell.edu/vcla).[8,9]

6.1. Experimental design

Three "Sentence Types" were tested in coordinate structures in this study, using the Elicited Imitation task. Table 1 summarizes the sentences used. The coordinated stimuli were all varied in "Conjunction Structure;" that is, they were tested in both sentential and phrasal forms. "Directionality" was also varied as a factor in Types I and III.[10,11]

Type I provides coordinations most similar to those tested previously (e.g., (3, 4)–(8, 9) above), ones that allow semantic equivalence between phrasal and sentential forms (e.g., "Mommy made the pie and the brownies" = "Mommy made the pie and Mommy made the brownies"), and appear to be susceptible to a conjunction reduction operation.[12] Thus, they provide a baseline for comparison to Type II and Type III with regard to our basic questions.

Type II and Type III did not allow such expansions. Type III involved predicates that do not allow sentential coordination paraphrases because they involve the "mix" verb, or combinatorial predicates like "make bubbles," "make a mud

---

8. It is not possible to precisely compare across this study and previous experiments as ages, language development levels, and sentence lengths varied across the studies. Further research should be conducted specifically to seek more precise cross-experimental comparisons than we can make here.

9. Original research was conducted by Barbara Krawiec in the Cornell Language Acquisition Lab, working with Suzanne Flynn and Yuchin Chien and resulting in an Honors Thesis (Krawiec 1980) at that time. The inter-rater reliability of data transcriptions was obtained by at least two transcribers. These data have now (in 2007) been rescored and statistically reanalyzed. Scoring criteria appear in the Experiment Bank cited.

10. Here 'forward' directionality refers to the case where the phrasal coordination appeared to the 'right' of the predicate (i.e., in object position) in a right-branching sentence structure; while 'backward' refers to the case where the phrasal coordination appeared to the 'left' (i.e., in subject position) in the clause.

11. For Type II, there are no expansions for the phrasal coordinations that can be related by reduction to the phrasal forms, only the paraphrastic types exemplified here. Type III sentential coordinations are the control sentences for those phrasal forms that do not have exact or paraphrastic expansion. Although these sentential coordinations can be reduced, and the corresponding phrasal coordinations can be expanded, these are not semantically equivalent in this type.

12. In fact, semantic equivalence may never be perfect between sentential and phrasal coordination forms, even in the 'classic' coordination types like our Type I, or examples (3, 4)–(8, 9) (i.e., the concept of simultaneity versus successiveness is susceptible to these formal variations).

Chapter 7. First language acquisition of coordination   **163**

Table 1. Sentences used in the Mud-Puddle study

Type I. Expandable coordinates

Sentential	*Phrasal*
Forward	Forward
1. Mom makes breakfast and Mom makes dinner.	1. Mommy made the pie and the brownies.
2. Jane ate candy and Jane ate ice cream.	2. Johnny pushes the car and the truck.
Backward	Backward
1. Boys throw balloons and Dads throw balloons.	1. The girl and the boy picked the flowers.
2. Liz ate cupcakes and Mom ate cupcakes.	2. The men and the ladies eat cupcakes.

Type II. Reciprocals: periphrastic expansion coordinates

Sentential	*Phrasal*
Forward	Backward
1. Tommy hit Mark and Mark hit Tommy.	1. The cat and the dog kissed each other.
2. Mommy kissed Jane and Jane kissed mommy.	2. Ernie and Big Bird pushed each other.

Type III. Mud-puddles: non-periphrastic coordinates

Sentential	*Phrasal*
Forward	Forward
1. Daddy mixed paint and Daddy mixed glue.	1. Mommy mixed the sugar and the milk.
2. Mom mixes soup and Mom mixes juice.	2. Dad mixes the soap and the water.
Backward	Backward
1. Mud makes a mess and sand makes a mess.	1. Some soap and some water make bubbles.
2. Dump trucks make noise and airplanes make noise.	2. Water and dirt make a mud puddle.

puddle," "make a mess," "make noise." For example, "Mommy mixed the sugar and the milk" (≠ "Mommy mixed the sugar and Mommy mixed the milk");[13] or, regarding combinatorial "make" predicates, "Water and dirt make a mud puddle" (≠ "Water makes a mud puddle and dirt makes a mud puddle").

Type II involved elementary reciprocal predicates (e.g., "Ernie and Big Bird pushed each other") that do allow sentential correlates, although only in a paraphrastic form (e.g., "Ernie pushed Big Bird and Big Bird pushed Ernie") but not in a form that would allow direct conjunction reduction or expansion between sentential and phrasal forms.

In a controlled experimental design, the coordination Types II and III were contrasted to the phrasal and sentential coordinate forms that do allow seman-

---

13. In fact, full sentential forms do allow a potential reading corresponding to the phrasal form, and phrasal forms do allow potential sentential correlates. For example, *Joan mixed water and flour with vinegar and sugar respectively* → *Joan mixed water with vinegar and Joan mixed flour with sugar*. Correspondingly, *Mommy mixed sugar and Mommy mixed milk* appears to allow the interpretation that they were mixed together, although it is not preferred.

tically parallel syntactically expanded sentential correlates in Type I. All sentences were regularized in word and syllable length (ranging from 7–9 words (mean = 7.25); all involved 9 syllables), and were presented in random order across two sentence batteries to young children. There were two replication items for each condition, as shown in Table 1. We tested 46 children between the ages of 2 years and 9 months to 4 years (with an overall mean age of 3 years and 6 months). The children were divided into three age groups (Mean age for each group: Group 1 = 35.8 months; Group 2 = 41.6 months; Group 3 = 46.7 months.)

This design allowed a test of several hypotheses that bear on the interface between semantic and syntactic representations in the grammatical structure of coordination, and on the interacting roles of syntactic computation and semantic predication in children's early language acquisition of coordination. If children's acquisition of expanded forms of coordination is based on a semantic representation and not a syntactic one, then when children are given reduced (phrasal) forms that have no semantic equivalent in expanded form, they should not show the same developmental effects as they do in Type I sentences. That is, they should not show that the development of the phrasal form required development of an expanded form, or that an expanded form was necessary to their acquisition of the phrasal form. They should not show the syntactic directionality effects that had been found in previous research (i.e., there would be no obvious reason why forward directionality would be preferred over backward in these forms if their representation was not, at least in part, syntactically determined). In particular, in Type II or Type III , in contrast to Type I, children's reformulations of the adult stimuli, when they occur, should not show attempts to *expand* these phrasal coordinations syntactically to sentential coordinations, since this syntactic expansion is not necessary to, or even applicable to, the meaning of the phrasal coordination.

6.2. Results: Quantitative analyses of correct imitations

Quantitative analyses, based on Analysis of Variance on variation in number of correct imitations across the different grammatical factors of the experimental design (i.e., "age group," "sentence type," "sentence (coordination) form," and "directionality") can be found in their entirety at: www.clal.cornell.edu/vcla. Here, in Table 2, we summarize the mean number of correct imitations (and the corresponding standard deviations inside the parentheses).

In general, the results reveal that children in all three age groups demonstrated competence for the coordinate structures tested. That is to say, although overall performance increased significantly from Group 1 to Group 3 ($F(2, 43) = 10.18, p <$ .01, partial $\eta^2 = .321$), even Group 1 children achieved more than 50% correct overall (with a mean of 1.11 on a score range of 0–2 over the two replication items for

Table 2. Mean number of correct imitations: (1) group (3 age groups) × sentence type (type I vs. type III) × sentence form (sentential vs. phrasal) × direction (forward vs. backward); (2) group (3 age groups) × sentence form (sentential vs. phrasal) for type II backward sentences

Age group	Sentential		Phrasal	
	Forward	Backward	Forward	Backward
Type I: Expandable coordinations				
Group 1 (n = 13) 2.09–3.02	1.31 (.75)	0.85 (.69)	1.62 (.65)	1.08 (.76)
Group 2 (n = 23) 3.03–3.08	1.17 (.83)	1.22 (.80)	1.61 (.58)	1.52 (.67)
Group 3 (n = 10) 3.10–14.00	1.70 (.48)	1.40 (.70)	2.00 (.00)	2.00 (.00)
TOTAL (n = 46) 2.09–4.00	1.33 (.76)	1.15 (.76)	1.70 (.55)	1.50 (.69)
Type II: Reciprocals: paraphrastic expansion coordinations				
Group 1 (n = 13) 2.09–3.02		1.00 (1.00)		1.31 (.75)
Group 2 (n = 23) 3.03–3.08		0.96 (.77)		1.70 (.56)
Group 3 (n = 10) 3.10–14.00		1.40 (.84)		1.90 (.32)
TOTAL (n = 46) 2.09–4.00		1.07 (.85)		1.63 (.61)
Type III: Mud-puddles: non-paraphrastic coordinations				
Group 1 (n = 13) 2.09–3.02	0.85 (.80)	0.92 (.64)	1.15 (.38)	1.08 (.76)
Group 2 (n = 23) 3.03–3.08	1.22 (.74)	1.30 (.82)	1.91 (.29)	1.74 (.45)
Group 3 (n = 10) 3.10–14.00	1.90 (.32)	1.50 (.53)	1.90 (.32)	1.90 (.32)
TOTAL (n = 46) 2.09–4.00	1.26 (.77)	1.24 (.74)	1.70 (.47)	1.59 (.62)

each condition).[14] Both Group 2 and Group 3 children performed significantly better than Group 1 children (Tukey HSD tests: G2 vs. G1, $p < .05$; G3 vs. G1, $p < .01$). There was no significant difference between overall success of Group 2 and Group 3 children (the overall mean number of correct imitations for G2 and G3 was 1.46 and 1.79, respectively). Even when the data of the six youngest children (under 3 years of age) were analyzed separately, all of them correctly produced at least some sentential and some phrasal coordinations, suggesting the essential competence for coordinate structure was already in place even in these very young children.

Overall, when Type I (expandable) coordinate structures were compared to the Type III (*Mud-Puddle*) coordinations, similar structural effects were found. There was generally greater success with phrasal forms of coordinations than sentential forms (Type I: 1.64 vs. 1.27; Type III: 1.61 vs. 1.28). Moreover, directionality affected both sentence types in a similar way (i.e., forward forms were more successful than backward ones; Type I: 1.57 vs. 1.34; Type III: 1.49 vs. 1.41). Direc-

---

14. The score range for each condition was 0–2. A score of '2' indicated the child had correctly reproduced the stimulus sentence over both replication items in a condition; a score of '1' indicated success on one item only; '0' indicated success on neither of the two replication items for that condition.

tionality also affected both coordination forms (sentential forward vs. backward: 1.36 vs. 1.20; phrasal forward vs. backward: 1.70 vs. 1.55). These results suggest that, in general, children are bringing similar structural factors to bear on coordinate structures over the different semantic variations tested in this study.

At the same time, the Type III (*Mud-Puddle*) predicates were the most inaccessible at the earliest ages, compared to the other coordination types. For example, when the six youngest children were analyzed, Type III phrasal forward coordinations revealed a mean of 1.00, and the sentential forward a mean of .83, as compared to a mean of 1.67 for both phrasal and sentential forward Type I sentences.

6.3. Results: Qualitative analysis of reformulations

Here we concentrate on qualitative analyses of the critical Type III (*Mud-Puddle*) and the Type II (reciprocal) coordinations.

6.3.1. *Type III: Mud-Puddle predicates*

Analysis of reformulations of Type III predicates by the youngest children showed that three of them revealed attempts at syntactic expansion of the Type III phrasal coordinations, as exemplified in (18)–(19),[15] and such attempts persisted through the first half of age 3.

(18) Adult stimulus: *Mommy mixed the sugar and the milk.*
      Child responses:
      a. *Mommy mixed the sugar and her mixed the milk.* (GK, 2.9)
      b. *Mom mixed the sugar, Mom mixed the milk.* (JB, 2.11)
      c. *Um Mommy ate... um mix the sugar and Mommy mixed the milk.*
          (MF, 3.0)

(19) Adult stimulus: *Dad mixes the soap and the water.*
      Child response: *Dad mixed soap and Dad mixed the water.* (JD, 3.4)

There were also some reductions of the related Type III forward sentential coordinations, like (20) or (21).

(20) Adult stimulus: *Mom mixes soup and Mom mixes juice*
      Child responses:
      a. *Mom mixes soup and juice.* (JC 3.0)
      b. *Mom mixes juice...and milk.* (AC, 3.1)

---

15. As noted previously, the 'preference' of the child for full sentential form is related to developmental stage and age; and it is related to direction of expansion.

Chapter 7. First language acquisition of coordination   **167**

(21)   Adult stimulus: *Daddy mixed paint and Daddy mixed glue*
       Child response: *Daddy mix glue and paint* (SR 3.1)

These elaborations and reductions signal that the child's syntactic operation on these sentences was, to some degree, independent of the semantic concepts involved and, to some degree, overrode the semantic representation of these coordinations. The preferred reading in the reduced forms in (20) or (21) differs from that in the unreduced form.

In addition, there were several indications of problems with the semantic concept involved in the 'mix' predicates. There were many conversions from 'mix' to 'make' (e.g., substituting 'make' in sentences with 'mix' as in the examples in (22) or (23)). It should be noted the 'make' predicate corresponds to a potential semantically equivalent sentential expansion.

(22)   Adult stimulus: *Mommy mixed the sugar and the milk.*
       Child responses:
       a.   *Mom make sugar and milk.* (SmcQ, 2.8)
       b.   *Mommy makes the sugar and the milk.* (MM, 2.11)
       c.   *Mommy make sugar and milk.* (CM, 3.2)

(23)   Adult stimulus: *Dad mixes the soap and the water.*
       Child responses:
       a.   *Dad make soap and the water.* (MM, 2.10)
       b.   *Dad, Dad make the soap and the water.* (BS, 3.3)

Several converted 'and' in these constructions to 'in', again, defying the coordination involved in the 'mix' predicate:[16]

       c.   Child response: *Dad mixes the soap in the water* (EL, 2.10)

The conversion of 'mix' to 'make' was a general one, also characterizing sentential coordinations, as in (24) or (25).

(24)   Adult stimulus: *Daddy mixed paint and Daddy mixed glue.*
       Child responses:
       a.   *Daddy mixed paint and...and Daddy make der glue.* (EL, 2.10)
       b.   *Daddy mix paint, Daddy makes glue.* (MM, 2.10)
       c.   *Daddy mixed...Daddy mixed paint and Daddy makes glue* (BS, 3.3)

(25)   Adult stimulus: *Mom mixes soup and Mom mixes juice.*
       Child response: *Mom make a soup and Dad make a soup* (SmcQ 2.8)

---

16. In fact, it was frequently impossible to distinguish whether the child was saying 'n' for 'and' or for 'in' (e.g., 'soap n water').

168   Barbara Lust, Suzanne Flynn, Yuchin Chien, and Barbara Krawiec

For Type III phrasal coordinations with a 'backward' structure, expansions, like (26) or (27) were less frequent, as they were for backward Type I coordinations (and as they were in previous research with backward Type I sentences like (8, 9)). Instead, children frequently converted these to sentences with agent subjects, possibly with the phrasal coordination moved to the 'forward' object location, or with the coordination eliminated in favor of a single referent.

(26)   Adult stimulus: *Some soap and some water make bubbles.*
Child responses:
    a.   *Some water makes some bubbles and...some what else? ...I don't know* (CK, 3.6)
    b.   *Mom makes some bubbles* (EL, 2.10)

(27)   Adult stimulus: *Water and dirt make a mud puddle.*
Child response: *Mommy make a dirt and a mudpie* (EL, 2.10)

The conversion to animate subjects was a general one, characterizing sentential coordinations as well as the phrasal coordinations of this type, as in (28):

(28)   Adult stimulus: *Mud makes a mess and sand makes a mess.*
Child responses:
    a.   *Mom...um Mom makes a mess and Sam makes a mess* (MF, 3.0)
    b.   *Sam make a mess, my mom make a mess* (SmcQ, 2.8)

Alternatively, for these structures, children created constructions that involved a conjoined product but achieved conjunction not by the verb itself but by the product itself (e.g., (29)).

(29)   Adult stimulus: *Water and dirt make a mud puddle.*
Child responses:
    a.   *Water make a mud puddle.* (MM, 2.10)
    b.   *Water make dirt puddle.* (SB, 2.10)

All of these reformation responses suggest that the child, in reconstructing these Type III coordinations, is consulting both the syntactic foundations of these sentences, including that of sentential coordination and directionality, as well as the combinatorial predicates involved.

6.3.2. *Type II: Reciprocals*

In contrast to Type III, children did not attempt to either expand or reduce the reciprocal Type II forms. Unlike in Type III, reformulations of 'reciprocals' sometimes characterized sentential forms (e.g., (30) and (31)), even while phrasal forms were accessible (e.g., (32) and (33)). Here the 'reciprocal' concept is shown not to

Chapter 7. First language acquisition of coordination **169**

automatically involve the sentential form of representation in the adult stimulus like (30) or (31) even when it was accessible in the phrasal form very early (e.g., (32) or (33)). In a response like (30a), the child maintains the sentential coordination syntactically, but has lost the semantic reciprocity involved; while in the phrasal coordination like (32), the child is simply correct, coordinating the reciprocity with the phrasal form through the lexical item 'each other' easily. However, often even the youngest children in the sample were frequently correct on both sentential and phrasal forms of the reciprocals. In general, the reciprocal phrasal forms like (32) or (33) are developed in close correlation with Type I backward phrasal forms, suggesting that elementary reciprocal constructions like (32) or (33) are available from the time the basic syntactic structure of the sentence is present (i.e., subject phrasal coordination).

(30) Adult stimulus: *Tommy hit Mark and Mark hit Tommy.*
      Child responses:
      a. *Mark hit Tommy and Mark hit Tommy.* (EL, 2.10)
      b. *Mark,...Tommy hit Mark and...and..Tom...and Mark hit Tommy.* (SB, 2.10)

(31) Adult stimulus: *Mommy kissed Jane and Jane kissed Mommy.*
      Child responses:
      a. *Jane kissed her and Jane kissed Mommy.* (EL, 2.10)
      b. *Jane..Mo..Mommy kissed Jane and Jane kiss Mommy.* (SB, 2.10)

(32) Adult stimulus: *Ernie and Big Bird pushed each other.*
      Child responses:
      a. *Ernie and Big Bird push each other* (EL, 2.10)
      b. *Ernie and Big Bird pushed each other* (SB, 2.10)

(33) Adult stimulus: *The cat and the dog kissed each other.*
      Child responses:
      a. *A dog and a cat kissed each other.* (EL, 2.10)
      b. *The dog and the cat kissed each other.* (SB, 2.10)

Children appeared to access the reciprocal 'each other' lexical item in coordinate structures very early and very easily.

7. Discussion

As was found in early studies, results from this *Mud-Puddle* study indicate the child's *competence* involves access to relations between full sentential and phrasal forms of coordination. Children pursued these links, elaborating phrasal Type III *Mud-Puddle* coordinations, even when there was no semantically equivalent correlate. At the same time, these results show that this relation is mediated by the semantic representation of the phrasal forms involved, as well as by syntactic factors, such as directionality. Coordination, in the human competence for language, as represented by the young child's early language acquisition, appears to involve both syntactic and semantic factors that are represented independently and continuously integrated over the course of language acquisition.

Ultimate acquisition of Type III (*Mud-Puddle*) coordinations was found to involve the necessary linkage of both syntactic and lexical predicate factors. In the absence of full access to the combinatorial lexical semantics related to a predicate like 'mix', children appear to fall back on a syntactic representation for these phrasal coordinations, as revealed through their sentential expansions, often semantically inappropriate or anomalous.

Acquisition of elementary reciprocal structures (like (32) or (33)) appear to depend on the development of the syntactic coordinate structure they involve (i.e., backward phrasal coordinations with subject coordination), at the same time that it depends on developing comprehension of reciprocity and its lexical expressions. Clearly, at least some elementary form of reciprocity appeared to be accessible very early, as was the ability to link the lexical form 'each other' to coordinate subjects, while verbal lexical combinatorial predicates like 'mix' took more time to develop in the coordinate frames of the Type III predicates.

In order to represent the early competence of the child, we can now move away from the postulation of an independent 'conjunction reduction' transformation as the sole explanation for the child's knowledge of the syntax of coordination (i.e., of the systematic and grammatical relation between sentential and phrasal forms of coordination). Both current theory and the acquisition data converge to motivate this shift. Now we are led to believe that this relation may best be cast in terms of an interface between syntactic representation involving sentential structure and the semantic representation of both sentential and phrasal forms. However, questions remain regarding the nature of the reconstruction involved in the derivation and interpretation of 'reduced' forms, such as phrasal coordinations, and their relation to full forms. More recent studies have begun to pursue the precise mechanisms by which this interface may be accomplished (e.g., Foley et al. 2003; Foley et al. in prep, Postman et al. 1997).

We are also led to new studies of the representation of predication involved in our Type III and Type II sentences, both in adult grammar and in the child's approach to these. Recent work by Langendoen and Magloire (2003) has begun to formulate a theory of how interplay of several factors can account for the semantic representation involved in structures like (12)–(17), and how these factors may interact with the syntax of conjunction reduction. (See also Langendoen 1978). These factors, they propose, involve a typology of predicate types in terms of plural properties of these predicates (note that coordinate structures necessarily involve plurality of sets) and a representation of the core semantics of reciprocity and/or reflexivity (unified as semantic "reciprocoreflexive" representation). This typology of reciprocity suggested in Langendoen and Magloire (2003) may lead the way in further research in this area, especially if this theory can be generalized to the Type III sentences.[17]

This *Mud-Puddle* study has only initiated study of the interaction between the syntactic representation and the semantic representation involved in the representation of coordination. However, its results appear to cohere basically with Langendoen and Magloire's (2003) typology in that they confirm that the semantic representations involved in the Type III sentences are partially localized in the lexicon (e.g., in 'mix' verbs) that we have seen are modified by the child as he or she strives to capture the representation of these sentences. However, the results also appear to implicate pragmatics. For example in sentences like 'water and dirt make mud puddles', it does not appear to be the lexicon (e.g., 'make') that controls the combinatorial concept they involve. That is, although the combination of water and dirt may result in mud puddles, it is not the simple lexical item 'make' that is solely responsible for this combinatorial meaning, but the general syntactic context in which the verb appears (involving a coordinate subject and unique predicate) and the pragmatic situation denoted by the sentence, as well as the particular interpretation of the verb. Although the verb 'make' can convey a combinatorial meaning, as in "Two and Two make four," the access of this meaning depends on the context of use.[18] It would appear that if a general theory is to relate Type II and Type III sentence structures, it must implicate pragmatics, as well as the lexicon, the coordinate syntax, and the relevant properties of plurality.

This preliminary study clearly deserves extension and replication. The results of this *Mud-Puddle* study indicate the need for further research with regard to

---

17. Indeed we lack a satisfactory term for the semantic representation of our '*Mud-Puddle*' type sentences, since they go beyond the 'reciprocoreflexive' concept, although they appear to be related to it. Some form of 'combinatorial' predication resulting in an end product that exists only because of the plural combination of or by the subject must be involved here. Further research can pursue more precise modifications of the semantic concepts reflected in our original design. For example, as one reviewer has noted, the 'mix' concept involved in "mix paint" and "mix soup" may involve different concepts of "mix;" indeed even any one of these is subject to multiple interpretations (e.g., "mix" = stir, or "mix" = combine ingredients, etc).

18. We owe this observation to an anonymous reviewer for this chapter. The general point we make here regarding the verb 'make', will apply to a wide range of verbs (e.g., *Lowering temperatures and condensation creates/forms storms*).

several empirical as well as theoretical issues. Further work must consider the specific semantic representation involved in the reciprocal and in different types of reciprocals along the Langendoen and Magloire (2003) typology. Animacy and stativity must be specifically evaluated as they clearly play a role in the child's access to these forms (as we know they might, cf.. Fiengo and Lasnik 1973) since children often changed the stative 'mudpie' sentences to active forms with animate subjects, as was seen above.

Several factors should be controlled in further experimental designs, including in particular, the age and developmental level of the sample.[19] With sentences as short as those used in this study, the most interesting and crucial results concerned the youngest children in the sample, signaling that further research should focus on an even younger age than the majority of our sample (i.e., the two year old age) and on earliest periods of syntactic productivity, in order to more precisely capture the developmental mechanisms involved in these interesting coordination forms. A research program that combined assessments of language production as well as language comprehension (e.g., Philip 2000; Matsuo 1999, 2000) would appear promising.

References

Ardery, G. 1980. On coordination in child language. *Journal of Child Language* 7:305–20.
Chomsky, N. 1995. *The Minimalist Program*. Cambridge MA: The MIT Press.
Cohen Sherman, J. & Lust, B. 1993. Children are in control. *Cognition* 46:1–51.
Comrie, B. 1988. Coreference and conjunction reduction in grammar and discourse. *Explaining Language Universals*, J. Hawkins (ed.), 3–28. Oxford: Blackwell.
DeVilliers, J., Tager-Flusberg, H. & Hakuta, K. 1977. Deciding between theories of development of coordination in child speech. *Papers and Reports on Child Language Development* 13: 128–37.
Dik, S. C. 1968. *Coordination*. Amsterdam: North-Holland.
Everett, D. L. 2005. Cultural constraints on grammar and cognition in Piraha: Another look at the design features of human language. *Current Anthropology* 46:621–46.
Fiengo, R. & Lasnik, H. 1973. The logical structure of reciprocal sentences in English. *Foundations of Language* 9:37–57.
Fitch, W. T., Hauser, M. & Chomsky, N. 2005. The evolution of the language faculty: Clarifications and implications. *Cognition* 97:1–32.
Flynn, S. 1993. Interactions between L2 acquisition and linguistic theory. *Confluence Linguistics, L2 Acquisition and Speech Pathology*, F. Eckman (ed.), 17–36. Amsterdam: John Benjamins.
Flynn, S. 1987. *A Parameter Setting Model of L2 Acquisition*. Amsterdam: Reidel.
Flynn, S. & Martohardjono, G. 1994. Mapping from the initial state to the final stage: The sepa-

---

19. Note that earlier studies found that acquisition of coordination correlated more strongly with the child's developing MLU than with his or her age (Lust 1977).

Chapter 7. First language acquisition of coordination **173**

ration of universal principles and language specific principles. In *Syntactic Theory and First Language Acquisition: Cross Linguistic Perspectives,* B. Lust, M. Suner & J. Whitman, 319–35. Hillsdale NJ: Lawrence Erlbaum.

Foley, C. Nuñez del Prado, Z. Barbier, I. & Lust, B. 2003. Knowledge of variable binding in VP ellipsis: Language acquisition research and theory converge *Syntax* 6: 52–83.

Foley, C. Pactovis, J. & Lust, B. In prep. Links between LF and PF: New evidence from first language acquisition of VP ellipsis ms. Cornell University.

Gentner, T. A. Fenn, K. M. Margoliash, D. & Nusbaum, H. 2006. Recursive syntactic pattern learning by songbirds. *Nature* 440: 1204–1207.

Gleitman, L. 1969. Coordinating conjunctions in English. *Language* 41: 260–93.

Hakuta, K. de Villiers, J. & Tager-Flusberg, H. 1982. Sentence coordination in Japanese and English. *Journal of Child Language* 9: 193–207.

Hankamer, J. & Sag, I. 1976. Deep and surface anaphora. *Linguistic Inquiry* 7: 391–428.

Harries, H. 1973. Coordination reduction. *Stanford University Working Papers on Language Universals* 11: 139–209.

Haspelmath, M. Dryer, M. Gil, D. & Comrie, B. (eds) 2005. *World Atlas of Language Structures.* Oxford: OUP.

Hauser, M. Chomsky, N. & Fitch, W. 2002. The faculty of language: What is it, who has it and how did it evolve? *Science* 298: 1569–1579.

Johannessen, J. B. 1998. *Coordination.* Oxford: OUP.

Johnson, K. 2000. When verb phrases go missing. In *The First GLOT International State-of-the-Article Book,* L. Cheng & R. Sybesma, 75–104. Berlin: Mouton de Gruyter.

Kayne, R. 1994. *The Antisymmetry of Syntax.* Cambridge MA: The MIT Press.

Krawiec, B. 1980. Development of Coordination in Preschool Children. Honors thesis Cornell University.

Krifka, M. 1990. Boolean and non-Boolean 'and'. In *Papers from the Second Symposium on Logic and Language,* L. Kálmán & L. Polos, 161–88. Budapest: Akadémiai Kiadó.

Lakoff, G. & Peters, S. 1969. Phrasal conjunction and symmetric predicates. In *Modern Studies in English: Readings in Transformational Grammar,* D. Reibel & S. Schane, 113–42. Englewood Cliffs NJ: Prentice Hall.

Langendoen, D. T. 1978. The logic of reciprocity. *Linguistic Inquiry* 9: 177–97.

Langendoen, D. T. & Magloire, J. 2003. The logic of reflexivity and reciprocity. In *Anaphora: A Reference Guide,* A. Barss (ed.), 237–63. Oxford: Blackwell.

Langendoen, D. T. & Postal, P. (eds). 1984. *The Vastness of Natural Languages.* Oxford: Blackwell.

Lasnik, H. 2000. Syntactic Structures Revisited. Cambridge MA: The MIT Press.

Lust, B. 1974. Conjunction Reduction in the Language of Young Children. PhD Dissertation, City University of New York, Graduate Center.

Lust, B. 1976. Gapped coordinate sentences: An examination of their logical form. Paper presented at Linguistic Society of America Annual Meeting, Oswego NY.

Lust, B. 1977. Conjunction reduction in child language. *Journal of Child Language* 4: 257–97.

Lust, B. 1981. On coordinating studies of coordination: Problems of method and theory in first language acquisition–a reply to Ardery. *Journal of Child Language* 8: 457–70.

Lust, B. 1994. Functional projection of CP and phrase structure parameterization: An argument for the strong continuity hypothesis. In *Heads, Projections, and Learnability,* Vol. 1, *Syntactic Theory and First Language Acquisition: Cross-Linguistic Perspectives,* B. Lust, M. Suner & J. Whitman, 85–118. Hillsdale NJ: Lawrence Erlbaum.

Lust, B. 2006. *Child Language. Acquisition and Growth*. Cambridge: CUP.

Lust, B. In prep. *Universal Grammar and the Initial State. Cross Linguistic Studies of Directionality*. Cambridge MA: The MIT Press.

Lust, B. & Chien, Y-C. 1984. The structure of coordination in first language acquisition of Mandarin Chinese. *Child Development* 56:1359–1375.

Lust, B., deAbrew, K. & Sharma, V. 1982. A cross-linguistic study of the acquisition of complex syntax in Hindi and Sinhalese: An argument for a universal. Paper presented at the Fourth South Asian Languages Roundtable. Syracuse University.

Lust, B., Flynn, S. Chien, Y-C. & Clifford, T. 1980. Coordination: The role of syntactic, pragmatic and processing factors in first language acquisition. *Papers and Reports on Child Language Development* 19:79–87.

Lust, B., Flynn, S. & Foley, C. 1996. What children know about what they say: Elicited imitation as a research method. In *Methods for Assessing Children's Syntax*, D. McDaniel, C. McKee & H. Cairns, 55–76. Cambridge MA: The MIT Press.

Lust, B., Flynn, S., Foley, C. & Chien, Y-C. 1999. How do we know what children know? Establishing scientific methods for the study of first language acquisition. In *Handbook of Child Language Acquisition*, W. Ritchie & T. Bhatia, 427–56. New York NY: Academic Press.

Lust, B. & Mazuka, R. 1989. Cross-linguistic studies of directionality in first language acquisition: The Japanese data response to O'Grady, Suzuki-Wei & Cho 1986. *Journal of Child Language* 16:665–84.

Lust, B. & Mervis, C. 1980. Coordination in the natural speech of young children. *Journal of Child Language* 7:279–304.

Lust, B. & Wakayama, T. 1979. The structure of coordination in children's first language acquisition of Japanese. In *Studies in First and Second Language Acquisition*, F. Eckman & A. Hastings (eds), 134–52. Rowley MA: Newbury House.

Lust, B., Solan, L., Flynn, S., Cross, C. & Schuetz, E. 1986. A comparison of null and pronoun anaphora in first language acquisition. In *Studies in the Acquisition of Anaphora*, B. Lust (ed.), 245–78. Dordrecht: Reidel.

Lust, B., Pinhas, J. & Flynn, S. 1980. Gapped coordinate sentences. Language of Young Children: A Psycholinguistic Study of the Interaction of Syntax and Processing. Paper presented at 5th Annual Boston University Conference on Child Language, Boston University.

Lust, B., Wakayama, T., Snyder, W. & Bergmann, M. 1980. The acquisition of complex sentences in first language acquisition of Japanese coordination. Paper presented at 5th Annual Boston University Conference on Child Language, Boston University.

Matsuo, A. 1999. Reciprocity and binding in early child grammar. *Linguistic Inquiry* 30:310–17.

Matsuo, A. 2000. Children's acquisition of reciprocal sentences with stative and active predicates. *Language Acquisition* 8:1–22.

Mazuka, R., Lust, B., Wakayama, T. & Snyder, W. 1986. Distinguishing effects of parameters in early syntax acquisition: A Cross-linguistic study of Japanese and English. *Papers and Reports on Child Language Development*:73–82.

Merchant, J. 2001. *The Syntax of Silence: Sluicing, Islands and the Theory of Ellipsis*. Oxford: OUP.

Munn, A. 1993. Topics in the Syntax and Semantics of Coordinate Structures. PhD Dissertation, University of Maryland.

Nuñez del Prado, Z., Foley, C. & Lust, B. 1993. The significance of CP to the pro-drop parameter: An experimental study of Spanish. In *The Proceedings of the Twenty-fifth Child Language Research Forum*, E. Clark (ed.), 146–57. Palo Alto CA: Stanford University.

Nuñez del Prado, Z., Foley, C., Proman, R. & Lust, B. 1994. Subordinate CP and pro-drop: Evidence for degree 'n' learnability from an experimental study of Spanish and English acquisition. In *Proceedings of NELS* 24, 2, M. Gonzalez (ed.), 443–60. Amherst MA: University of Massachussetts.

O'Grady, W., Suzuki-Wei, Y. & Cho, S.-W. 1986. Directionality preferences in the interpretation of anaphora: Data from Korean and Japanese. *Journal of Child Language* 13:409–20.

Philip, W. 2000. Adult and child understanding of simple reciprocal sentences. *Language* 76: 1–27.

Pinker, S. & Jackendoff, R. 2005. The faculty of language: What's special about it? *Cognition* 95: 201–36.

Postman, W., Foley, C., Santelmann, L. & Lust, B. 1997. Evidence for strong continuity: New experimental results of children's acquisition of VP ellipsis and bound variable structures. In *MIT Working Papers in Linguistics: Proceedings of the 8th Student Conference in Linguistics*, B. Bruening, 327–44. Cambridge MA: MITWPL.

Progovac, L. 1998a. Structure for coordination. Part I. *Glot International* 3:3–6.

Progovac, L. 1998b. Structure for coordination. Part II. *Glot International* 3:7–9.

Reibel, D. & Schane, S. (eds). 1969. *Modern Studies in English: Readings in Transformational Grammar*. Englewood Cliffs NJ: Prentice-Hall.

Sag, I. 1976. Selection and Logical Form. PhD Dissertation, MIT.

Sag, I. 1980. *Deletion and Logical Form*. New York NY: Garland.

Seuss, Dr. 1965. *Fox in Socks* [Beginner Books]. New York NY: Random House.

Slobin, D. & Welsh, C. 1973. Elicited imitation as a research tool in developmental psycholinguistics. In *Studies of Child Language Development*, D. Ferguson & D. Slobin (eds), 485–96. New York NY: Holt, Rinehart and Winston.

Smith, C. 1969. Ambiguous sentences with AND. In *Modern Studies in English: Readings in Transformational Grammar*, D. Reidel & S. Schane, 75–9. Englewood Cliffs NJ: Prentice-Hall.

Williams, E. 1977a. Discourse and logical form. *Linguistic Inquiry* 8:101–39.

Williams, E. 1977b. On deep and surface anaphora. *Linguistic Inquiry* 8:692–6.

Zwart, J-W. 2005a. On headedness and coordination: Noun phrase conjunction in head-final languages. Paper presented at LAGB Annual Meeting, Cambridge, UK.

Zwart, J-W. 2005b. Some notes on coordination in head-final languages. In *Linguistics in the Netherlands 2005*, J. Doetjes & J. van de Weijer (eds), 1–13. Amsterdam: John Benjamins.

CHAPTER 8

Frequency effects in children's syntactic and morphological development*

Cecile McKee and Dana McDaniel

University of Arizona/University of Southern Maine

We have long loved Langendoen (1970) — a paper on the theoretical justification of "transformations, their effects on the structure of sentences, and the conditions under which they are optional or obligatory" (p. 102). In that paper, Langendoen argued that acceptability and grammaticality are "partially independent [and] partially dependent notions" (p. 103). We are struck by the implications of this contrast for language learning. If the learner's grammar is a set of probabilistic patterns and not (also or instead) a set of grammatical rules, one might expect high frequency elements to be 'grammatical' and low frequency elements to be 'ungrammatical.' In other words, grammaticality and acceptability should be similar if frequency is the determining factor. But Langendoen (1970) hypothesized that grammatical competence contributes to grammaticality while processing factors contribute to acceptability. Our research shows clearer effects of frequency on the latter than the on former and thus relates to Langendoen's observation.

This chapter explores the role of frequency in children's syntactic and morpho-phonological development. One study compares relative clauses involving different extraction sites, which constructions vary considerably in their frequency of occurrence. Children's production of these relatives suggests that frequency affects sentence planning, but their judgments of the same relatives are out of synchrony with the frequency rates. The other study presented here concerns the *a* and *an* forms of the indefinite article, which distinction is acquired relatively late even though the forms occur frequently. These studies show that frequency cannot be the whole story. We conclude that children's mastery of a system of rules proceeds — at least to some extent — independently of frequency patterns in the input.

1. Relative clauses

Children's syntactic development is critical to the debate on learning and frequency. Recent findings clearly show that infants can apply statistical learning mechanisms to language (e.g., Maye, Werker, & Gerken (2002) on the discovery of phonetic categories; see also Ellis (2002) for review of other domains). But sentences are

---

* We gratefully acknowledge the help of our longtime collaborators Wayne Cowart at the University of Southern Maine and Merrill Garrett at the University of Arizona.

interestingly different from sounds and words (Jackendoff 2006). Syntax is both abstract and combinatorial, relying on type categories like *subject* and *noun* and hierarchical organization of such elements. These categories combine to generate an *infinite* product. One way to capture this combinatorial system is via rules. Take the phrase *red fish* and consider the information in (1). The words in (1a) are arranged by the rule in (1b), which operates over type categories. An important aspect of English that this rule captures is that the adjective *red* precedes the noun *fish* in a noun phrase. Linguists attribute no special status to this ordering. Indeed, other possibilities are easily found. For example, Spanish has the rule in (2) for the phrase *pez rojo*.

(1) a. fish = N (or noun)
        red = A (or adjective)
    b. NP (or noun phrase) → A N

(2) a. pez = N
        rojo = A
    b. NP → N A

It is not always necessary to search across languages to find variation in such rules. English has other NPs. The rule in (3) describes relative clause modifiers of nouns. It orders elements like in (2b) with the post-nominal modifier. A further complexity is relevant to our study: Relative clauses can be differentiated by the grammatical function of the head. Compare the four types of relatives in (4), which all have the same head *the pizza*. But *the pizza* has a different role in each relative clause. In the subject relative in (4a), the head of the relative is the subject of the relative clause's verb. Another way of putting this is that the head corresponds to a subject gap in the relative clause. Similarly, *the pizza* is related to the object of the relative's verb in (4b), the object of the preposition *on* in (4c), and the determiner of the genitive phrase in (4d).

(3) NP → N S

(4) a. S: the pizza that ___ fell on the floor
    b. O: the pizza that Bert hit ___
    c. OP: the pizza that Bert danced on ___
    d. G: the pizza whose sauce Bert tasted ___

Interestingly, strings of elements that violate syntactic rules are easily perceived as ungrammatical, as illustrated by (5). Crucially, it is not something inherent in a particular ordering of elements that makes a phrase ungrammatical since what is fine in one language can be problematic in another (and vice versa). Grammatical rules are — to some degree — arbitrary. And to the extent that they account for people's linguistic behavior, linguists conclude that they are real. But we only see them indirectly — deducing their existence from systematicity in people's behavior.

(5) a. *the fish red
    b. *that was hit the pizza

To learn the syntax of English relative clauses, children have to combine many different abstract categories. How do they learn to do this? An extreme version of a possible answer maintains that syntactic rules per se do not exist. They are only linguistic shorthand for statistical patterns. That position makes some interesting and testable predictions about acquisition. For one thing, learners whose 'syntax' is a set of statistical patterns should perform differently on structures that vary in how often they occur in the target language. To illustrate, we return to the relative clauses exemplified above and note their frequencies according to Yamashita (1994), which was a study of the explicitness of relative clauses.[1]

(6) a. S: the pizza that fell on the floor (62%)
    b. O: the pizza that Bert hit (16%)
    c. OP: the pizza that Bert danced on (7%)
    d. G: the pizza whose sauce Bert tasted (2%)

A couple of observations about frequency of syntactic structures are important to emphasize here. First, the numbers noted above are *not* percents of the total utterances in a child's input. Instead, these are percents of the relative clauses that Yamashita studied. Thus, the 2% noted above represents only six utterances. Yamashita exemplifies that type with a non-restrictive relative, which leads us to think children work with even less data when learning the syntax of relatives like (6d). Keep this in mind as we move through our arguments. Second, we cannot consciously access *intuitions* about which sentence types occur more frequently. But, as illustrated above, we *easily* recognize whether a sentence fits the rules of English syntax.

The 36 children in this study ranged in age from 3;5 to 5;11 (mean age 4;9). They participated in the experiments reported in McDaniel, McKee, and Bernstein (1998), one designed to elicit their production of relative clauses and the other their judgments of the grammaticality of relative clauses. Details of the experimental procedures can be seen in McDaniel et al. (1998), as well as in McDaniel, McKee, and Cairns (1996). Briefly, the production task manipulated pragmatics.

---

1. These percents come from Yamashita's analysis of 330 relative clauses from a variety of speech samples in the Lancaster/IBM Spoken English Corpus. He included restrictive and non-restrictive relatives in this analysis, while we analyzed only restrictive relatives.

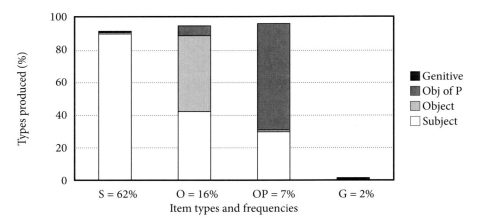

Figure 1. Comparison of targeted item types to percent of utterances of each type

For example, a trial targeting a subject relative like *the pizza that fell on the floor* introduced two identical pizzas, and one of them fell on the floor. An experimenter pointed to that pizza, and the child told a second experimenter, who was blindfolded during this part of the trial, to pick up the designated pizza. A trial targeting an object relative like *the pizza that Bert hit* also included two identical pizzas, but in this case a character named Bert hit one of them. Thus, a story involving pizzas could be manipulated so that one of the pizzas met different grammatical functions in some proposition.

Figure 1 shows the types of relatives that children produced in items designed to elicit the constructions in (6). We report here the percent of communicative, restrictive relative clauses of each type that were produced out of a total of 108 opportunities (three items targeting each relative clause type X 36 children). The frequencies given below each bar are the percentages reported by Yamashita (1994).

Children (and adults) did produce other utterances in this study, some communicative to a blindfolded interlocutor (e.g., *the one on the floor*) and some not (e.g., *that one*). But alternatives to the target were rare. What we find most striking in these data is that children used subject relatives both when the pragmatics called for them and when a different construction would have fit the communicative context as well or better. In contrast, they used object and object-of-preposition relatives only in situations specific to those constructions. In other words, the construction that occurs most frequently was also most often produced. Children in this study were capable of producing the rare constructions, but they did so only when in proscribed circumstances and, even then, only some of the time. They clearly avoided the even rarer *whose* genitive, even in these proscribed circumstances.[2] The production pattern of the relative clause types in our experiment thus corresponds with the frequency data reported for adult spontaneous speech. If this is a frequency effect, it can be interpreted as involving a processing system.

Let us briefly consider the 'extra' subject relatives — the ones that children produced in items designed to elicit object and object-of-preposition relatives, as exemplified in (7). These are interesting, in part, because the passive construction is also rare. These children substituted one *in*frequent construction for another. Thorough discussion of why speakers do this takes us too far afield. But briefly, English-speakers get a lot of practice with subject relatives. The execution of the plan for generating this construction is probably fast and smooth because of that. On a related note, it is worth asking why subject relatives are more frequent. This may also reflect properties of the sentence planning system. For example, the load on working memory may be less for the production of a filler-gap construction where the filler and its associated gap are close together.

(7) a. the pizza that was hit by Bert (O target: the pizza that Bert hit)
    b. the pizza that got danced on by Bert (OP target: the pizza that Bert danced on)

Our judgment data come from the same children. Again, details of the experimental procedures can be seen in McDaniel et al. (1998), as well as in McDaniel et al. (1996). Briefly, in the judgment task, the experimenter first set up a scenario with props and then asked the child to judge the grammaticality of a series of different sentences referring to that scenario.[3] The experiment included the constructions exemplified in (6), as well as some related items of interest. Items targeting judgments of grammatical and ungrammatical responses were balanced, to the extent this could be done before eliciting adult judgments. Unsurprisingly, children (like

---

2. As might be expected given the infrequency of this construction, adults in our experiment did not produce many of these relatives either (i.e., 53% of their utterances in the genitive items). See McDaniel et al. (1998) for details regarding what speakers said instead of the *whose* relatives, and McDaniel, Stickney, Fowler, and McKee (2002) for a follow up of the *thats* genitives. McDaniel et al. (1998) also has details regarding the adult subjects mentioned here.

3. This task followed the production task for two reasons. First, we wanted to avoid modeling the very constructions that we were asking to see whether speakers would produce on their own. Second, we wanted children to judge some of their own utterances (e.g., ones that were ungrammatical or pragmatically odd). Analysis of those judgments reveals children's awareness of speech errors. It also buttresses a methodological point we have made elsewhere — namely, that children's non-target utterances should be treated exactly like adults' non-target utterances. See McKee, McDaniel, and Snedeker (1998) for further discussion of this point. We take production data to reflect both grammatical competence and processing factors, in both adults and children. To analyze children's utterances as if they reflected only linguistic competence seems misguided.

adults) accepted most of what they themselves said. They also easily accepted sentences that they hear frequently. And, that makes sense since it is a system that surely cares about practice.

But what about a construction so rare that (some) children might not have heard it? To address this question, we compared the least frequent of the relatives introduced above — the object-of-preposition relatives and the genitive relatives. The object-of-preposition relatives were judged to be grammatical by 94% of the children.[4] Note that these *same* children rejected sentences of the same type that do *not* obey syntactic rules (and are also rare). The pair in (8) exemplifies this point.

While the data on the genitive relative are messier, they make the same point. See (9) and (10). The genitives also show us what children think about what they do *not* say.

(8) a. OP: This is the pizza that Bert danced on – 94% accepted
    b.   ungrammatical counterpart: This is the pizza that Bert danced – 3% accepted (one child, aged 3;7)

(9) a. G: the girl whose chair Bert sat in – 81% accepted
    b.   ungrammatical counterpart: * the girl whose Bert sat in chair – 11% accepted

(10) a. G: the boy whose cat Miss Piggy likes – 79% accepted
     b.   ungrammatical counterpart: * the boy whose Miss Piggy likes cat – 19% accepted

Our results would be very different if children's responses depended only on the statistical frequency of these constructions: They would *not* produce or accept rare sentence types. Instead, children accepted rare and yet grammatical sentences, while they rejected *un*grammatical (and rare) sentences. We claim that young children have knowledge of complex and rule-governed syntax, and that their syntax is not determined by frequency alone. Their production system, on the other hand, does seem to be influenced by frequency.

2. Indefinite articles

Children's morpho-phonological development also bears on questions regarding learning and frequency. This study examines a case where children have difficulty

---

4. Each child was given two or three opportunities to judge each type of relative clause (three when a child was inconsistent on the previous two). We classified the children as accepting or rejecting a sentence type based on a two-out-of-three criterion.

Chapter 8. Frequency effects in development   **183**

acquiring an apparently simple and frequently attested rule — namely, the *a–an* rule exemplified in (11).

(11) a. I have a bicycle.   *I have an bicycle.
      b. I have an umbrella.   *I have a umbrella.

We characterize the *a–an* rule as simple for two reasons. First, it applies without exception. The plural rule of English, in contrast, is not simple in the same sense because of the existence of irregular nouns. Second, a simple rule applies in an environment designated by a single linguistic distinction. The plural rule is not simple in this sense either, since voicing and sibilance are both relevant to its operation. The *a–an* rule is simple in both of these senses. The rule applies without exception and the factor in the environment determining its application is the fundamental vowel–consonant distinction: *a* is used before consonant-initial words, and *an* is used before vowel-initial words.[5]

In addition to the *a–an* pattern being simple, the relevant forms are frequently attested in the input. According to Francis and Kucera (1982), *a* is the fifth most frequent word in English. Although *an* occurs only around one sixth as often as *a*, that form is also highly frequent (i.e., the 30th most frequent word). If language acquisition reflects only statistical patterns in the input, then simple and frequent patterns should be easy to master and should be instantiated early on.[6]

The 84 children in this study ranged in age from 3;3 to 8;4. They attended private schools in Portland, Maine. The assumption was that children attending these

---

5. The *a–an* distinction is clearly part of the natural native dialect of many speakers. Unlike the prestige rules determining the distribution of *who* and *whom*, for example, which some speakers make an effort to obey, the *a–an* rule is effortlessly and accurately obeyed by a large proportion of speakers. Speech error data support this claim. When speakers produce errors that change the consonant/vowel status of the first sound in a word, the form of the indefinite article agrees with the new form of the word, such as 'an arrent curgument' for 'a current argument' and 'a meeting arathon' for 'an eating marathon' (Fromkin 1971:41).

In some dialects of English, there is no *a–an* alternation; only *a* is used. McDaniel and Cowart (2002) used a text corpus to examine the primary target dialect of the children in this study. The corpus included 743 student postings to an online discussion board for a lower division undergraduate course at the University of Southern Maine. Generally USM students come from white, working-class, native English-speaking families. The postings were casually composed; they included relatively frequent misspellings, sentence structure anomalies, non-standard punctuation and spacing, and neglect of capitalization. This 56,000-word corpus had over 1,500 uses of indefinite determiners. The standard *a–an* pattern was followed in 99.5% of these cases (six errors). By contrast, spelling errors on the 1,500 words following each occurrence of *a–an* were five times more frequent than anomalies in *a–an*. There was no evidence in this corpus that the *a–an* distinction is unstable or thinly represented in the speech community.

6. See McDaniel and Cowart (2002) for a more detailed discussion of the *a–an* distinction and of the study we describe here.

Table 1. Mean percentage of correct responses on the consonant- and vowel-initial words for each age group. Standard deviations are given in parentheses

Age Group	Consonant-initial (*a*)		Vowel-initial (*an*)
Group 1, N=26 3- and 4-year-olds	100	(0)	12.8 (.33)
Group 2, N=42 5- and 6-year-olds	100	(0)	50.8 (.46)
Group 3, N=16 7- and 8-year-olds	97.9	(.08)	79.2 (.38)

schools, which charge relatively high tuitions, were from middle- or upper-class families where the adults speak Standard American English. For this analysis, the children were divided into three age groups. Group 1 had 26 3- to 4-year-olds (range 3;3–4;11; mean 4;2); Group 2 had 42 5- to 6-year-olds (range 5;0–6;8; mean 5;11); and Group 3 had 16 7- to 8-year-olds (range 7;3–8;4; mean 7;7).

A production task was used to elicit the indefinite article. Children were shown six pictures of objects. Three of the objects corresponded to words beginning with consonants: a cow, a pumpkin, and a bicycle; and three corresponded to words beginning with vowels: an owl, an apple, and an umbrella. The children were asked to respond in a full sentence to the question "What's this?" in reference to each picture.

With one exception, the responses to the consonant-initial items were correct, with *a* preceding the noun. The exception was from a child aged 8;1, who used *an* instead of *a* in "an bicycle". Children did not perform nearly as well on the vowel-initial items. Table 1 shows the mean percentage of correct responses on the vowel- and consonant-initial items for each age group.

The results were analyzed by way of the difference between each participant's mean success rate on *a* and *an* (i.e., the difference between the second and third columns in Table 1). There was a reliable increase in the success rate on *an* across the age groups.[7]

The data can also be analyzed by categorizing children according to response patterns. With respect to the three vowel-initial items, children manifested three response patterns. The 32 children who correctly used *an* on all three items (mean age, 6;6) will be referred to as '*an* children.' The 41 children who *incorrectly* used *a* on all three *an* items (mean age, 5;0) will be referred to as '*a* children.' Finally, the 11 children who used *an* for some, but not all, of the *an* items (mean age, 6;2) will be referred to as 'mixed children.' Figure 2 shows the breakdown of *an* children, *a* children, and mixed children by the three age groups.

There was a reliable shift in the number of *an* and mixed children as age increased.[8] Only two of the youngest children used *an* consistently. Most, but not all,

---

7. $F(2,81) = 14.9, p < .001$

8. $\chi^2 = 22.95$, df = 2, $p < .001$. The *an* children and the mixed children were combined for this

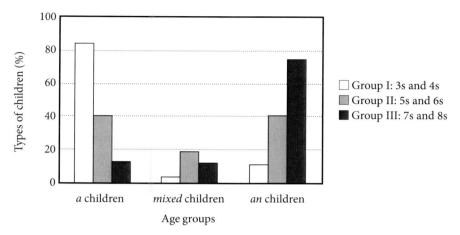

Figure 2. Breakdown of response categories by age

of the oldest children correctly made the *a–an* distinction. The middle age group, Group 2, is split between children who made the distinction and children who did not. Group 2 also contains the highest percentage of mixed children.

Children also completed a sentence with the nonsense word *ogal*. Children's performance on this word paralleled their responses on the real words. The *an* children said "an ogal", whereas the *a* children said "a ogal". Seven of eight mixed children said "an ogal"; the other mixed child said "a ogal". Children's parallel performance on the real and nonsense words suggests that they are not storing phrases like *an apple* individually at a point when they are in the process of acquiring the *a–an* distinction. This would lead to better performance on real words than on nonsense words (as in the case of the plural allomorphs in Berko (1958). In particular, some of the *an* children would have responded incorrectly to the nonsense item.

At the end of the experiment, an item was modeled. The experimenter used the phrase "an eagle" in asking the child the question, "Does this look to you more like an ostrich or an eagle?" in reference to a picture of an eagle. Even in this context, only three of the 41 *a* children said "an eagle". In contrast, only one of 30 *an* children said "a eagle". Six of 10 mixed children said "an eagle"; the other four 'mixed' children said "a eagle". The *a* children's responses to this modeled item suggest that they 'ignore' or 'resist' *an* when they hear it in running speech. Otherwise, they would have been more successful on this item, where their answer consisted of a partial repetition of what they had just heard.

---

analysis to prevent some of the expected frequencies from going too low; the result is the same with the *a* children and the mixed children combined, $\chi^2 = 17.1$, df = 2, $p < .001$.

The 32 *an* children and five of the mixed children (those who correctly produced *an* on two of the three vowel-initial words) were asked at the end of the experiment whether they knew about the *a–an* distinction and whether they had learned about it in school. None of them indicated any awareness of the distinction. The children's responses suggest that the *a–an* rule is acquired naturally. There was no evidence for any kind of explicit instruction.

This study confirms the informal observation that the *a–an* distinction is difficult for children. Its mastery seems to occur relatively late, between ages 5 and 9. Until then, children avoid *an* in their speech. Despite the high frequency of the indefinite article, one might still attempt to explain children's difficulty with *a–an* in terms of frequency. One possibility is that the greater frequency of *a* relative to *an* causes children to overuse *a*. Note, however, that *an* is not an exception to a pattern in the way that an irregular past tense form is exceptional. Instead, *an* is one of two completely regular forms. The overuse of *a* is therefore not comparable to overregularization. Further, our data reflect the avoidance of *an* rather than the overuse of *a* in children's production. Even though *a* is used more than *an* in adult speech, *an* is still one of the most frequent words in the language. The higher relative frequency of *a* should not cause children to omit *an* in their speech.[9]

3. Conclusions

To summarize, our study of relative clauses examined the role of frequency in children's syntax, while our *a–an* study examined the same in children's morpho-phonology. The findings from both studies are puzzling for an account of language acquisition that relies exclusively on probablistic learning mechanisms. Generally, claims are not this extreme. But accounts of this type should predict that high frequency elements are easy to learn and low frequency elements are hard to learn. This seems too simple for the aspects of linguistic competence that are abstract and combinatorial. Even children's morpho-phonology seems to require a more complex account. Crucially though, we are not anti-learning, and we do not dismiss frequency as an essential signal to the language learner. Our findings on relative

---

9. A reviewer suggests that *a* and *an* may be difficult to distinguish in running speech because they are unstressed function words. This is unlikely, in our view, to account for the late acquisition of *an*, however. If children were unable to perceive this distinction, they would also miss quite a few other aspects of language. Further, the presence of the nasal consonant is relatively salient, since it affects nasality on surrounding vowels and optionally results in the following word being pronounced with the nasal as an onset, as suggested by examples like *a whole nother N* (instead of just the word's initial vowel or a glottal stop onset). Finally, in slower speech, *an* is pronounced [aen], and *a* is sometimes pronounced [e], which are quite distinct.

clauses suggest that frequency does play a role in the real-time process of language production. It would also make sense for frequency to play a similar role in comprehension. One of the most interesting challenges ahead of us then will be to better understand the role that frequency plays in language development. What is its role in children's mastery of grammatical competence? And, what factors interact with frequency in the development of the processing systems that support production and comprehension?

We end, as we started, with Langendoen's (1970) observations about the independence of acceptability and grammaticality. Regardless of the theories relating to language acquisition, it will be useful to distinguish grammaticality from acceptability. If Langendoen is right, grammatical competence contributes to grammaticality while processing factors contribute to acceptability. Factors like the frequency of a form might affect acceptability more than grammaticality.

References

Berko, J. 1958. The child's learning of English morphology. *Word 14*: 150–77.
Ellis, N. 2002. Frequency effects in language processing: A review of implications for theories of implicit and explicit language acquisition. *Studies in Second Language Acquisition 24*: 143–88.
Francis, N. and H. Kucera (1982). *Frequency Analysis of English Usage: Lexicon and Grammar*. Boston: Houghton Mifflin.
Fromkin, V. 1971. The non-anomalous nature of anomalous utterances. *Language 47*: 27–52.
Jackendoff, R. 2006. Commentary on linguistic structure and connectionist models. Linguistic Society of America Annual Meeting, 6 January 2006, Albuquerque NM.
Langendoen, D. T. 1970. The accessibility of deep structures. In *Readings in English Transformational Grammar*, R. Jacobs & P. Rosenbaum, 99–104. Waltham MA: Ginn and Company.
Maye, J., Werker, J. & Gerken, L. A. 2002. Infant sensitivity to distributional information can affect phonetic discrimination. *Cognition 82*: B101–B111.
McDaniel, D. & Cowart, W. 2002. Late acquisition of the *a–an* distinction: A problem for frequency-based accounts. Ms, University of Southern Maine.
McDaniel, D., McKee, C. & Bernstein, J. 1998. How children's relatives solve a problem for Minimalism. *Language 74*: 308–34.
McDaniel, D., McKee, C. & H. S. Cairns (eds). 1996. *Methods for Assessing Children's Syntax*. Cambridge MA: The MIT Press.
McDaniel, D., Stickney, H., Fowler, S. & McKee, C. 2002. What's thats? *English Studies 83*: 53–69.
McKee, C., McDaniel, D. & Snedeker, J. 1998. Relatives children say. *Journal of Psycholinguistic Research 27*: 573–96.
Yamashita, J. 1994. An analysis of relative clauses in the Lancaster/IBM Spoken English Corpus. *English Studies 1*: 73–84.

CHAPTER 9

Abstract linguistic representations and innateness

The development of determiners*

Virginia Valian
Hunter College and CUNY Graduate Center

This paper uses the syntactic category of determiner to address the issue of innateness in language acquisition. Reviewing data from infants and toddlers, I propose that categories are innate and that children show continuity in category acquisition. As development proceeds, children learn the individual words in each category in the target language and the specific syntactic properties of those words, but they do not construct the categories themselves.

1. Nativism and syntactic categories

This paper addresses the issue of innateness in language acquisition, using the syntactic category of determiner as the example. The nature-nurture controversy is alive and well, despite attempts to recast it or eliminate it (Elman, Bates, Johnson, Karmiloff-Smith, Parisi, & Plunkett 1996; Thelen & Smith 1994). It deserves to be alive and well because of the importance of the central question — whether and in what way the child's mind has content independent of experience (Spelke & Newport 1998). Since the focus of this paper is on syntax, when I speak of nativism and empiricism, I will be doing so with respect to syntax only. It is possible to be an empiricist in one domain, like syntax, but a nativist in another domain, such as semantics or cognition. Braine (1992), for example, proposed the absence of any specifically syntactic innate ideas but at the same time proposed the existence of innate ideas concerning the structure of logic, such as the notion of an argument.

---

* This work was supported in part by an award from the National Science Foundation to Hunter College (SBE-0123609). An early version of this paper was presented in 2006 at the Symposium on The role of function words in early language development at the International Conference on Infant Studies, Kyoto, Japan. I thank the contributors to that symposium for their papers and I thank the following contributors for their comments and suggestions about this manuscript: R. Shi, E. Johnson, P. Hallé, and A. Christophe. I also thank Sandeep Prasada and two anonymous readers for their comments.

The distinction between process or mechanism nativism and content nativism will help focus the discussion (Braine 1992). Process nativism claims that there are innate mechanisms for absorbing, learning, and remembering information. Humans are more sophisticated learners and users of information than any other species and may well use special processes unavailable to other species. Process nativism is not a locus of controversy and is not discussed here. Related to process nativism, and here subsumed underneath it, is what might be called architecture nativism (Braine 1992; Elman et al. 1996). By architecture I am not referring to how the brain is wired, but to how the mechanisms for learning and remembering are structured. Is the learning system, for example, an algorithm or is it connectionist? Architecture nativism is also not discussed here.

Both mechanisms and architecture require content. That is, the mechanisms for learning and remembering operate over content. The issue I address is whether any of that content is syntactic from the start. The controversy over nativism in syntax acquisition is thus not whether children innately have semantic or cognitive concepts, nor whether they have dispositions, nor whether they have one or another learning mechanism, nor whether language is used primarily for communicative purposes. The controversy is whether humans have innate ideas with specific syntactic content.

The nativist position with respect to syntax is that there are innate syntactic concepts; the empiricist position is that there are not. Thus, modern models that go by the names constructivism, interactionism, and emergentism are empiricist with respect to syntax. Claims to the contrary notwithstanding, such models do not stake out some neutral ground between nativism and empiricism (Elman et al, 1996; Thelen & Smith, 1994).

Categories are a good place to start in trying to choose between empiricism and nativism. That is because, on both positions, the final state includes syntactic categories and features, such as noun, verb, adjective/adverb, preposition (the lexical categories), and tense, person, determiner, and complementizer (among the functional categories and features). (Not all languages use articles like *the*, but all seem to use quantifiers, possessive pronouns, and demonstratives; they are functional categories that I am treating here as in the same class as articles.) For some areas of syntax, nativists and empiricists disagree about the nature of the final state; if there is disagreement about the final state, there is no point in comparing the theories with respect to the initial state. But, at least for English, there is agreement that the final state includes basic syntactic features and categories. Both positions also largely agree about the learning process: it is a form of pattern learning. The agreement about the endpoint and learning mechanism helps localize the areas of disagreement.

The argument concerns whether pattern learning operates over uncategorized words and yields categories as an outcome or whether pattern learning operates to match uncategorized words to categories. Empiricism takes the first position: categories are constructed. Nativism takes the second: words are mapped onto categories.

On syntactic empiricism, children create syntactic categories with no syntactic foundation: they use whatever non-syntactic concepts they possess plus the input they hear to create syntactic categories. *Lexical learning* — the term I will use for proposals that children have lexically-specific formulae (e.g., Pine & Lieven, 1997; Pine & Martindale, 1996), pivot-open grammars (Braine, 1963), or verb islands (Tomasello, 1992) — is an empiricist proposal that abjures an innate syntactic basis. According to *lexical learning*, the child has particular knowledge about particular words but each piece of knowledge is isolated from other similar pieces of knowledge and is tied to a particular lexical item. The child begins at the bottom with particulars and works her way up — at some point and in some manner — first to lexical categories, such as nouns, and after that to functional categories such as determiners. On this proposal, children around 24 months do not have any syntax. Their representations are category-free and consist of frames, such as *that's a*, into which words are slotted. The problem children face is not a mapping problem but a creation problem: creating categories from words.

On syntactic nativism, the child begins with an abstract representation of syntactic categories and has the task of mapping the input to those categories (Grimshaw 1981; Pinker 1984). Syntactic nativism is abetted by *semantic bootstrapping*. Semantic bootstrapping gives the child an entry point into the syntactic system which is already innately specified but is present at too abstract a level to allow direct mapping. The semantic correlates of words help the child map a word to an innate abstract syntactic characterization of a category. Children's first categorized words are likely to be those with clear external referents or semantic/cognitive correlates — such as nouns (Pinker 1984). Once the system has been cracked open, the child can use distributional regularities to map new words to categories and include functional categories like determiners, the category I will focus on in this chapter.

Nativism does not specify any particular set of syntactic features, though linguists in the generative tradition often assume that whatever features are part of universal grammar are innate. The nativism that I will propose here has two main claims: 1) syntactic categories are innate; 2) the general form of the grammar is innate. Although I am presupposing, for the sake of convenience, a generative type of grammar, what I am saying could be reformulated for any syntactic theory. With respect to determiners, the claims imply that the child innately knows that a Determiner Phrase (DP) has a determiner as its head and takes a noun as its complement. Once the child has identified a noun — perhaps via semantic boot-strapping — she then has to identify items that can serve as the head of a DP. She knows that there will be heads, but not what they are.

Prosodic phrase boundaries and edges, which provide data about the beginnings and ends of phrases (Christophe, Guasti, Nespor, & van Ooyen 2003; Christophe, Millotte, Bernal, & Lidz 2008; Morgan 1996; Seidl & Johnson 2006), can help the child establish whether determiners precede or follow nouns. Not all important syntactic boundaries correspond to prosodic boundaries (Selkirk 1984), but prosodic boundaries do correspond to major syntactic boundaries and even newborns are sensitive to them (Christophe, Dupoux, Bertoncini, & Mehler 1994). Prosodic boundaries can help limit the processing of distributional regularities to clause-internal boundaries (Morgan 1996) and can help the child work out directionality patterns in her language (Christophe et al. 2003).

A lot is at stake in the controversy over whether children's early categories are syntactic. First, if categories are abstract from the earliest point at which we can measure, they are either innate (as I will argue) or acquired before child is stringing words together. Second, if categories are abstract, there is continuity in language acquisition, i.e., use of the same theoretical vocabulary in children's and adults' grammars. I will argue that there is no suggestion at any point in a child's development that there is a qualitative shift in her syntactic representations. Third, if categories are syntactic, evidence that has been claimed to show item-specific learning in early combinatorial speech is deceptive and does not really reveal lexical formulae. What counts as evidence for or against item-specific learning will have to be rethought.

How can we decide whether nativism or empiricism is a better account of category acquisition? The argument will take the form of an inference to the best explanation because there is no knock-down proof available for either position. To choose between the two positions we also need to agree on the domain of the theories, what they explain. Otherwise, we cannot compare them. I will assume that we want to explain how the child achieves the final state of category acquisition, and that that involves specifying the initial state, the role of input, and the mechanism. I will be taking a piece of that domain here: what can we infer about the initial state and the mechanism from the data available?

2. Determiners

I focus on determiners because they are less likely to benefit from semantic correlates or acoustic salience than lexical categories. Lexical categories — especially

Chapter 9. Innateness and determiners **193**

nouns, verbs, and prepositions — contribute to the determination of semantic roles. Semantic roles are related to the cognitive structure of events and might thus be more accessible to children at an early age. Of the four lexical categories, two of them — nouns and adjectives — often have referential correlates: you can point to a ball or to something that is red (though not, of course, to virtue or to something that is ineffable). Of the four lexical categories, three of them — nouns, verbs, and adjectives/adverbs — are acoustically salient thanks to a combination of stress, duration, vowel character, syllable structure, and position in the sentence (see, e.g., Monaghan, Chater, & Christensen 2005; Shi, Morgan, & Allopenna 1998). Even prepositions, the fourth lexical category, receive stress in some contexts, such as when used as a final particle: "pick this up". There is thus a weak correlation between referentiality and stress: many words with a referential correlate receive high stress, especially nouns. That cluster of properties should make lexical categories salient. For infants to both perceive and mentally represent determiners would, in contrast, be surprising: unlike lexical categories but like most functional categories, determiners have little meaning, seldom have clear referential correlates, do not participate directly in assigning thematic roles, and are "hard to hear". Compared to nouns, verbs, and adjectives, determiners have little acoustic substance (though they contribute to rhythm and coarticulation). Thus, if any categories should show late development, it is functional categories like determiners.

A key property of spoken English is the extremely high frequency of some determiners. For example, *the* and *a* account for almost 10 % of all word tokens in a sample of English texts (Kucera & Francis 1967) and in the British National Corpus, *the* is the most frequent word and *a* is the fifth most frequent word (forms of *be* are second, *of* and *and* are third and fourth). A frequency analysis of mothers' speech to 21 children from the Valian corpus (e.g., Valian 1991) shows that *you* is the most frequent morpheme, followed by *'s*, *what*, *the*, *that*, *it*, and *a* (together accounting for more than 20 % of all tokens).

Frequency matters: children attend more to high-frequency items than low-frequency items (see, e.g., the review by Werker & Yeung 2005). Adults in language experiments are notoriously sensitive to frequency (making psycholinguists' lives a nightmare). A beginning learner could, then, use determiners to establish word boundaries, to make predictions about the next word, identify new nouns, and distinguish nouns from verbs.

In an artificial language learning experiment with adults, Valian and Coulson (1988) proposed that high-frequency markers, akin to functional categories like determiners, serve as anchor points for distributional analysis. They help the learner tabulate co-occurrences (what occurs immediately after or before a marker), substitutions (what a given marker is in complementary distribution with), and other distributional phenomena. In two versions of an identically-structured language, which differed only in how frequent a marker was relative to a content word, learners acquired the fine-grained dependency linking a marker type with a content word type *only* in the version with highly frequent markers. High frequency alone helps learners with structure. High frequency also helps whether a reference field is present or not: reference helps distinguish phrase types, but high frequency is independently helpful (Valian & Coulson). High frequency markers also help learners when they hear sentences rather than read them, and help whether intonation is list-like or phrasal (Valian & Levitt 1996).

When phonologically coherent cues for content words are combined with high- or low-frequency for content words, the two have separate but interdependent effects. Monaghan et al. (2005) adapted Valian and Coulson's (1988) language, manipulating phonological coherence of the two noun-like classes and manipulating lexical frequency within each class. In one version, each of the two classes of content words had a distinct group of phonological properties; in the other version, each class had mixed properties. In each version, each class of content words had some frequent tokens and some infrequent tokens. High frequency — now of content words rather than markers — aided learners, as did a phonologically coherent demarcation of content words, especially for low-frequency tokens. Adult learners can make use of multiple sources of information simultaneously, especially if they are in different domains (frequency, phonology, reference).

Word or frame frequency has also been manipulated in computer simulations of category acquisition (e.g., Mintz 2003; Monaghan et al 2005). Frequency has been moderately to very successful in accurately isolating at least some categories. Thus, frequency provides benefits to adults learning an artificial language and to computer simulations of category learning. This notion of frequency differs from transitional probability (though is often co-extensional with it), which infants are also responsive to (Saffran, Aslin, & Newport 1996). Frequency is not the be-all and end-all of processing, even in infancy: when speech cues to grouping conflict with transitional probability grouping cues, for example, 8-month-olds follow the speech cues, such as stress and co-articulation (Johnson & Jusczyk 2001). But highly frequent words — like determiners — can serve as anchor points around which structural analyses can take place.

3. Two-year-olds' knowledge of determiners

Some of the most skeptical claims about children's categories concern children between the ages of 2–4: they don't represent determiners, they don't represent verbs, they don't represent abstract syntactic structures like the passive. One reason for skepticism is that children frequently leave out functional categories like determiners and tense, at least in English. Even though young children's understanding of syntactic categories has been studied for decades, there is no agreement about when children have genuine categories rather than lexically-based formulae or local information about what precedes and follows individual words. The timing of the first evidence of genuine categories is an important aspect of the debate. The earlier in time that children provide evidence of categories, the better the evidence for nativism. The later, the better the evidence for empiricism.

But in neither case — early or late learning — is the evidence definitive. With respect to early learning, say age 2, there is the possibility that in an earlier period the child may have learned about categories, leaving nativism under-determined. With respect to later learning, say age 3, there is the possibility that the mapping problem for some categories is difficult and thus more extended in time, leaving empiricism under-determined. The overall pattern of the data will help make the inference to the best explanation.

On the basis of *distributional tests* of spontaneous speech from six 2-year-olds, whose Mean Length of Utterance (MLU) measured in morphemes ranged between 3–4, I have argued that 2-year-olds' grammars contain the categories determiner, adjective, noun, noun phrase, preposition, and prepositional phrase (Valian 1986). The evidence for determiners was of several sorts. One was that the children distinguished between determiners and adjectives. If children thought that determiners and adjectives were a single category — a modifier of some sort — they should use them in either order if they were both included in a phrase: "the red truck" and "red the truck" should be equally likely. But children always sequenced them correctly.

Similarly, adjectives can be repeated but (most) determiners cannot: "the green green green truck" (an actual child production) is permissible but "the the the truck" is not; "the tiny little truck" is permissible but "the my truck" is not (in English). Adjectives were infrequent, and sequenced adjectives were rarer still, but they occurred. In contrast, despite the high frequency of determiners, combinations of determiners never occurred. There was a possible exception, phrases like "this the truck". Such phrases were analyzed as missing a copula rather than as an illicit noun phrase with two determiners. The basis for the analysis was that such phrases never acted like phrases: they never occurred as either the subject of a sentence, the object of a verb, or the object of a preposition. Legitimate sequences, on the other hand, like "this truck" or "the truck" did occur in all possible positions. Although such reasoning is unexceptional linguistic reasoning, it is likely to strike the skeptic as excusing away errors. (My word-processing software puts a wavy green line under phrases like "this the truck"; it can only perform very superficial linguistic analyses.)

The children frequently failed to include a determiner when one was required. If one used a criterion like Brown's 90 % appearance in obligatory contexts as a necessary and sufficient condition for demonstrating mental representation of a category, two-year-olds would appear not to show evidence of determiners (Brown, 1973). I have argued that inconsistent use of a category or relation does not by itself argue for absence of a category (Valian 1991; Valian & Aubry 2005; Valian, Hoeffner, & Aubry 1996; Valian, Prasada, & Scarpa 2006). Instead, inconsistent use can be attributed to limitations in the child's planning and sequencing abilities, cognitive limitations, the information value of different constituents, and prosodic templates (Demuth 2001, Gerken 1996).

The child's utterances are the result of several different forces acting simultaneously (Valian & Eisenberg 1996). The child, like the adult, has a message to convey, a grammar she can use to give syntactic form to the message, and a limited set of resources. Resource allocation operates at the joint behest of message characteristics, grammar characteristics, and task characteristics. Children are, as Brown implicitly suggested, cognitive misers (Brown & Bellugi 1964; Brown & Fraser 1963). Depending on the message, the child's current grammar, and the discourse context, different parts of the message will be privileged.

The skeptic's view of the appeal to performance limitations is that they have not been demonstrated (Tomasello 2000). But the evidence does support the idea of performance limitations. For example, in an elicited imitation task, two-year-olds with low MLUs include subjects more often from short than long sentences, whereas two-year-olds with higher MLUs include subjects equally from short and long sentences (Valian et al. 1996). Longer sentences tax the child's sentence-processing abilities, leading to omission. As another example, children include more pronominal subjects in their imitations when they have a second opportunity to imitate a sentence (Valian & Aubry 2005). Having performed a partial analysis on the first attempt, children have more resources available on the second attempt, resources which are now directed toward less informative elements like pronominal subjects. As another example, children include more constituents when imitating sentences that have a predictable compared to an unpredictable direct object (Valian et al 2006). A predictable direct object requires less processing than an unpredictable one.

Are adults any different? Studies of adult processing suggest continuity: the adult processor, like the child's, is incremental and sensitive to a variety of sources of information. Message characteristics, grammar characteristics, real world knowledge, and task characteristics all play a role (e.g. MacDonald, Pearlmutter, & Seidenberg 1994; Trueswell & Tanenhaus 1994; Tanenhaus, Spivey-Knowlton, Eberhard, & Sedivy 1995; Kamide, Altmann, & Haywood 2003). The limitations of the adult processor are less obvious during spontaneous speech than those of the child's because there are few "super"-adults (such as Henry James) whose extended resources would make the average adult look limited.

Another objection on the skeptic's part is that claims about categories are interlocked: claims for determiners, say, involve claims about adjectives and nouns. The skeptic wants evidence for each category that is independent of the evidence used for any other category. From a linguistic perspective, this is impossible. The category system *is* an interlocking system and it *is* impossible to talk about one of its components in complete isolation from its other components. Similarly, knowledge of one element in the system cannot be independent of knowledge of every other element in the system. Part of understanding any individual element is understanding how that element fits into the system as a whole.

Subsequent observations have replicated Valian's (1986) category results. A longitudinal investigation of a child aged 27 months at the beginning of observations corroborated Valian's analysis, finding that early determiners were distributed across a variety of nouns and showed no semantic localization (Ihns & Leonard 1988). A second longitudinal study of the spontaneous speech of 17 children, beginning at 18 months, similarly found that children used determiners from the onset of combinatorial speech and made very few errors other than omissions (Abu-Akel, Bailey, & Thum 2004).

Elicited imitation data likewise suggest that very young children both attend to and understand determiners. Two-year-olds are more likely to repeat an English noun if it is preceded by an English determiner than if it is preceded by a short nonsense word (Gerken, Landau & Remez 1990: high MLU children, Experiment 1; low MLU children, Experiment 2). A child who hears "Pete push-o na car", for example, is less likely to repeat *car* than a child who hears "Pete pushes the car". Genuine determiners help in parsing unknown lexical categories. Children are also more likely to repeat nonsense words that occupy the determiner slot than to repeat English determiners, indicating that even very young children distinguish between English and nonsense determiners that have the same prosodic and segmental characteristics (Gerken et al. 1990). The fact that children preferentially omit genuine determiners demonstrates that they know what such words are and know that they are less important than other parts of the sentence.

Comprehension data similarly demonstrate an early sensitivity to determiners. Seventeen-month-old girls are able to choose one or another animal or doll depending on whether a determiner is used before a nonsense word to guide the child's choice (Katz, Baker & MacNamara 1974). In a later, better-controlled, experiment, children aged 31 months used the presence or absence of a determiner to guide their choice of a stuffed animal or block (Gelman & Taylor, 1984).

In sum, children who are just beginning to string words together seem to have grammars that include the abstract category determiner. But a skeptical rejoinder is that children's achievements are more apparent than real and are due to lax criteria (Pine & Lieven, 1997; Pine & Martindale, 1996). If a child had lexically specific formulae, for example, she might appear to meet the distributional tests, but only because her repertoire consisted of stored frames extracted from the input, such as *the ball* and *a horse*. Pine and colleagues instead propose an overlap test for determiners. If the child is using frames, then *ball* will occur only with *the* and *horse* will occur only with *a*. If the child has the category determiner, *ball* should occur with both *the* and *a*, as should *horse*. The overlap test requires children to use more than one determiner (in their analyses, *the* and *a*) with the same noun. Without such overlap, they argue, the child is not operating with a category but only with lexically-specific formulae. In their analyses of children's speech, the children showed little or no overlap, in contrast to their mothers.

Valian, Solt, and Stewart (in press) agree with the overall reasoning. A child who knows that *a* and *the* are determiners should, *ceteris paribus*, use both of them before singular count nouns. But we think that Pine and colleagues' implementation of the test was faulty. Most importantly, the implementation did not take into account how often a child used a given noun with a determiner. Consider the limiting case, where a child uses a noun only once with a determiner: overlap is impossible by definition. With a small sample per child, or with children who produce many nouns only once or twice, overlap will be difficult for the observer to detect, purely on statistical grounds. We stratify the child's and parent's nouns according to how often each occurs with a determiner (and run additional tests as well). Across 21 children aged 22–32 months, and ranging in MLU from 1.53 to 4.38, there is no difference between the children and their mothers: both show overlap to the same degree.

Thus, two-year-olds, even those who are producing utterances that average less than two morphemes in length, have the determiner category. That finding undermines lexical learning — at least if the theory is offered, as it has been, as a theory for children up to the age of three. So far, nativism has the edge. In addition, the finding raises the possibility that other evidence thought to support lexical learning is also flawed, and that properly-implemented tests will reveal abstract categories across the board.

4. Infants' perception of determiners

If we accept the claim that 2-year-olds have the determiner category, we can use continuity — not simply as an argument in the abstract but empirically by demonstration. Continuity has always been a strong argument in principle. Continuity is the thesis that the child's grammar is commensurate with the adult's. As I am using the term, it means that the child's set of theoretical categories does not differ from the adult's in kind, only in degree: infants' categories are underspecified phonetically, morphologically, and syntactically. The infant begins knowing no language-specific facts about her language (other than those she acquired in utero). She has only abstract characterizations of categories and knowledge of what features they could include. She acquires language-specific information, such as which features actually are included in the language she is acquiring and what words are members of the category, after she is exposed to it. The category becomes fleshed out and mapped to lexical items but does not change its fundamental character. If the category is innate, continuity, rather than discontinuity, should be evident.

Discontinuities are costly in terms of extra theoretical apparatus: they require the introduction of different concepts and different mechanisms. If there is no good theory to account for the discontinuities, continuity is the best working assumption. To reiterate an earlier point, categories are a good domain in which to have an argument about the abstractness of children's representation because everyone agrees that children eventually do acquire categories. Eventually, determiners are part of an English speaker's grammar. In a discontinuous theory, you have to explain how they arise. Tomasello (2000) has suggested that lexically-specific learning evades the discontinuity problem, because the child goes not from one system to a different system but from no system to a system. Unfortunately, going from nothing to something is also a discontinuity. Without a mechanism in hand that succeeds in getting from one system to another, or from no system to a system, how to establish continuity remains an unsolved problem.

Although it is hard to say exactly how infants should perform if the determiner category is innate rather than constructed, we can make some educated guesses. If the child has abstract, underspecified categories, as I propose here, her errors should look like underspecification errors. If the child has lexically-specific categories, she should not make errors of underspecification because, by definition, she has encoded a specific form. The infant data I review support underspecification more than lexical specificity. Although high frequency items like determiners are, by hypothesis, underspecified phonetically and morphosyntactically, that should not interfere with their ability to serve as anchor points, as Valian & Coulson (1986) proposed. As long as they have few sound-alike competitors and are very frequent, determiners should help infants process speech, and that is what happens.

That any high-frequency item can help segment words is suggested by data on six-month-olds. They can use their own name or their mother's in possessive form to isolate nouns (Bortfeld, Morgan, Golinkoff, & Rathbun 2005). A child named Maggie who hears *Maggie's cup* is later more likely to recognize *cup* in isolation than if she had earlier heard *Hannah's cup*. Hearing *Mommy's cup* provides a similar benefit. But whether the high-frequency items directly help parse the following word or whether the motivational importance of the child's and mother's names recruits more attention to the sentence, indirectly benefiting parsing, is not clear. Real determiners and similar sounding nonsense words provide more information.

For infants at 8 months, determiners are underspecified with respect to phonetic content. A detailed study compared 8- and 11-month-olds' ability to use real vs nonsense determiners to segment a nonsense noun from its preceding determiner, manipulating determiner frequency (Shi, Cutler, Werker, & Cruickshank 2006). Infants heard determiner-noun pairs half the time with a high-frequency real determiner (e.g., *the tink*) and half the time with a phonologically similar nonsense determiner (e.g., *kuh breek*). Other infants heard a low-frequency determiner, *her* vs *ler*.

If infants' first representations are tied to specific words, then they should be equally unable to segment words like *tink* and *breek* (i.e., equally unable to recognize them when they are presented in isolation), whether they are preceded by *the* or *kuh* during familiarization trials. Since they have never heard *tink* before, they have also never heard the sequence *the tink* before. Although the infants have heard *the* before, if *the* is tied in their representations only to nouns they have previously encountered, the sequence *the tink* should be perceived as a single two-syllable word. Since the children have never heard *kuh* before, they should similarly perceive *kuh tink* as a single two-syllable word.

Importantly, the 8-month-olds did not distinguish *the* and *kuh*, indicating that *the* is not fully specified phonetically. Eight-month olds *were* sensitive to frequency: infants who heard *the* or *kuh* were more likely to segment the accompanying nonsense noun (treating it as something they had heard before) than infants who heard *her* or *ler*. Thus, 8-month-olds can use the high-frequency determiner *the* to segment speech, but they represent it in an underspecified fashion that does not distinguish it from its phonologically similar mate *kuh*.

The 11-month-olds showed a different pattern. They distinguished between *the* and *kuh*, with the result that only *the* isolated the following nonsense noun. The other three items — *kuh*, *her*, and *ler* — did not help isolate the following noun. The step from 8 to 11 months was to develop a specific representation for the high-frequency determiner *the*, enough to distinguish it from *kuh*. The low-frequency determiner *her* was still undifferentiated from its phonologically similar nonsense mate.

Infants thus do not begin with a highly-specific representation. Instead, they have an underspecified representation of a very highly frequent form and can initially use that form to segment new words. By 11 months, the infant has phonetically specified *the* but not *her*. Infants appear to be working with the most highly frequent forms first. The 11-month-olds seem not to know just what items are included in the determiner category beyond its most frequently encountered member. They have yet to construct an equivalence class of elements that populate the determiner category. What they are missing, on this analysis, is not the category, but knowledge of all the specific elements that make up the category.

With a similar task but a different set of materials (Shi, Werker, & Cutler 2006), only 13-month-olds showed a reliable preference for a sequence of determiner-nonsense noun pairings that used real determiners (*the, his, her, their, its*) over nonsense determiners with similar sounds (*kuh, ris, ler, lier, ots*). Although it is possible that the 13-month-olds preferred the real determiners solely because they recognized *the*, that seems unlikely. Since 11-month-olds distinguish *the* and *kuh*, they would have shown the same performance as 13-month-olds if only recognition of *the* were driving the results. By 13 months, then, the infant has mapped out the phonetic form of more than one real determiner, but we do not know which ones. (English-speaking 11-month-olds demonstrate via brain responses that they distinguish a set of English words that play a functional role from phonologically similar nonsense words (Shafer, Shucard, Shucard, and Gerken 1998) but here it is possible that only *the* (out of a list consisting of *was, is, the, a, of, with,* or *that*) was responsible for the effect. The same caveat holds for preference data for 11-month-olds (Shady 1996).

Eleven-month-old French infants prefer real determiner-noun sequences over nonsense determiner-noun sequences when the noun is monosyllabic, whether the noun is familiar (*chat*) or unfamiliar (*dôme*) (Hallé, Durand, & de Boysson-Bardies 2008). When the noun is disyllabic, the infants prefer the sequence with real determiners for familiar (*canard*) but not unfamiliar (*soutard*) nouns. Since six different determiners were used, possible frequency differences among the determiners could not be determined. The overall pattern of data suggests that 11-month-olds recognize at least some familiar determiners and use them to segment monosyllabic nouns, data consistent with the reports for English that I reviewed earlier.

French 11-month-olds also prefer familiar nouns to unfamiliar nouns — but only if the noun is preceded by a real determiner, not if it is preceded by a nonsense determiner (Hallé et al. 2008). A preference for familiar nouns requires a mechanism to register frequency: a familiar noun cannot become familiar if each perception of it is erased. Infants are thus tabulating noun frequencies as well as determiner frequencies.

The acquisition sequence for specifying determiners phonologically seems, then, to have three steps: step 1) make use of very high frequency markers like determiners to segment them from content words, but (probably) use only the vowel to specify the marker; step 2) refine the representation of the marker to specify it in more phonetic detail; step 3) proceed similarly with other markers that are still highly frequent relative to content words but less frequent than *the*.

That infants 14–16 months of age have some idea of what items constitute the class of determiners comes from a head-turning experiment with German-speaking infants. When children had familiarization trials with the indefinite article *ein* followed by a nonsense word (*glamm* or *pronk*), they subsequently showed a novelty effect, listening more to passages where the nonsense word was in a verb context rather than a noun context featuring a different determiner, such as the definite article *das* or the demonstrative *dieses* (Höhle, Weissenborn, Kiefer, Schulz & Schmitz 2004). Although several interpretations of this experiment are possible, it suggests that children recognize that *ein glamm* implies that *glamm* is a noun and accept other determiners, but not personal pronouns, as syntactically legitimate contexts.

Determiners receive a rich phonetic representation before they are fully specified morphosyntactically. Dutch-learning 24-month-olds, for example, cannot use the difference between *de* (common gender definite determiner) and *het* (neuter gender definite determiner) to guide eye gaze, indicating that gender is not well-specified (Johnson & Diks 2005). Fine-grained morphosyntactic detail concerning determiner features is thus a later occurrence than fine-grained phonetic detail. Again, the infant appears to be fleshing out a category rather than creating one *de novo*.

Dutch-learning infants at even 19 months, however, understand instructions better if they hear *de* or *het* rather than a nonsense determiner *se* (van Heugten 2006). Similar data exist for English (Gerken & McIntosh 1993; Kedar, Casasola, & Lust 2006; Zangl & Fernald 2007): 18-month-olds and older infants parse a speech stream better if they hear a genuine determiner than a nonsense form or function word from a different class (such as *and*), and, often, better than if they hear no determiner. Even though children at 18 months seldom produce determiners, their comprehension is improved when they hear real determiners, indicating that they have a determiner slot which they expect to be filled appropriately.

The final set of data suggesting underspecification comes from children who produce filler syllables, which are usually (though not always) syllables with reduced vowels (see, for example, Bottari, Cipriani, & Chilosi 1993/1994; Peters 2001; Tremblay 2005; Veneziano & Sinclair 2000). Not all children produce them, and not all children who produce them use them in exactly the same way, but there is a pattern. They appear to be positioned like syntactic markers, especially before nouns. The first function of these filler syllables may be completely prosodic — to make the child's output sound like the target language. But, later, around 19–22 months, the syllables before nouns appear to be serving a determiner-like syntactic function in European French (Veneziano & Sinclair 2000), Canadian

French (Tremblay 2005), and Italian (Bottari, Cipriani, & Chilosi 1993/1994). The existence of filler syllables is easy to explain on an underspecification model, because the child has not mastered the specific knowledge about just which determiner precedes just which noun. An underspecified form meets the syntactic requirement of supplying a determiner without indicating features like number or gender. The contrasting model of lexical-specificity cannot account for filler syllables. If the child is learning, item by item, what combinations are possible, she should only produce combinations she has heard before. Filler syllables should not exist.

5. Conclusion

By age 2, there is clear evidence that children's grammars include the syntactic category determiner. Between early infancy and age 2, children's perception and comprehension of determiners and their production of filler syllables suggest that the determiner category is part of the child's grammar, but in unspecified form. The data on determiners now extend from no later than 11 months to 36 months. Determiners and their role in parsing have been more fully documented than any other functional category and as much as nouns. The data suggest that continuity is empirically true. Children never look as if they are abandoning one system for another. They never look as if they only have knowledge about individual, specific words and construct a category. Instead, they look as though they are fleshing out a category more and more fully, acquiring more and more specific details, mapping more and more items.

Where do determiners and nouns come from? This is where we came in. The inference to the best explanation is that categories are there from the beginning. The child's job is to find out what the members of those categories are in the target language she will become a speaker of and what the language-particular characteristics of those categories are. She accomplishes those tasks by age 2 for determiners.

References

Abu–Akel, A. Bailey, A. & Thum, Y.–M. 2004. Describing the acquisition of determiners in English: A growth modeling approach. *Journal of Psycholinguistic Research* 33: 407–24.

Bortfeld, H. Morgan, J. Golinkoff, R. & Rathbun, K. 2005. Mommy and me: Familiar names help launch babies into speech-stream segmentation. *Psychological Science* 16: 298–304.

Bottari, P. Cipriani, P. & Chilosi, A. 1993/1994. Protosyntactic devices in the acquisition of Italian free morphology. *Language Acquisition* 3: 327–69.

Braine, M. D. S. 1963. The ontogeny of English phrase structure; the first phrase. *Language* 39: 1–13.

Braine, M. D. S. 1992. What sort of innate structure is needed to bootstrap into syntax? *Cognition* 45: 77–100.

Brown, R. 1973. *A First Language*. Cambridge MA: Harvard University Press.

Brown, R. & Bellugi, U. 1964. Three processes in the acquisition of syntax. *Harvard Educational Review* 34: 133–51.

Brown, R. & Fraser, C. 1963. The acquisition of syntax. In *Verbal Behavior and Learning: Problems and Processes*, C. Cofer & B. Musgrave (eds). New York NY: McGraw Hill.

Christophe, A. Dupoux, E. Bertoncini, J. & Mehler, J. 1994. Do infants perceive word boundaries? An empirical study of the bootstrapping of lexical acquisition. *Journal of the Acoustical Society of America* 95: 1570–1580.

Christophe, A. Guasti, M. T Nespor, M. & van Ooyen, B. 2003. Prosodic structure and syntactic acquisition: The case of the head–complement parameter. *Developmental Science* 6: 213–22.

Christophe, A. Millotte, S. Bernal, S. & Lidz, J. 2008. Bootstrapping lexical and syntactic acquisition. *Language and Speech* 51: 61–75.

Demuth, K. 2001. Prosodic constraints on morphological development. In *Approaches to Bootstrapping: Phonological, Syntactic and Neurophysiological Aspects of Early Language Acquisition* [Language Acquisition and Language Disorders 24]. 3–21, J. Weissenborn & B. Höhle (eds). Amsterdam: John Benjamins.

Elman, J. Bates, E. Johnson, M. Karmiloff–Smith, A. Parisi, D. & Plunkett, K. 1996. *Rethinking Innateness: A Connectionist Perspective on Development*. Cambridge MA: The MIT Press.

Gelman, S. & Taylor, J. 1984. How two–year–old children interpret proper and common names for unfamiliar objects. *Child Development* 55: 153 –1540.

Gerken, L. A. 1996. Prosodic structure in young children's language production. *Language* 72: 683–712.

Gerken, L. Landau, B. & Remez, R. 1990. Function morphemes in young children's speech perception and production. *Developmental Psychology* 26: 204–16.

Gerken, L. & McIntosh, B. 1993. Interplay of function morphemes and prosody in early language. *Developmental Psychology* 29: 448–57.

Grimshaw, J. 1981. Form, function, and the language acquisition device. In *The Logical Problem of Language Acquisition*, C. Baker & J. J. McCarthy. Cambridge MA: The MIT Press.

Hallé, P. Durand, C. & de Boysson–Bardies, B. 2008. Do 11–month–old French infants process articles? *Language and Speech* 51: 23–44.

Höhle, B. Weissenborn, J. Kiefer, D. Schulz, A. & Schmitz, M. 2004. Functional elements in infants' speech processing: The role of determiners in the syntactic categorization of lexical elements. *Infancy* 5: 341–53.

Ihns, M. & Leonard, L. 1988. Syntactic categories in early child language: Some additional data. *Journal of Child Language* 15: 673–8.

Johnson, E. & Diks, M. 2005. On-line processing of grammatical gender in Dutch-learning toddlers. Paper presented at the Xth International Congress for the Study of Child Language, Berlin.

Johnson, E. & Jusczyk, P. 2001. Word segmentation by 8–month–olds: When speech cues count more than statistics. *Journal of Memory and Language* 44: 548–67.

Kamide, Y. Altmann, G. & Haywood, S. 2003. The time–course of prediction in incremental sentence processing: Evidence from anticipatory eye movements. *Journal of Memory and Language* 49:133–56.

Katz, N. Baker, E. & Macnamara, J. 1974. What's in a name? A study of how children learn common and proper names. *Child Development* 45:469–73.

Kedar, Y. Casasola, M. & Lust, B. 2006. Getting there faster: 18- and 24-month-old infants' use of function words to determine reference. *Child Development* 77:325–38.

Kucera, H. & Francis, W. 1967. *Computational Analysis of Present–Day American English*. Providence RI: Brown University Press.

MacDonald, M. Pearlmutter, N. & Seidenberg, M. 1994. The lexical nature of syntactic ambiguity resolution. *Psychological Review* 101:676–703.

Mintz, T. 2003. Frequent frames as a cue for grammatical categories in child directed speech. *Cognition* 90:91–117.

Monaghan, P. Chater, N. & Christiansen, M. 2005. The differential role of phonological and distributional cues in grammatical categorization. *Cognition* 96:143–82.

Morgan, J. 1996. Prosody and the roots of parsing. *Language and Cognitive Processes* 11: 69–106.

Peters, A. 2001. Filler syllables: What is their status in emerging grammar? *Journal of Child Language* 28:229–42.

Pine, J. & Lieven, E. 1997. Slot and frame patterns and the development of the determiner category. *Applied Psycholinguistics* 18:123–38.

Pine, J. & Martindale, H. 1996. Syntactic categories in the speech of young children: The case of the determiner. *Journal of Child Language* 23:369–95.

Pinker, S. 1984. *Language Learnability and Language Development*. Cambridge MA: Harvard University Press.

Saffran, J. Newport, E. & Aslin, R. 1996. Word segmentation: The role of distributional cues. *Journal of Memory and Language* 35:606–21.

Seidl, A. & Johnson, E. 2006. Infant word segmentation revisited: Edge alignment facilities target extraction. *Developmental Science* 9:565–73.

Selkirk, E. 1984. *Phonology and Syntax: The Relation between Sound and Structure*. Cambridge MA: The MIT Press.

Shady, M. 1996. Infants' Sensitivity to Function Morphemes. PhD Dissertation, SUNY-Buffalo.

Shafer, V. Shucard, D. Shucard, J. & Gerken, L. 1998. An electrophysiological study of infants' sensitivity to the sound patterns of English speech. *Journal of Speech, Language & Hearing Research* 41:874–86.

Shi, R. Cutler, A. Werker J. & Cruickshank, M. 2006. Frequency and form as determinants of functor sensitivity in English–acquiring infants. *Journal of the Acoustical Society of America* 119: EL61–EL67.

Shi, R. Morgan, J. & Allopenna, P. 1998. Phonological and acoustic bases for earliest grammatical category assignment: A cross-linguistic perspective. *Journal of Child Language* 25: 169–201.

Shi, R. Werker, J. & Cutler, A. 2006. Recognition and representation of function words in English–learning infants. *Infancy* 10:187–98.

Spelke, E. & Newport, E. 1998. Nativism, empiricism, and the development of knowledge. In *Handbook of Child Psychology*, 5th edn, Vol.1, *Theoretical Models of Human Development*, W. Damon & R. Lerner (eds), 275–340. New York NY: John Wiley.

Thelen, E. & Smith, L. 1994. *A Dynamic Systems Approach to the Development of Cognition and Action*. Cambridge MA: The MIT Press.

Tomasello, M. 1992. *First Verbs: A Case Study of Early Grammatical Development*. Cambridge MA: Cambridge University Press.

Tomasello, M. 2000. Do young children have adult syntactic competence? *Cognition* 74: 209–53.

Tanenhaus, M. Spivey-Knowlton, M. Eberhard, K. & Sedivy, J. 1995. Integration of visual and linguistic information in spoken language comprehension. *Science* 268: 1632–1634.

Tremblay, A. 2005. On the status of determiner fillers in early French: What the child knows. In *Proceedings of the 29th Annual Boston University Conference on Language Development*, A. Brugos, M. Clark-Cotton & S. Ha, 604–15. Somerville MA: Cascadilla.

Trueswell, J. & Tanenhaus, M. 1994. Toward a lexicalist framework of constraint –based syntactic ambiguity resolution. In *Perspectives on Sentence Processing*, C. Clifton, L. Frazier & K. Rayner. Hillsdale NJ: Lawrence Erlbaum Associates.

Valian, V. 1986. Syntactic categories in the speech of young children. *Developmental Psychology* 22: 562–79.

Valian, V. 1991. Syntactic subjects in the early speech of American and Italian children. *Cognition* 40: 21–81.

Valian, V. & Aubry, S. 2005. When opportunity knocks twice: two–year–olds' repetition of sentence subjects. *Journal of Child Language* 32: 617 –641.

Valian, V. & Coulson, S. 1988. Anchor points in language learning: The role of marker frequency. *Journal of Memory and Language* 27: 71–86.

Valian, V. & Eisenberg, Z. 1996. Syntactic subjects in the speech of Portuguese-speaking children. *Journal of Child Language* 23: 103–28.

Valian, V. Hoeffner, J. & Aubry, S. 1996. Young children's imitation of sentence subjects: Evidence of processing limitations. *Developmental Psychology* 32: 153–64.

Valian, V. & Levitt, A. 1996. Prosody and adults' learning of syntactic structure. *Journal of Memory and Language* 35: 497–516.

Valian, V. Prasada, S. & Scarpa, J. 2006. Direct object predictability: Effects on young children's imitation of sentences. Journal of Child Language 33: 247–69.

Valian, V. Solt, S. & Stewart, J. In press. Abstract categories or limited — scope formulae? The case of children's determiners. *Journal of Child Language*.

van Heugten, M. 2006. Dutch-learners' use of definite articles in speech processing. MA Thesis, Radboud Universiteit, Nijmegen, The Netherlands.

Veneziano, E. & Sinclair, H. 2000. The changing status of 'filler syllables' on the way to grammatical morphemes. *Journal of Child Language* 27: 1–40.

Werker, J. & Yeung, H. 2005. Infant speech perception bootstraps word learning. *TRENDS in Cognitive Science* 9: 519–27.

Zangl, R. & Fernald, A. 2007. Increasing flexibility in children's online processing of grammatical and nonce determiners in fluent speech. *Language Learning and Development* 3: 199–231.

PART 3

Language as a formal system

CHAPTER 10

One-level finite-state phonology*

Michael Hammond
University of Arizona

Finite state approaches to phonology usually make use of transducers to model the mapping of input to output forms. This applies to both rule-based approaches and more recent approaches inspired by Optimality Theory. Here, we develop an alternative approach based on automata where phonological generalizations and lexical regularities are encoded as regular expressions and these expressions are combined by intersection and concatenation. The system that results captures the full range of phonological systems, but does so with simpler automata, rather than transducers. In addition, the resulting system bears interesting similarities to Optimality Theory. We also compare the approach to other finite state approaches.

1. Introduction

Traditional phonological theory (Chomsky and Halle 1968) maintains that phonological generalizations should be described in terms of a mapping from lexical representations to phonetic representations, essentially pronounced forms. For example, the fact that word-initial voiceless obstruents are aspirated can be described in terms of a rule that maps input voiceless obstruents to output aspirated elements.

$$(1) \quad \begin{bmatrix} -\text{sonorant} \\ -\text{voiced} \end{bmatrix} \rightarrow [+\text{aspirated}]/_{\text{word}} [\underline{\hspace{1cm}}$$

The input representation encodes what is idiosyncratic about a lexical item, while the rule encodes what is regular across items. For example, in the case at hand, the rule says that *all* word-initial voiceless obstruents are aspirated, thus encoding both the context of the generalization and a configuration that must hold after the rule applies. Lexical entries would then include a specification for *whether* there is a word-initial voiceless obstruent, e.g. the difference between words like *toe* [tʰo] and *know* [no].

---

* Thanks to Adam Baker, Jordan Brewer, Lynnika Butler, Erin Good, Mans Hulden, Naomi Ogasa-wara, Diane Ohala, Dan Siddiqi, Ben Tucker, Yuko Watanabe, and Gwanhi Yun for much useful discussion. Thanks also to the reviewer and editors for useful feedback. All errors are my own.

Since a typical phonological system contains more than one rule, there is the possibility of rule interaction; the mapping produced by one rule can affect the mapping produced by another. For example, English can be described as having a rule nasalizing vowels before nasal consonants, e.g. in *ran*[ræn] or *banned* [bænd]. English also has a generalization whereby nasal consonants may be deleted before a voiceless stop, e.g. in a word like *rant* [ræt] or *bank* [bæk]. Notice that in words like *rant*, the vowel is nasalized even if the nasal consonant is deleted. We return to rule-ordering below.

There are several finite state implementations of rule-based phonology, e.g. Johnson (1972); Kaplan and Kay (1994); Karttunen (1983); Koskenniemi (1984). All of these approaches involve treating the mapping from input to output in terms of finite state transducers, cascaded, composed, or in parallel. The explicit claim of such formalizations is that phonological generalizations are instances of regular relations.

Optimality Theory (OT henceforth; Prince and Smolensky 1993) alters this picture somewhat. There is still an input-output mapping, but now that mapping is achieved by constraints. The basic idea is that an input form is paired with every possible output pronunciation. There is a finite set of universal constraints that are prioritized or "ranked" in a language-particular fashion: all languages then have the same constraints, but prioritize them in different ways. These constraints select the optimal output candidate. In the case at hand, there would be a markedness constraint penalizing word-initial voiceless unaspirated obstruents (ASPIRATION). There would also be a faithfulness constraint penalizing mismatches in aspiration between input and output (FAITHFULNESS). In English, where aspiration occurs in this environment, the markedness constraint outranks the faithfulness constraint (Table 1). This has the effect of allowing aspiration at the expense of a mismatch between the lexicon (/to/) and what is pronounced ([tʰo] *toe*).

In French, on the other hand, where aspiration does not occur, the same constraints occur, but the faithfulness constraint outranks the markedness constraint

Table 1. Aspiration in English

	/to/	ASPIRATION	FAITHFULNESS
☞	[tho]		*
	[to]	*!	

Table 2. No aspiration in French

	/to/	FAITHFULNESS	ASPIRATION
	[tho]	*!	
☞	[to]		*

(Table 2). This has the effect of insuring that the output ([to] *tôt* 'early') matches the input (/to/) at the expense of aspiration.

Thus OT has an input-output mapping, though it is mediated by universal constraints (ranked on a language-particular basis), rather than language-particular rules. There are finite state implementations of OT as well, e.g. Ellison (1994); Hammond (1995); Karttunen (1998). Like the implementations of rule-based phonology, these make use of finite-state transducers.

In this chapter, we take a different approach. Rather than treat phonological generalizations as mappings — and therefore as transducers — we view them as regular expressions directly and therefore as finite-state automata. If we make this move, we are committed to a number of consequences as far as implementing it. First, treating phonological generalizations as regular expressions commits us to using intersection as a mechanism to combine generalizations and as a mechanism to "apply" generalizations to lexical material. Second, using intersection commits us to representing the alternate pronunciations of segments as unions. Third, if those alternate pronunciations are general over the lexicon, we are compelled to view lexical entries as composed of more primitive concatenative elements drawn from an inventory of such elements. These components of the proposal will each be explained and elaborated below.

We are certainly not the first to propose a monostratal phonological theory. One very important early effort here is Wheeler (1981). Subsequent influential proposals include Scobbie (1991), Russell (1993), and Walther (1992). Our approach is explicitly finite-state in orientation and is thus similar in spirit to the monostratal finite-state approach of Bird and Ellison (1994) and Bird (1995). The proposal presented here differs in several ways, as will be explained in Section 6 below.

We will show that there are several desiderata of our approach. First, on computational grounds, it naturally allows us to replace transducers with more compact and more constrained automata. Second, on linguistic grounds, it allows us to do away with input representations, which have always had a controversial status in the theory.[1] Third, it allows for a fully representation-neutral constraint-based approach. Fourth, it allows for a separation of markedness and faithfulness.

The chapter is organized as follows. First, we review a sample of the kinds of generalizations that any phonological model must be able to describe. Second, we review the necessities of finite state automata. Third, we show how these general-

---

1. The controversy goes all the way back to questions of abstractness, raised in response to Chomsky and Halle (1968), through the various concretist phonological theories, e.g. Hooper (1976), Tranel (1981), Stampe (1973), through theories of underspecification, e.g. Archangeli (1988), Steriade (1995). The issue comes up in modern OT as well, e.g. Golston (1996), Hammond (2000), Russell (1995).

izations can be implemented in the system outlined. Fourth, we review the desiderata of the system presented and discuss what is left to accomplish. Finally, we compare the system with that proposed by Bird and Ellison (1994) and Bird (1995).

2. Phonology

Phonological theory characterizes the sound system of any language and describes the range of variation possible for these systems.

In this section, we very briefly review the kinds of data that our implementation must account for. These include phonological inventories, distributional regularities, natural classes, and patterns of alternation. Our characterization is general, as the goal is to outline the central facts at issue for any theory of phonology.

First, any theory of phonology and any implementation thereof must be able to account for the fact that the set of sounds that a language uses is (i) finite, and (ii) language specific. For example, English has the sound [æ] as in *cat* [kʰæt], but not the sound [y], as in French *rue* [ʁy] 'street'. Thus [æ] is in the inventory of sounds in English, but [y] is not.

Second, any theory of phonology must account for the fact that the distribution of sounds varies in a language-particular fashion. For example, English allows word-initial consonant clusters that begin with [s], but Spanish does not. For example, *strap* [stræp] is well-formed in English, but illegal in Spanish. On the other hand, French allows stop-nasal clusters, but English does not. Thus French *pneu* [pnø] 'tire' is illegal in English.

A third fact that any theory must describe is that phonological generalizations refer to natural classes. For example, the set of sounds thatare aspirated word-initially in English are the voiceless stops: [p], [t], and [k]. This set is defined in terms of the physiology of speech articulation and in terms of parameters that recur in generalizations of different sorts in many other languages. A language that was otherwise identical to English, but where [p], [s], and [k] underwent word-initial aspiration is ruled out. This set does not share a physiological characterization and does not occur in other languages.

Finally, any account of phonological patterning must accommodate alternations in the pronunciation of morphemes. For example, there is a distributional regularity in American English that disallows [t] and [d] between vowels when the second vowel is stressless and allows [ɾ] (flap) in precisely that context.[2] This

---

2. The full range of facts is quite complex and factors involving stress, morphological structure, identity of adjacent consonants, word frequency and length, etc. all play a role. The traditional analysis of this is given by Kahn (1980); see Hammond (1999) for a more recent account. Note too that flapping does not occur in all dialects of English and is optional in some.

Chapter 10. One-level finite-state phonology   **213**

distributional regularity triggers alternations in the case of morphemes like *write* [rayt] and *ride* [rayd] when they are suffixed with a vowel-initial form like *-ing* or *-er*, e.g. *writing* [ráyɾɪ̃ŋ],*writer* [ráyɾr̩], *riding* [ráyɾɪ̃ŋ], and rider [ráyɾr̩].

Phonological patterning can get much more complex than this, but these general categories will suffice to outline the general properties of the system.

3. General finite state machinery

In this section, we review the necessary formal preliminaries. In particular, we define what a finite state automaton is. We explain what a regular expression is and how it is equivalent to an automaton. We also explain various additional closure properties of the regular languages: intersection and complementation.[3]

Finite state automata have a long history and very well-understood properties. The broader class of Turing machines was originally proposed in Turing (1936). The general logic of finite automata per se was developed in McCulloch and Pitts (1943), and then fleshed out mathematically in Kleene (1956). Hopcroft and Ullman (1979), Lawson (2004) and many others provide overviews.

We define a finite state automaton (FSA) in the usual fashion: $(\Sigma, S, s_0, \delta, F)$ where Σ is a finite alphabet of symbols, S is a finite set of states, s_0 is the designated start state, δ is a mapping from $S \times \Sigma$ to 2^S, and F is a subset of final states from S. FSAs can be deterministic or non-deterministic. A deterministic automaton is one where there is at most one path through the automaton for any string composed of Σ, e.g. Σ^*. Deterministic and non-deterministic automata are equivalent, in that the set of languages that can be accepted by the set of non-deterministic automata is identical to the set of languages that can be accepted by the set of deterministic automata.

For example, Figure 1 shows a simple non-deterministic automaton. This automaton accepts any string composed of zero or more instances of *a* followed by a single *b*, e.g. *b*, *ab*, *aab*, etc. Figure 2 shows an equivalent deterministic automaton that accepts the same strings.

We define a regular expression as a characterization of a set of strings over some finite alphabet making use only of concatenation, union, and Kleene star.[4] For example, the regular expression accepted by the automata in Figure 1 and in Figure 2 is a^*b. We assume that any regular language is accepted by some FSA and any language accepted by an FSA can be cast as a regular expression. Regular ex-

---

3. Readers familiar with formal language theory—as presented, for example, by Hopcroft and Ullman (1979)—can safely skim or skip this section.

4. We use $(a|b)$ to express the union of a and b.

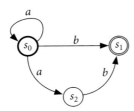
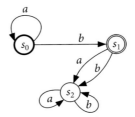

Figure 1. A simple non-deterministic automaton

Figure 2. A simple deterministic automaton

pressions are, of course, closed under concatenation, union, and Kleene star, but they are also closed under complementation and intersection.

Finally, we define a notion of abbreviation for expressing phonological generalizations and regular expressions in a perspicuous fashion. Specifically, any regular expression $ab\ldots$ can be defined as an abbreviation α, e.g. α $= ab\ldots$, where α is a symbol not in Σ. Abbreviations can then be used in subsequent regular expressions and subsequent abbreviation definitions. For example, if we define α $= abc$, then we can use α in subsequent expressions. Thus (α|d) is equivalent to (abc|d).

An abbreviatory system of this sort runs the risk of introducing expressions that go beyond regular languages. To avoid this consequence, we impose the restriction that, while abbreviations may make use of other abbreviations, the set of abbreviation definitions may not "cycle". That is, if α is defined in terms of β, then β may not be directly or indirectly defined in terms of α. It will then follow that regular expressions making use of abbreviations are still regular.[5]

Theorem 1 *Regular languages augmented with "non-cyclic" abbreviations are still regular.*

This can be shown straightforwardly.[6] First, a regular language without abbreviations is by definition regular.

Second, a regular language with a single abbreviation α is regular. This follows from the fact that any instance of α can simply be replaced with its equivalent regular expression. Since any expression containing α is otherwise regular, substituting a regular expression for α does not alter that.

---

5. There are other ways of insuring regularity of course.

6. The logic of the proof is analogous to the logic of the proof that the regular languages are closed under homomorphisms (Hopcroft and Ullman 1979).

Chapter 10. One-level finite-state phonology   215

Assume that some language with some number of "non-cyclic" abbreviations $\alpha_1, \ldots, \alpha_{n-1}$ is regular. We can add an additional abbreviation α_n that is defined in terms of existing abbreviations. To confirm that any expression built using α_n is regular, we replace α_n with its regular expression. We now have a regular expression with only $\alpha_1, \ldots, \alpha_{n-1}$, which, by assumption, is regular.

4. How it works

Now that the finite state machinery is in place, we turn to implementing phonology in these terms. Recall that we require the model to account for the following kinds of generalizations: inventories, distributional regularities, natural classes, and alternations.

We will present several smaller examples, and provide a more in-depth account of flapping in English at the end.

4.1. Inventories

The first property of phonological systems that we need to account for is that speakers are aware of what sounds comprise their language. We can capture this with the definition of Σ. In particular, if a speaker of a language knows that their inventory is composed of, for example, [p], [t], [k], [r], [a], [i], and [u], then we define Σ ={p, t, k, r, a, i, u}. The simplest phonology consistent with this inventory would be (p|t|k|r|a|i|u)*. We will refer to this as the Basic Phonological Automaton (BPA).[7]

4.2. Distributional regularities

Distributional regularities can be expressed as simple regular expressions that can be intersected with the BPA. Recall that English does not allow word-initial stop-nasal sequences, e.g. [pn], [bn], [kŋ], etc. The set of patterns that are excluded can be expressed as follows: (p|t|k|b|d|g)(m|n|ŋ)Σ*. To get the effect that these strings are ruled out in English, we intersect the complement of this expression with the BPA for English.

(2) $\overline{\text{(p|t|k|b|d|g)(m|n|ŋ)}\Sigma^*} \cap$ BPA

This has the effect of ruling out the offending sequences.

---

7. Notice that this is quite different from the notion of feasible pair in two-level phonology. A feasible pair is a possible input–output mapping, but we are taking the knowledge of phonological inventory to be entirely surface-based: the set of sounds that can occur in the language.

4.3. Natural classes

Chomsky and Halle (1968) make a distinction between *formal* and *substantive* universals. The system we have outlined so far falls in the former category. The definition of abbreviation is also a formal restriction. The precise abbreviations we define fall into the latter category. We can use the mechanism of abbreviation to capture traditional feature categories and prosodic constituents. Capturing the former means that the substantive abbreviation categories we allow will do the work of feature theory. Capturing the latter means that these categories will do the work of syllables, feet, etc.

Consider again the restriction on word-initial stop-nasal sequences. We can define an abbreviation for stops as follows.[8]

(3)   STOP = (p|t|k|b|d|g)

We can define the set of nasals as follows.

(4)   NASAL = (m|n|ŋ)

These allow us to recast the restriction on word-initial stop-nasal sequences as follows.

(5) $\overline{\text{STOP NASAL } \Sigma^*} \cap \text{BPA}$

To capture the substantive restrictions of traditional phonology, we simply define equivalent abbreviations and require that our system make use of them in analogous fashion.

The system of abbreviations can also be used to capture prosodic restrictions. For example, consider a language where syllables are defined as CV(C), with obligatory onsets and optional codas. In addition, the language is subject to the usual restriction that all words must be exhaustively parsed into syllables.

Let us assume that V and C are abbreviations defined for consonants and vowels. We define syllables as follows.

(6)   SYLLABLE = CV(C|ε)

The restriction that all words are parsed into syllables can be expressed like this:

(7)   SYLLABLE SYLLABLE*

To impose this restriction on the language, we intersect this expression with the BPA for the language.

---

8. Abbreviations will always be expressed with capital letters here.

Chapter 10. One-level finite-state phonology 217

Table 3. No flapping next to a consonant

V_V	V_C	C_V
ready [rɛɾi]	admit [ədmít]	anecdote [ǽnəkdòt]
coda [kóɾə]	codfish [kádfiš]	candy [kǽndi]
pity [píɾi]	outcast [áwtkæ̀st]	active [ǽktɪv]
data [déɾə]	suitcase [sútkès]	optic [áptɪk]

Table 4. No flapping before a stressed vowel

V_V	V_V́
coda [kóɾə]	codeine [kódìn]
adder [ǽɾər]	adapt [ədǽpt]
motto [máɾo]	veto [vító]
data [déɾə]	attack [ətǽk]

4.4. Alternations and flapping

Phonological alternations require some additional machinery. The key idea is to separate the representation of the alternation from the representation of distributional regularities.

Recall again the simplified description of flapping from above: flapping disallows [t] and [d] between vowels when the second vowel is stressless and allows [ɾ] in precisely that context. One additional complication is that an [r,y,w] will count as a vowel as well.

This generalization allows for both distributional skewing and alternations. Let's first consider the distributional regularities. First, we find [t,d] when one of the adjacent segments is a consonant (Table 3), or when the following vowel is stressed (Table 4). We also find [t,d] when the preceding consonant is an [l], but not when it's an [r] (Table 5).

The generalization is also responsible for alternations. Some of these occur because a word-final [t,d] can become intervocalic because of a vowel-initial suffix (Table 6) or because of a shift in stress due to suffixation (Table 7).

There are three components to the analysis. First, we must have in place suitable abbreviations so that we can refer to the relevant classes of sounds. Second, we

Table 5. No flapping after a lateral

r_V	l_V
border [bórɾər]	bolder [bóldər]
mordant [mórɾənt]	seldom [séldəm]
party [párɾi]	sultan [sʌ́ltən]
portal [pórɾəl]	delta [déltə]

Table 6. Flapping and suffixation

| write [rayt] | writing [ráyɾɪŋ] | writer [ráyɾər] |
| ride [rayd] | riding [ráyɾɪŋ] | rider [ráyɾər] |

Table 7. Flapping and stress shift

vortex [vórtèks]	vortices [vórɾəsiz]
atom [ǽɾəm]	atomic [ətámɪk]
autumn [ɔ́ɾəm]	autumnal [ɔtʌ́mnəl]
adore [ədór]	adoration [æ̀ɾəréšən]
cadence [kéɾəns]	cadential [kədénšəl]

must have regular expressions that express the surface distribution of the relevant segments. Finally, we must also have combinatorial units from which lexical items can be assembled that express the range of alternations possible.

The abbreviations we need are vowels, consonants, stressed vowels, stressless vowels, and coronal stops. These are all straightforwardly defined as unions of the relevant segments. We also need something to accommodate the behavior of [r] and [l]; the former behaves like a vowel, but the latter does not. This is actually a matter of phonology proper and there are several routes we could take.

One possibility is to attribute the special behavior of [r] to the fact that it is more like a vowel than a consonant, e.g. that it is really a glide, rather than a liquid like [l]. There is flapping after an [r] because it is, in essential respects, like a vowel. If we go this route, we'd define and use abbreviations for liquid and glide.

Another possibility is to attribute the absence of flapping after [l] to the fact that it is an apically produced segment, unlike [r], and that this prevents flapping. If we went this route, we'd define an abbreviation for apical.

The data at issue here are insufficient to decide the question and so, for concreteness sake, we'll take the first choice, employing liquid and glide.

We will represent these abbreviations as in Table 8 in the expressions that follow. Let's now turn to the constraints on distribution that are required.

Table 8. Relevant abbreviations for flapping

Class	Examples	Symbol
vowels	a, e, ə, etc.	V
consonants	p, t, s, l, etc.	C
stressed vowels	á, ó, é, etc.	V́
stressless vowels	ă, ĭ, æ̆, etc.	V̆
coronal stop	t, d	T
liquid	l	L
glide	y, w, r	G

Chapter 10. One-level finite-state phonology **219**

Coronal stops in English cannot occur intervocalically whenthe second vowel is stressless. In addition, flap [ɾ] cannot occur in any other environments. These are distributional regularities that can be expressed as described above. First, we have the restriction on coronal stops.

(8) $\overline{\Sigma^*(V|G)T\breve{V}\Sigma^*}$

Then we have the restriction on [ɾ]; it cannot occur after something that is not a vowel or before something that is not a stressless vowel.

(9) $\overline{\Sigma^*((V|G)ɾ|ɾ\breve{V})\Sigma^*}$

These are, of course, intersected with the BPA of English. They express—in an independent fashion—these two restrictions on the sound system of English.

The distributional regularities are only part of the story, however. In particular, we must also account for how the pronunciations of particular morphemes are altered to satisfy these regularities.

As these stand, we have no way of accounting for why morphemes exhibit different pronunciations. Consider a form like *write*. If we represent this as is, e.g. as /rayt/, then the prediction of the model thus far is that adding a vowel-initial suffix like -*er* results in an ungrammatical form.

While this is not what we want for flapping, this kind of behavior is required for other situations. For example, there is a well-known restriction on the deverbal nominalizer -*al* in English: if it attaches to a verb, then that verb must have final stress, e.g. *renéwal, avówal, appróval, arríval, deníal, espóusal*, etc. Forms that would violate this pattern are not repaired, but are simply excluded, e.g. **edítal* or **édital*.

We capture the fact that words like *write* and *ride* exhibit alternating pronunciations by positing a separate lexicon, represented as an FSA as well.

The individual elements of the lexicon are concatenated from more basic elements that represent the phonemic inventory of the language. The fact that certain sounds can exhibit multiple pronunciations is represented by the union of those pronunciations. For example, the lexical representation of *write* is composed as follows:

(10) /r + a + y + (t|ɾ)/

Here, only the final segment alternates and the available pronunciations are indicated with a union. The correct pronunciation is chosen by intersecting lexical (regular) expressions with the fully intersected BPA of the language.

On this view, the behavior of these items is not an idiosyncratic fact about these items, but about the fact that the lexical alphabet of English includes (t|ɾ) and (d|ɾ).

If we choose, the entire lexicon can be represented as the union of all of its entries, which are—as just indicated—composed of more basic concatenative units. This is not a necessary part of the theory, however.

This model of phonological alternations has a number of properties that are worth emphasizing. First, the set of possible alternations of the language is defined *not* by the lexical entries of the language, but by the set of basic concatenative elements from which those entries are composed. Thus, the set of alternations is defined separately from the lexicon and serves to restrict the language generally. Any new lexical entry must be composed from the same set of basic concatenative units.

Second, the system proposed separates the set of distributional regularities from the set of alternation possibilities. This is, in fact, required by phonological systems. For example, we see that there are alternations in English that are triggered by the regularities of (8) and (9) that describe the distribution of coronal stops and flap respectively. On the other hand, there are no alternations triggered by (5) which governs word-initial stop-nasal sequences.[9]

5. Desiderata

The system developed is quite simple. First, there is a system of "non-cyclic" abbreviation that can be used to encode the substantive universals of phonological theory. Second, there is an FSA that represents the distributional regularities of the language. This is composed of smaller expressions that represent individual distributional regularities that are intersected together. Third, there is a set of basic concatenative units that represent the available lexical building blocks of the language. These are composed of elements of Σ and union is used to allow multiple pronunciations of the same element. The basic units are concatenated together to make lexical entries. The latter can be intersected with the BPA to produce surface pronunciations.

We've given several examples of how the system works: flapping, vowel nasalization, and some of the restrictions on syllable onsets in English.

There are a number of nice properties to the model. First, it is a monostratal model that does not require transduction. Hence it enjoys the full restrictiveness of finite state automata over transducers.[10] The mechanism by which it does this is

---

9. This separation of distributional regularities shows up in a number of phonolog-ical theories, e.g. Kisseberth (1970); Paradis (1988); Prince and Smolensky (1993).

10. For example, regular expressions (automata) are closed under intersection while regular relations (transducers) are not (Kaplan and Kay 1994).

effectively trading in input-output pairings for intersection. Where previous models map from input /t/ to output [t] and [ɾ], the model here intersects (t|ɾ) with other regular expressions to achieve the same effect.

Second, on the phonological front, the model is inspired by ideas from Optimality Theory. First, OT posits a frequently misunderstood notion of *Richness of the Base*, which holds that the distributional regularities of a language must be fully expressed by the constraint ranking of that language, not by any restrictions on the input. Richness of the Base does, however, allow the input to play a role in selecting the appropriate pronunciation for elements that alternate. We have taken a similar tack here, separating the fully intersected BPA from the set of alternating elements.[11]

Our position takes us even further down the path away from relying on the input. On the proposal developed here, the input for a word like *write* is not a single specific pronunciation, but an automaton (10) which allows for several different pronunciations. The contextually appropriate pronunciation is selected by intersecting this automaton with the BPA.

If we want to interpret this in the context of some notion of psychological reality, the claim is that speakers don't store a form like *write* in terms of a single abstract pronunciation, but in terms of a representation of the set of possible pronunciations of the word.

Third, the same distinction between the BPA and the concatenative elements of the lexicon can be seen as extending the separation of markedness and faithfulness constraints in OT. Markedness for us is instantiated in the fully intersected BPA. Faithfulness is expressed in the set of basic lexical concatenative units.

Fourth, the current model is explicitly non-representational, following the logic of earliest OT that we put as much into the constraint system as possible. In the years before the rise of Optimality Theory, there had been a tremendous focus on nonlinear representations in phonology, metrical and syllabic structure and autosegmental representations. OT turned the field's attention to constraints on phonological representations and much of the work of nonlinear representations could be viewed as a function of appropriately formulated constraints. Our approach continues the development of a fully representation-neutral constraint-based framework in that any work done in previous frameworks by non-linear representations and featural specification is done by our notion of abbreviation.

---

11. There have been radical versions of OT that have entirely eschewed input representations, e.g. Hammond (2000); Russell (1995). The present work can be seen as extending this line of investigation drawing on the richness and restrictiveness of finite state phonology. Another revision of input representations in OT is Golston (1996), which bears interesting similarities to the current model.

6. Comparison

How does the model proposed here differ from previous approaches? There are a number of finite-state transducer-based approaches, e.g. Kaplan and Kay (1994), Karttunen (1983), Karttunen (1998), Ellison (1994). Our approach differs from these in that it is based on intersection, rather than transduction.

There have been previous attempts at a phonology that is monostratal: Wheeler (1981), Bird (1995), Bird and Ellison (1994), Russell (1993), Walther (1992), Scobbie (1991), etc. How is the current model different from these?

There are a number of differences between these models and so we focus our comparison on the very interesting proposals of Bird (1995) and Bird and Ellison (1994), the most similar to the current approach. Their model is monostratal like the current proposal and explicitly finite-state in terms of computational power.

One perhaps superficial difference between the current proposal and Bird (1995) is that the latter develops a rich logical formalism along the lines of HPSG. The current proposal is built exclusively on regular expressions enriched with our notion of abbreviation. In both cases, the model is constrained to be finite state, so it is not clear that this is more than a notional distinction.

Another difference is that Bird and Ellison (1994) and Bird (1995) were advanced in the representational era of generative phonology, when the nature of the phonological representation constrained phonological generalizations. Hence, these models spent a fair amount of time developing finite state encodings of autosegmental and metrical formalisms. The current proposal seeks to accommodate nonlinear representations and featural distinctions all with the notion of abbreviation.

Finally, Bird and Ellison and Bird explicitly reject destructive processes, those that neutralize contrasts like flapping in English. This is necessary in any monostratal framework, of course. It's a little unclear how such generalizations are to be handled then in those frameworks. In other work, Bird et al. (1992) provides analyses for some of these phenomena.[12] In particular, Bird et al. propose two solutions.

For Chumash harmony, their analysis is superficially similar in structure to our analysis of flapping. The range of alternations allowed for harmony are defined in terms of a separate automaton. They do not, however, go down the route we go of proposing that lexical entries must be composed from a set of basic combinatorial units that represent what alternations are possible.

However, for the Pasiego dialect of Montañes Spanish, they propose that a neutralizing harmony process can be handled as a morphological relationship.

---

12. This chapter is a combination of several smaller sections each written by one of the co-authors; the relevant section for us is the one written by Bird.

Chapter 10. One-level finite-state phonology **223**

Table 9. Pasiego dialect of Montañes Spanish

sEnt-		*sintáis*	*sentémus*	*sintí:s*
feel		2PL PR SUB	1PL PR IND	2PL PR IND
bEb-		*bebámus*	*bebémus*	*bibí:s*
drink		1PL PR SUB	1PL PR IND	2PL PR IND

Bird et al. cite the data in Table 9; the facts are taken from McCarthy (1984). The basic generalization is that non-low vowels of verb roots must agree in height with a stressed vowel in the suffix; low vowels are transparent. They treat this in morphological terms: roots that exhibit this alternation are marked for two pronunciations triggered by the pronunciation of the suffix.

This unfortunately misses the generalization that the phenomenon in question is not morphological in nature. Rather, any root with the appropriate vowel will exhibit the generalization before any suffix with the appropriate vowels.

Our analysis would be just as in our analysis of flapping above. The basic concatenative units of the language include (e|i). This element can be concatenated with other vowels and consonants to make morphemes. In the BPA of the language there would be a constraint that rules out disharmonic vowel sequences (assuming appropriate abbreviations are already defined).

(11) $\overline{\text{MID } C^*(\text{HIGH} \cap \text{STRESSED})}$

The advantage of our approach is twofold. First, we treat this process with the same machinery we use to treat everything else. Second, we make the prediction that the process is general and not morphologically restricted.

The reason why this option is available to us and was not available to Bird et al. is that we view lexical entries as concatenations of more basic regular expressions. Hence the generality of the process is ensured by the requirement that those concatenative elements be general.

7. Remaining questions

There are a number of outstanding questions. First, we have only treated very simple phonological processes and there are many other processes that may require richer computational power, e.g. metathesis, metrical structure assignment, reduplication and prosodic morphology generally. Language games arguably require much more computational power than finite state (Baker 2007), and it may be that the same is true for reduplication and prosodic morphology generally (Culy 1985).

A second open question is how to treat rule interactions. For example, we have not treated the classical problem of vowel lengthening before voiced consonants in English. This produces a contrast in vowel length between *write* [rayt] and *ride* [ray:d]. This length difference is preserved in flapping environments (in some dialects), e.g. *writer* [ráyɾɾ] vs. *rider* [ráy:ɾɾ]. Notice how the vowel in *writer* is short, even though the following flap is voiced. The traditional analysis of this is to posit a lengthening rule that precedes the flapping rule.

Such an account is not possible in the current analysis since generalizations are combined by intersection. There are two possible ways to go here. One is to deny any version of the rule-ordering account and merge the relevant constraints. Another possibility is to combine constraints by something more complex than intersection, to achieve the same effect. A similar problem arises in finite state implementations of OT and is resolved in this fashion (Karttunen 1998).

8. Conclusion

We have seen how a treatment of phonological generalizations is possible in a one-level finite-state framework. This framework is maximally simple using simple and well-behaved regular operations: intersection, union, concatenation, abbreviation.

In effect, the current system is finite state phonology, updated with insights from radical versions of OT. There is no input representation. There is a separation of markedness and faithfulness. Representations are maximally impoverished.

There are a number of other issues that arise as well that we cannot treat fully in the space available. Nonetheless, the system developed has interesting properties that are worth pursuing further.

References

Archangeli, Diana. 1988. "Aspects of underspecification theory." *Phonology* 5: 183–207.
Baker, Adam. 2007. "Language games and the theory of computation." U. of Arizona.
Bird, S., Coleman, J., Pierrehumbert, J., and Scobbie, J.M. 1992. "Declarative phonology." A. Crochetière, J.-C. Boulanger, and C. Ouellon (eds.), *Proceedings of the Fifteenth International Conference of Linguists*, Québec: Presses de l'Université Laval.
Bird, Steven. 1995. *Computational Phonology*. Cambridge: Cambridge University Press.
Bird, Steven and Ellison, T. Mark. 1994. "One-level phonology: autosegmental representations and rules as finite automata." *Computational Linguistics* 20: 55–90.
Chomsky, Noam and Halle, Morris. 1968. *The Sound Pattern of English*. New York: Harper & Row.
Culy, C. 1985. "The complexity of the vocabulary of Bambara." *Linguistics and Philosophy* 8: 345–51.

Ellison, T. Mark. 1994. "Phonological derivation in Optimality Theory." *COLING* 94: pp. 1007–13.

Golston, C. 1996. "Direct Optimality Theory: representation as pure markedness." *Language* 72: 713–48.

Hammond, Michael. 1995. "Syllable parsing in English and French." ROA #58.

Hammond, Michael. 1999. *The Phonology of English*. Oxford: Oxford University Press.

Hammond, Michael. 2000. "There is no lexicon!" *Coyote Papers* 10: 55–77, ROA #43.

Hooper, J. 1976. *An Introduction to Natural Generative Phonology*. New York: Academic Press.

Hopcroft, J.E. and Ullman, J.D. 1979. *Introduction to Automata Theory, Languages, and Computation*. Reading: Addison-Wesley.

Johnson, Douglas C. 1972. *Formal aspects of phonological description*. The Hague: Mouton.

Kahn, D. 1980. *Syllable-based Generalizations in English Phonology*. New York: Garland, 1976 MIT doctoral dissertation.

Kaplan, R. and Kay, M. 1994. "Regular model of phonological rule systems." *Computational Linguistics* 20: 331–78.

Karttunen, L. 1983. "KIMMO: a general morphological processor." *Texas Linguistic Forum* 22: 163–86.

Karttunen, Lauri. 1998. "The proper treatment of optimality in computational phonology." *The Proceedings of FSMNLP '98: International Workshop on Finite-State Methods in Natural Language Processing*, pp. 1–12, Ankara, Turkey: Bilkent University.

Kisseberth, Charles. 1970. "On the functional unity of phonological rules." *Linguistic Inquiry* 1: 291–306.

Kleene, S. C. 1956. "Representation of events in nerve nets and finite automata, automata studies." *Ann. Math. Studies* 34: 3–41.

Koskenniemi, Kimmo. 1984. "A general computational model for word-form recognition and production." *COLING 84*, pp. 178–81.

Lawson, Mark V. 2004. *Finite Automata*. Boca Raton: Chapman & Hall/CRC.

McCarthy, John. 1984. "Theoretical consequences of Montañes vowel harmony." *Linguistic Inquiry* 15: 291–318.

McCulloch, W.S. and Pitts, W. 1943. "A logical calculus of the ideas immanent in nervous activity." *Bulletin of Mathematical Biology* 5: 115–33.

Paradis, Carole. 1988. "On constraints and repair strategies." *The Linguistic Review* 6: 71–97.

Prince, Alan and Smolensky, Paul. 1993. "Optimality Theory." U. Mass and U. of Colorado.

Russell, K. 1993. *A constraint-based approach to phonology*. Ph.D. thesis, USC.

Russell, Kevin. 1995. "Morphemes and candidates in Optimality Theory." ROA #44.

Scobbie, J. 1991. *Attribute-value phonology*. Ph.D. thesis, University of Edinburgh.

Stampe, David. 1973. *A Dissertation on Natural Phonology*. Ph.D. thesis, University of Chicago, 1979, New York: Garland Publishing Company.

Steriade, D. 1995. "Underspecification and markedness." *Language* pp. 114–74.

Tranel, Bernard. 1981. Concreteness in Generative Phonology: Evidence from French. Berkeley: University of California Press.

Turing, A.M. 1936. "On computable numbers: with an application to the Entscheidungsproblem." *Proceedings of the London Mathematical Society* pp. 230–265.

Walther, M. 1992. *Deklarative Silbifizierung in einem constraintbasierten Grammatikformalismus*. Master's thesis, University of Stuttgart.

Wheeler, D. 1981. *Aspects of a Categorial Theory of Phonology*. Ph.D. thesis, University of Massachusetts-Amherst.

CHAPTER 11

Biolinguistics today and Platonism yesterday

T. G. Bever
University of Arizona

This contribution expounds on ideas put forth by a group of New York City generative grammarians that language possesses certain essential features that are uncaused
and adhere to an abstract ideal form. An analogy of the situation with language is
made with certain natural properties of numbers. It is also noted that this situation
contrasts with that of the functional structure of human color vision. This idea is
viewed alongside recent work in biolinguistics and is compared to the neoplatonist view of language, namely that language is discovered by the child learner and
not triggered. The main consequences of this idea are discussed both within the
historical context and with respect to current theories on language acquisition.

During the 1980s, an extreme idea about the ontology of language emerged amongst
a group of New York City generative grammarians. Jerry Katz wrote several articles
and then a book, "Language and other abstract objects" (1981). In this work, he outlined his arguments for the notion that certain aspects of the essential features of
language have a natural form, and hence are uncaused in the usual sense of causation. He likened this view to Plato's notions of ideal form, and suggested that certain
aspects of language exhibit such an ideal form.

The obvious analogy is to properties of number. There is no physical cause that
explains why/how functional relations between numbers have particular properties: why/how 2+2 = 4, why/how the square root of 4 is 2, why/how the difference
between 0 and 2 is the same as between 2 and 4, etc. Most important, the number
of numbers is not countable but transfinite: a fact like that clearly suggests (and
for many, proves) that, wherever numbers come from, it is not from human cognition — we can imagine counting to the highest immediate infinity, given enough
time: but human notions of time in which to count are transcended by the number
of numbers.

This situation contrasts with the cause of the functional structure of human
color vision: red is the opposite of green and blue the opposite of yellow (in each
case they merge to grey) for neurochemical reasons, which may in turn have an
interesting evolutionary basis (see Shepard 1997). The point is that the functional
structure of certain biological or physical phenomena can be codified and understood, even used practically, long before the physical basis is determined or at
least given a mechanistic theory (notorious cases include the gene theory and the

periodic table of elements). But the fact that these theories have an articulated and predictive functional structure does not mean that they are inevitably abstract or uncaused — the 'true' cause is eventually unearthed. But in the case of numbers, the 'true' cause appears intractably abstract. Our intuition insists that 2+2 = 4, or that the right triangle's hypotenuse is the root of the sum of the squares of the other two sides, long before humans discovered such facts, and will persist without possible counter demonstration, after humans have disappeared. In the case of the essence of language, Katz applied roughly the corresponding form of argument for Platonism used in mathematics: Natural language has formal properties independent of us, it is abstract, and we come to know it via intuition.

Langendoen and Postal (1984) were interested in the idea, and developed a form of proof that language has properties independent of us. Their achievement was to show that the number of sentences is not countable, but is transfinite, just as in the case of numbers themselves. Chomsky had often used the idea that the number of sentences is countably infinite to show that what people know when they know a language has to be governed by learned generative rules, not a finite list of sentences. Langendoen and Postal's took their formal demonstration to argue that the situation is even more extreme: the number of sentences is not merely countably infinite, it transcends any human counting mechanism, just like numbers. Thus, language has its own properties, properties that existed before humans discovered and applied some of those properties for their own purposes, and properties that will persist after humans have disappeared.

I lived in the same milieu as Katz, Langendoen and Postal (albeit further uptown than the first two) and added my own contribution to the 'Platonic' idea by exploring some psychological implications of the notion of language structure as uncaused. The idea was particularly intriguing because it cast a distinct light on the problem of language acquisition relevant for the zeitgeist: the current view was that the child re-creates language based on critical cues from the speech that it hears, which trigger options on a number of innately predefined dimensions. This model (basically an early version of parameter setting) was (and is) extremely elaborate, since the kind of linguistic model to be accounted for — government and binding - was a complex set of distinct 'theories' (e.g., case theory, government, theta role theory...) and levels of representation, (DS, SS, Logical form...). and complex movement rules organizing the relation between levels. Meaning was in part read off of the logical form, in part off the surface form. Parameter setting is a model that attempts to show how learning such a complex architecture is possible in the absence of clear cues to that structure in what the child hears. Parameter setting today remains to be developed even as a logically possible model, although recent investigations have made substantial progress in outlining the nature of the data that the child must experience and note for such a program to work. (Fodor 1998, 2001; Fodor and Sakas 2004).

The neoplatonist view proposed by Katz, Langendoen and Postal seemed to cut through this complexity. On the neoplatonist view, language is *discovered* by the child, not *triggered*: Just as the child (allegedly) discovers the concept of number or naïve physics or the moon because those entities exist outside the child, the child discovers the true essence of language because it is real and external to the child. This framed the language acquisition problem quite differently from the idea that the child has it already innately prefigured and is only waiting for specific cues to clarify which of the innate parametric options are relevant for its particular language. At the time, I noted that this has several consequences (Bever 1982):

(a) The 'poverty of the stimulus' presented to the child remains the central problem of language acquisition. If language is to be discovered and learned (not automatically triggered), the child must have learning mechanisms more constructive than associative connectionism. It may also have innate mechanisms that point it to the correct kind of grammatical structures, while not causing those structures.
(b) Conversely, the language learning child may be capable of making false *kinds* of hypotheses about the language it is learning. That is, if possible languages are not pre-configured within the child's cognition, it may create impossible hypotheses on its way to mastering its language correctly.
(c) There must be structurally possible languages that are not attested because they cannot be learned via normal language learning mechanisms.

To answer (a), I suggested an hypothesis-testing model of acquisition which accesses abstract concepts to resolve conflicts in representation. The flagship model was the acquisition of the concept of number. Since the 1930s, it was known that children go through several phases of mastery of numbers. At one point, they are confused about the relationship between the number of objects in an array and the apparent size of the array — they accept the view that if an array is changed to look larger (to adult eyes), it is assessed as having 'more' than before: at the same time if you take one of the objects away, now the child volunteers that it has 'less' than before. This is a representational conflict: stretching an array makes it have more, taking one object away makes it have less. The ultimate resolution is to access the concept of the invariance of number under physical transformation of shape. At the time, I argued that since the properties of numbers are not caused, the child is discovering an abstract and 'real' set of properties. Since then, cognitive neurologists such as S. Dehaene (1997) have elucidated many demonstrations that the number *concept* itself has innate neurological foundations in humans which he claims both enable and circumscribe its possible forms. Dehaene suggests that the biologically based simple number concept — available in similar inchoate form to some animals — evolved as a functional capacity adapted to a world that our perceptual system resolves into discrete objects. In fact, he argues directly that the basic number concept *is* exactly like color vision — humans are innately wired to segment the world into objects and to differentiate amongst small numbers of those objects.

This casts a new light on the claim that children discover an abstract platonic form for numbers — it is now arguable that children *apply* a neurologically predisposition to categorize the world not only in terms of objects in it, but in terms of number of similar objects. But it leaves open what the critical experiences are that stimulate the child to access that capacity. It remains the case that children go through a phase of mathematical inconsistency before arriving at a stable number concept: hence, we can still infer that the concept is accessed as a resolution of conflicting representations.

What are the implications of all this for language acquisition? Dehaene's discoveries of specific brain areas devoted to the early development of number concepts may be elegant and surprising science, but we already knew well that there are specific brain areas devoted to language. What we do *not* know is whether these areas are predisposed to cause language, or are special mechanisms available to discover it. The basic learning issue remains — is there a special learning device for language, or is it the outcome of the combination of a general hypothesis testing model, in combination with a large symbolic capacity and special tuning to access particular linguistic architectures that provide consistent cognitive representations of languages?

The other two implications of language as an abstract object for learning also remain. Children may come to false kinds of hypotheses about their language — for example that every phrase is a sentence, or that there are only nouns and verbs. And it remains the case that there are many languages allowed by today's syntax, which are not learnable or usable, for various reasons.

What is the situation today? The notion of 'biolinguistics' has crystallized the idea that language has an essential structure, and that attested languages result from the interaction of that structure with interfaces, such as mechanisms for thought, acquisition, perception, production and associative memory (Hauser et al. 2002). The 'essential structure' of language has shrunk from the elaborate — almost Byzantine — GB architecture, to a single recursive tree-building process — recursive merge — almost everything else about attested languages is being explored as the result of interfaces, abstract categories and the lexicon. If this proposal is correct, it opens up a different way of thinking about acquisition from triggering settings on innate parameters. In fact, it makes more plausible the idea that the child's attested language is discovered via hypothesis testing, using variations on combinations of merge to reject and verify hypotheses created at the language interfaces.

Indeed, the greater reliance on interface constraints confirms the importance of the largely unstudied range of mental and neurological filters that can substantially narrow the search space for possible languages. It is interesting that Terry and I spent some time four decades ago exploring the role of statistically valid perceptual strategies in constraining attested languages — a radical notion at the time. We suggested that the counterpoint between systems of behavior such as perception, and systems of grammatical knowledge can explain certain dynamics of historical language change. Our major case study was the the emergence of the restriction on deleting the subject relative pronoun (who) in subject relative clauses. In old English the equivalent could be deleted when the inflection and agreement on the verb blocked a garden path in which the subject relative could be taken as the main independent clause. When the inflectional system of English was basically leveled, initial subject relative clauses became compelling garden paths, blocked only by requiring the subject relative pronoun to be explicit (but not the object relative pronoun, since deleting that did not create a substantial perceptual garden path) (Bever and Langendoen 1971, 1972). As part of our exploration of the role of behavioral systems, we also suggested that certain apparently grammatical constructions are actually ungrammatical, but allowed in the attested language because they are transparently interpretable speech errors created by normal processes of speech production (Langendoen and Bever 1973). Finally, together with Jerry Katz, we collected a set of reprinted and new articles outlining different ways in which behavioral and learning mechanisms constrain attested languages: presciently, we called the book "An integrated theory of Linguistic Ability", just because each article discussed the impact of one or another system of language use — what today are called 'interfaces', on apparent language structures. (Bever et al. 1976).

More recently, I have suggested that an important general role of many interface structures is to compile statistical regularities as the child experiences them: the statistical regularities create an internalized bank of potential sentences with paired meaning and form, against which the child can test his/her syntactic hypotheses about their derivational structure. This alternation between hypothesis formation at the interface and filtering via a derivational model is spelled out a bit more in several current papers (Bever in press a, b). It has the possible implication of greatly reducing the impact of the poverty of the stimulus arguments in favor of passive parameter setting. (Bever in press a, b).

Thus, from the psychological viewpoint, the notion of language as an abstract object does not change the idea of how it might be learned, from the current formal architecture. In either case, hypothesis formation and verification is a possible model. In either case, interface constraints may account for a great deal of the appearance of attested languages. This leaves the prior arguments for platonic linguistics from Katz, Langendoen and Postal as they were: for better or for worse.

References

Bever, T. G. 1970. The cognitive basis for linguistic structures. In *Cognition and Language Development*, R. Hayes, 277–360. New York NY: Wiley & Sons.

Bever, T. G. 1982. Some implications of the non-specific bases of language. In *Language Development - The State of the Art*, L. Gleitman & E. Wanner, 429–49. Cambridge: CUP.

Bever, T. G. In press a. Minimalist behaviorism: The role of the individual in explaining language universals. In *Language Universals*, M. Christiansen, C. Collins & S. Edelman. Oxford: OUP.

Bever, T. G. In press b. Remarks on the individual basis for linguistic structures. In *Of Minds and Language: The Basque Country Encounter with Noam Chomsky*, M. Piattelli-Palmarini (ed.). Oxford: OUP.

Bever, T. G. & Langendoen, T. 1971. A dynamic model of the evolution of language. *Linguistic Inquiry* 2. (Reprinted in *An Integrated Theory of Linguistic Ability*, T. G. Bever, J. J. Katz & D. T. Langendoen (eds), 115–47. New York NY: T. Y. Crowell.

Bever, T. G. & Langendoen, T. 1972. The interaction of perception and grammar in linguistic change. In *Historical Linguistics in the Perspective of Transformational Theory*, R. Stockwell & R. MacCaulay, 32–95. Bloomington IN: Indiana University Press.

Bever, T. G., J. J. Katz & Langendoen, D. T. (eds). 1976. *An Integrated Theory of Linguistic Ability*. New York NY: T. Y. Crowell.

Dehaene, S. 1997. *The Number Sense. How the Mind Creates Mathematics*. Oxford: OUP.

Fodor, J. 1998. Unambiguous triggers. *Linguistic Inquiry* 29: 1–36.

Fodor, J. D. 2001. Setting syntactic parameters. *The Handbook of Contemporary Syntactic Theory*, M. Baltin & C. Collins, 730–8. Oxford: Blackwell.

Fodor, J. D. & Sakas, W. G. 2004. Evaluating models of parameter setting. *BUCLD 28: Proceedings of the 28th Annual Boston University Conference on Language Development*, A. Brugos, L. Micciulla & C. E. Smith, 1–27. Somerville MA: Cascadilla.

Hauser, M. D., N. Chomsky & W. T. Fitch. The faculty of language: What is it, who has it, and how did it evolve? Science 298: 1569–79.

Katz, J. 1981. *Language and Other Abstract Objects*. Lanham MA: Rowman and Littlefield.

Langendoen, D. T. & Bever, T. G. 1973. Can a not unhappy man be called a not sad one? In *A Festschrift for Morris Halle*, S. R. Anderson & P. Kiparsky, 392–409. New York NY: Holt, Rinehart and Winston.

Langendoen, D. T. & Postal P. M. 1984. *The Vastness of Natural Languages*. Oxford: B. Blackwell

Shephard, R. 1997. The perceptual organization of colors. An adaptation to regularities of the terrestrial world? In *Readings on Color*, Vol. 2, A. Byrne & D. R. Hilbert, 311–56. Cambridge MA: The MIT Press.

PART 4

Standards

CHAPTER 12

Linguistics as a community activity

The paradox of freedom through standards

Gary F. Simons
SIL International

The Internet has given us a new playing field for global collaboration. It could transform the practice of linguistics through universal access to huge quantities of digital language documentation and description. But this transformation can happen only if certain aspects of community practice are formalized by defining and adhering to shared standards. After expanding on the vision for what linguistics could be like in the twenty-first century, this essay attempts to clarify the role of standards by considering two case studies of life with and without standards — using solar time versus standard time, and using language names versus language identifiers. The essay then develops two metaphors that seek to put standards in a positive light: "linguistics as community" and "development as freedom." The ultimate conclusion is that only by submitting to the constraints of shared standards will the community be free to develop the riches of knowledge it is seeking.

The man whom we honor with this volume is well-known for his contributions to formal linguistics in the usual sense of formal approaches to the description of language. In recent years, Professor Langendoen has also given attention to formalizing linguistics more broadly — that is, to developing formalisms that will empower the practice of linguistics in community. My collaborations with him, first in the TEI (Text Encoding Initiative, www.tei-c.org) and then in the E-MELD project (Electronic Metastructures for Endangered Language Data, www.emeld.org), have centered around a vision for how the practice of linguistics could be transformed by the universal availability of digital language documentation and description that are encoded in a standardized and interoperable way. Time and again, however, we have encountered the less-than-enthusiastic response of colleagues who are not keen on being constrained by standards.

This essay addresses the place of standards in the formalization of community practice. After expanding on the vision for what linguistics could be like in the twenty-first century, the essay attempts to clarify the role of standards by considering two case studies of life with and without standards — using solar time versus standard time, and using names versus codes to identify languages. The essay then develops two metaphors that seek to put standards in a positive light: "linguistics as community" and "development as freedom." The ultimate conclusion is that only by submitting to the constraints of shared standards will the community be free to develop the riches of knowledge it is seeking.

1. Linguistics in the twenty-first century

In the last two decades, some fundamental changes in the world have had a profound impact on the way business is conducted. These same changes are likely to have an equally profound effect on the way we do linguistics. In a recent book, *The World is Flat*, Thomas Friedman (2005) explains what is happening. Five centuries ago, when Columbus put his conviction that the world was round to the test by sailing west to reach "the countries of India," he thought he had reached part of the Indies, but in fact he had run into America. Friedman (2005: 3–5) recounts how in 2004 he flew east to make his own voyage of discovery to Bangalore, the "Silicon Valley" of India. When he actually got to India, he was surprised to find parts of America — billboards touting American companies, software firms using American business techniques, people using American names and American accents at large call centers. His conclusion: the world must be flat.

Freidman goes on to describe "the ten forces that have flattened the world" (2005, chapter 2). The first of these was the fall of the Berlin wall in 1989, which almost overnight removed barriers that were keeping half of the world from collaborating with the other half. The second was the emergence of the World Wide Web in the mid 1990s and the shift of focus in the personal computing platform from the desktop to the Internet. The other eight flatteners have been new approaches to collaboration on a global scale that the first two flatteners have made possible: work flow software, open-sourcing, outsourcing, offshoring, supply-chaining, insourcing, in-forming (e.g. Google), and the wireless technologies that make it possible to collaborate while on the move.

These ten flatteners have produced a Web-powered playing field for global collaboration. The flattening did not happen as soon as the Internet became available; rather, it took a decade or so for business processes to change in order to achieve the great productivity breakthroughs made possible by the new technologies. By the time the new processes were in place, three billion people (of China, India, Russia, Eastern Europe, Latin America, and Central Asia) who had been frozen out of the playing field only two decades ago, found themselves with the potential to plug into the field and play with the rest of the world. Friedman (2005: 181–2) offers the following conclusion:

> It is this triple convergence — of new players, on a new playing field, developing new habits and processes for horizontal collaboration — that I believe is the most important force shaping global economics and politics in the early twenty-first century. ... The

> scale of the global community that is soon going to be able to participate in all sorts of discovery and innovation is something the world has simply never seen before.

The triple convergence will shape far more than economics and politics; a global community of unprecedented scale is poised to participate in linguistic discovery and innovation as well.

Friedman (2005: 9–10) summarizes the history of globalization in terms of three eras. In Globalization 1.0, which began with the voyage of Columbus, a handful of countries drove global integration as they sailed the seas to establish colonial empires. In Globalization 2.0, which began in the nineteenth century and was fueled by the Industrial Revolution with its falling transportation costs, multinational companies were the main force driving global integration. Now at the turn of the twenty-first century, fueled by the technologies of the Information Age, Globalization 3.0 brings us a new dynamic force — the power of individuals to collaborate and compete on a global scale.

This new era of the flattened playing field is having its effect on the academic world. In the previous era, the institutions of learning with global reach were the world-class universities. Just a generation ago, in order to access the information riches of the world, one had to physically enter the libraries and archives of such institutions. Today, the center of gravity has shifted from institution to individual. Whether you are a professor logging in from an Ivy League campus in North America or a peasant logging in from an Internet cafe somewhere in the developing world, you have access to the same indexed collection of billions of information resources from around the globe. For the linguist, these resources include not just the secondary works of description and the tertiary works of theory that are typically found in libraries, but also the primary data that have traditionally been found in archives, plus a new form of primary data that is cropping up on the web as hundreds (and soon thousands) of language communities start posting materials in their own language.

This is the context for doing linguistics in the twenty-first century. All linguists will have finger-tip access to materials in and about thousands of languages, not just the materials they may have personally collected for a handful of languages. Linguists, educators, and native speakers from different corners of the globe will be able to form virtual communities around a particular language of interest as they collaborate to document, describe, preserve, and promote that language. Typologists and theorists will be able to form other virtual communities as they collaborate with each other and with particular language-specific virtual communities to test their hypotheses across a larger body of data than has ever been possible.

The field of linguistics is at a crossroads where it has a choice between two possible futures. The enormous quantity of materials on the new digital playing field could either hold the promise of unprecedented access to interoperable information, or, the specter of unparalleled frustration and confusion as the materials fail to interoperate. The outcome will depend on how we choose to act — whether we act in community in order to define and follow common standards of practice that will make it possible to index and search the wealth of materials, or, act in isolation so as to proliferate idiosyncratic practices that will make it impossible to find and compare resources. In the end, achieving the ultimate vision of unprecedented access to information will require defining and following standards. This essay focuses on the role of standards in achieving the vision; elsewhere I have given a sketch of what the cyberinfrastructure for linguistics might look like (Simons 2007).

2. Life without standards

The average linguist does not immediately warm up to the idea of standards. After all, one makes a mark in the world of academics by demonstrating the uniqueness of one's contribution, not by being like every one else. Thus we face an up hill battle in convincing linguists that standards are a good idea.

In fact, standards are an indispensable aspect of every day life. When we transact business in the marketplace, we are relying on federally set standards for weights and measures and for the regulation of money. When we switch on a light in the office, we are taking advantage of standards that specify the mating of bulbs with light sockets and of plugs with wall sockets, that govern the wiring of light fixtures to switches and the source of power outside the building, and that regulate the wider power grid for moving electricity from suppliers to consumers on a regional scale. When we perform a web search with Google, we are depending on a host of standards covering issues like physical connections between machines, addressing of internet nodes, transmission of data as signals on physical lines, execution of transmissions as a sequence of logical packets, reliable reassembly of those packets, formats for representing different types of information, schemes for encoding characters, and more. All the standards mentioned in this paragraph are things we simply take for granted. We will know that we have arrived in the twenty-first century of linguistics when the standards needed to achieve the vision described in section 1 are also taken for granted.

It is instructive to consider an example of life without standards. In medieval times (and earlier), the time was regulated by the position of the sun in relation to the individual's position on earth. Noon was defined as the moment when the sun was directly overhead. This standard worked fine as long as wind and muscle power constrained the distance that could be traveled in a day. But the advent of train travel in the nineteenth century changed all of that. In the most populated latitudes of North America, the earth rotates at a rate of twelve and a half miles a minute (Blaise 2000: 30). Thus rail passengers could journey 100 miles in a couple hours, only to find that their pocket watches were eight minutes off when they arrived.

Today it is hard for us to imagine life without standard time, but just 150 years ago in North America there were 144 official times based on local solar noon (Blaise 2000: 34). The rail network grew up in this context; each railroad set and published its schedules in terms of the official time of its headquarters, rather than of the city in which the train was stopping. Thus in a station that serviced more than one railroad, it was simultaneously a different time on each road (Blaise 2000: 70). Rail passengers had to travel with a big book of time conversions in order to plan their connections, and it was still easy to miscalculate and miss the train. What's worse, sharing the same tracks among railroads employing different official times could lead to disastrous results — train wrecks were a daily occurrence (Blaise 2000: 72).

These problems were finally solved in 1884 when the nations of the world gathered at the Prime Meridian Conference. In addition to establishing the zero meridian at Greenwich, this conference established the International Date Line and the system of universal time with 24 standard time zones stretching around the globe. For the first time in history, it was possible to answer the question "What time is it?" with a single global answer, rather than with a myriad of local answers.

3. Examples from linguistics

In the world of linguistics, an analogous act of international standardization has just taken place. For millennia, the standard means of identifying languages has been by name. This has worked well when the people communicating are members of the same local community who use the same naming conventions. But languages do not have just one unique name — the preferred name for a language may change over time, the same language may have different names in different languages, and different outsiders may refer to the same language by different names (especially before they learn what the speakers of the language actually call it). Nor do languages have unambiguous names — different languages (in different parts of the world) may have the same name, or a name used for a language may refer to something that is not the language in other contexts.

When we move from the context of a closed local community to the context of an open global community where billions of once isolated information resources are being brought together into a single World Wide Web, we see that using names to identify languages is like using solar time to run the railroads. If we fail to modernize that practice, the passengers of the web will miss the information train when they use just one name to query for a language that has many names, and they will experience an information wreck of global proportions when they use an ambiguous name and retrieve all the irrelevant occurrences on the web mingled with the relevant.

For instance, *Ega* is the name of a language spoken in Côte d'Ivoire, but when searching for "Ega dictionary" in Google one quickly discovers that EGA is an acronym for Enhanced Graphics Adapter and Enterprise Grid Alliance. *Santa Cruz* is the name of a language spoken in Solomon Islands, but searching for "Santa Cruz dictionary" yields descriptions of a city in California and other places around the world that bear the same name. *She* is the name of a language in China, but searching for "She dictionary" uncovers the *Woman-Speak Dictionary* among other things.

Joseph Grimes anticipated this kind of problem over 30 years ago when he developed the database for managing the *Ethnologue*, a comprehensive reference work listing all known languages of the world — the most recent edition identifies 6,912 living languages (Gordon 2005). As Grimes explained at the time: "Each language is given a three-letter code on the order of international airport codes. This aids in equating languages across national boundaries, where the same language may be called by different names, and in distinguishing different languages called by the same name" (Grimes 1974:i). These three-letter codes became widely known when the *Ethnologue* was published on the web and became a *de facto* standard for groups like the Open Language Archives Community that needed unique identifiers for all known languages in order to catalog their collections of language resources (Simons 2000, 2002b; Bird and Simons 2003).

In 2002 a subcommittee of the International Organization for Standardization (specifically TC37/SC2) formally invited SIL International to prepare a new standard that would reconcile the complete set of codes used in the *Ethnologue* with the approximately 400 codes already in use in the earlier ISO standard for language identification. In addition, codes developed by Linguist List to handle ancient and constructed languages were to be incorporated. The result is a standard named ISO 639–3 that provides unique and unambiguous codes for identifying nearly 7,500 languages (ISO 2007). In 2006, the final revision of the standard was successfully submitted to the subscribing national standards bodies for their vote on full adoption, and official publication occurred in February 2007.

Two other examples of information standards for linguistics deserve mention. The first regards standardizing the encoding of characters in textual data. All digital information ultimately reduces to a sequence of binary numbers. In the early days of computing, there was no standard for how to represent writing in a data stream. Each hardware manufacturer developed a different scheme for mapping letters to numbers; it soon became apparent that the resulting impediment to information interchange between computers was not in any company's best interest. The leading manufacturers in the United States therefore got together to work out a common standard and in 1963 ASCII, or the American Standard Code for Information Interchange, was adopted (Brandel 1999). That standard says, for instance, that the number 65 will be used in a digital data stream to represent a capital A, 66 to represent B, and so on. It was elevated to the status of international standard, as ISO 646, in 1972. In all, only 95 printable characters were standardized (upper- and lower-case Roman letters, digits, punctuation, and a few other symbols), but this was enough to launch ubiquitous applications like email and the World Wide Web.

ASCII solved the character encoding problem for English, but what about the other languages of the world? In the ensuing decades, dozens of other character sets were formalized through national and international standards processes. With so many standards in use, however, it was not possible to correctly interpret the numbers into characters without knowing which standard had been followed to encode the information. With the advent of personal computers, linguists jumped on the bandwagon (e.g. Simons 1989) and developed clever system-specific solutions for building their own fonts that would redefine selected characters to meet the requirements of the language they were studying. However, the inevitable train wreck occurred whenever a linguist tried to share data with someone who used a different system, and even worse, when the original creator upgraded to a new system on which the special font solution no longer worked. Linguists began to learn the hard way that one must follow a common standard in order to ensure not only the interchange of information in the present, but also its survival far into the future (Simons 2006). Fortunately, the same problem was plaguing the software industry, so in the late 1980s a group of leading software companies got together to define Unicode — a single standard for encoding the characters in all the major writing systems of the world. The first version was published in 1991 and by the time the next version appeared in 1993 it had attained the status of international standard (as ISO 10646). The current version standardizes the encoding of nearly one hundred thousand characters (Unicode Consortium 2007). Work is on-going to add to the inventory of writing systems and characters that are covered.

The final example I want to mention, GOLD (General Ontology for Linguistic Description), is the brainchild of Langendoen and two of his students (Farrar, Lewis, and Langendoen 2002; Farrar and Langendoen 2003). Inspired by the Semantic Web activity of the World Wide Web Consortium (Berners-Lee and others 2001; Hendler 2003), GOLD seeks to provide a formal description of the concepts (and relationships between concepts) that exist within the problem domain of linguistic description. By mapping the terminology and markup vocabularies used in actual linguistic descriptions to their nearest equivalents in the linguistic ontology, it would become possible to support smart searching for linguistic concepts across a large collection of descriptive materials (Langendoen, Farrar, and Lewis 2002).

Each concept as defined in GOLD is like a standardized time zone — the manifestation of a concept in any given language is like the idiosyncratic solar noon of a particular locality, but by overlooking slight local differences in order to capture the greater similarities it becomes possible for data from disparate sources to operate in a coordinated fashion over the same information processing tracks. For instance, identifying a tense in a particular language with the GOLD concept "Past-Tense" is not saying that it is exactly the same as tenses identified in the same way in other languages, but only that all of them are in the same zone for the purposes of comparison across languages.

One result of Langendoen's early experience with digital standards in linguistics, as first author of chapters in the TEI guidelines about the linguistic analysis of text (Sperberg-McQueen and Burnard 1994: chapters 15, 16, 21), was a conclusion that developing a single prescriptive system of markup for linguistics was not going to work. Thus, as leader of the E-MELD project's work on linguistic markup he conceived of GOLD as a standard for interpreting markup rather than for prescribing it. The approach is to take the descriptive work of linguists (with whatever terminology and markup they originally used), then to formally map the terms and markup into the standardized zones of GOLD, and finally to perform cross-linguistic search across the regularized interpretations (Simons 2002a). Langendoen was part of the team that did proof-of-concept implementation of the approach for search across lexicons from three different languages that were encoded with different markup schemas (Simons and others 2004b) and for search across interlinear glossed texts from seven languages that were originally encoded with different markup schemas and glosses (Simons and others 2004a). Though GOLD (at www.linguistics-ontology.org) is still under development, it holds tremendous promise as a foundational part of the cyberinfrastructure for twenty-first century linguistics — but only if it can become firmly grounded in the community.

4. Metaphors to live by

The general reaction to the notion of standards within the linguistics community is not particularly enthusiastic. Typical reactions run the gamut from wariness to skepticism to hostility. The idea of conforming to standards, it would seem, is counter to the ideal of academic freedom. What can be done to change this perception?

In pondering this problem, I've been inspired by George Lakoff's work on metaphor (Lakoff and Johnson 1980) and its application to contemporary politics (Lakoff 1995, 1996). In the latter work, Lakoff points out that conservatives (with their "strict father" model) have gotten the upper hand over liberals (with their "nurturant parent" model) through the deft use of metaphor in the public discourse. How might metaphor be used to inform the discourse about standards among linguists? What metaphors could linguists live by that would cast standards in a nurturant light rather than a strict one?

I've identified two. The first is "linguistics as community;" it highlights the role of standards in allowing the body of linguists to function as a community. The second, "development as freedom," highlights the role of the shared constraints embodied in standards in freeing the community to develop the riches of knowledge it is seeking. These ideas are developed in the following two sections.

5. Linguistics as community

Science is "an inescapably cooperative, social activity" — so concludes chemist Henry H. Bauer (1992:52) in *Scientific Literacy and the Myth of the Scientific Method*. It is generally believed that the essence of science is the "scientific method," which involves making systematic observations, formulating hypotheses to explain what has been observed, and then validating or invalidating those hypotheses through further observation. Bauer observes that although the method has a place in science, it does not explain how science really works (Bauer 1992: 19–41). The subfields of science differ in the extent to which they are data-driven or theory-driven, data-rich or data-poor, experimental or observational, quantitative or qualitative, and so on. They are consequently characterized by different methodologies.

Science is best understood, not in terms of a method, but in terms of social activity. Bauer argues that the unity of science derives from a shared commitment to certain kinds of cooperative action. In a chapter named "How science really works," he uses two metaphors to explain the cooperative activities that lie at the heart of science. These metaphors help to shed light on linguistics as a community activity and how standards fit into the picture.

The first metaphor is the jigsaw puzzle (Bauer 1992:42–4; after Polanyi 1962). Doing science is like putting together a large jigsaw puzzle with a group of people. One strategy might be to give each puzzler an equal share of the pieces and have them work independently, but this approach would be doomed to failure since few of the pieces given to any one puzzler would actually fit together. Alternatively, one could give each puzzler a copy of all the pieces, and eventually combine their separate, partial results. This approach at least has a chance of completing the puzzle, but would lead to large-scale duplication of effort and may not be significantly faster than a single puzzler working in ideal conditions.

The only effective way to put multiple puzzlers to work at once is to have them all work together on a single copy of the puzzle in sight of each other. In this way, as one puzzler fits in one more piece, all the others will see the resulting state of the puzzle and will potentially adjust their next step in response to the new state. These puzzlers take individual initiative in determining what part of the puzzle they will work on and how they will go about doing it. The result of the adjustment and self-coordination that occurs as they observe the outcomes achieved by their fellows is a joint achievement that could not be equaled by any single puzzler working in isolation.

When we apply this metaphor to the puzzle of human language, we see that it is a huge puzzle indeed — in fact, the number of pieces is unbounded (Langendoen and Postal 1984). There are tens of thousands of people around the world who are working professionally on this puzzle; countless others are interested in observing and even contributing, especially native speakers of the languages being described. The Internet offers the potential — for the first time in history — for all of the puzzlers to see all the available pieces and to watch each other as they fit them together; Simons (2007) sketches a vision of what such a cyberinfrastructure might look like.

The challenge is for the community to align its practices so as to make that potential into a reality, and standards are a key part of achieving such alignment. A standard like Unicode (for character encoding) is needed so that every puzzler who looks at a particular piece sees the same thing. A standard like ISO 639–3 (for language identification) is needed so that the puzzlers interested in a particular language can locate all the relevant pieces. A standard like GOLD (for identifying the concepts used in linguistic description) is needed so that the puzzlers interested in a particular linguistic phenomenon can locate all the relevant pieces. In order to encode the puzzle pieces for digital interoperation, we also need standard ways of representing common linguistic data types (like lexicons, interlinear glossed texts, paradigms, recordings with time-aligned transcription, and even descriptive write-ups). Without all these standards, linguistic practice in the Internet age cannot be community-wide and community-based, but will resemble the scenarios in which individual puzzlers work separately or in small groups.

The second metaphor is that of the filter (Bauer 1992: 44–8). The process by which a scientific community generates scientific knowledge is like a process of putting ideas through a multistage filter. Each stage is manifest by social institutions that the scientific community has developed over time. The first stage is undergraduate and graduate training in which aspiring scientists learn to align their thinking and behavior with the norms of a particular scientific community. The second stage is research, or frontier science, in which a vast array of ideas get formed and tested. But the array of ideas is not unconstrained; the institution of grant funding (with its attendant mechanisms of proposal writing and peer review) serve to limit those ideas that actually get worked on. The results of research cannot contribute toward scientific knowledge until they enter the third stage, namely, the primary literature. Here the key institutions are conferences and journals and the primary mechanisms are peer review and editing. The review process serves not only to filter out poor work but also to ensure that authors frame their ideas in light of established knowledge.

The fact that an idea is published does not make it scientific knowledge; it just makes it widely available. The next stage in the filter is for published ideas to be tested and used by others. In the process some ideas will ultimately be rejected by the community; others will be refined and extended and eventually make their way into the secondary literature of review articles, monographs, and graduate-level textbooks. After the passage of even more time and testing, we reach the final stage of textbook science in which the consensus of the community gets expressed as scientific knowledge in undergraduate textbooks. But even textbook knowledge is never completely correct, and it slowly changes over time as newer discoveries eventually make their way to the bottom of the knowledge filter.

The filter metaphor helps us to understand the rightful place of standards like ISO 639–3 and GOLD within the linguistics community. They are meant to be a formalization of current textbook knowledge. As Langendoen (personal communication) is fond of saying with respect to GOLD, "We aren't trying to make the search engine into an expert linguist; we are just trying to bring it up to the level of an undergraduate student in linguistics." This means that researchers working on the frontier of a particular issue would always see something in a relevant standard that they would want to change, while the parts of the standard in which they are not expert would look okay to them. Standards will never align fully with frontier knowledge. They are necessarily slow to change, evolving only as knowledge works its way through the multistage filter to become the shared consensus of the community. In the meantime, even if a standard proves to be incorrect on a particular point, it has served its purpose in enabling the global community to organize and share its knowledge in a consistent and repeatable way.

6.   Development as freedom

Freedom in the pursuit of knowledge is a high ideal within the halls of academe. As a doctrine of higher education, academic freedom is defined more narrowly as "the ability to teach, research, and write without fear of repercussion because the subject or conclusions are considered unacceptable by other faculty, administration, community organizations, state or local governments or religious groups" (Kant 2004). Nevertheless, the doctrine may at times be invoked more broadly to embody the notion of intellectual independence, which can in turn lie behind the eschewal of standards that would constrain one's approach to research and writing. But, in fact, such standards are commonplace in academics — each institution involved in the knowledge filter (including every funding agency, journal, and book publisher) imposes standards that define its operation and thereby constrain participation.

Every community requires constraints on the behavior of its members. While the ability to do whatever one wishes may seem like the ultimate of freedom, in fact the resulting anarchy leads to anything but freedom in the end. As Jean-Jacques Rousseau, the great social theorist of the eighteenth century, concluded: "The mere impulse of appetite is slavery, while obedience to a law which we prescribe to ourselves is liberty" (Rousseau 1762, chapter 8).

This paradox of freedom through constraint should make sense to linguists, of all people, since this principle lies at the very heart of language. What is it that empowers the free interchange of ideas between two people who speak the same language? It is mutual conformance to a shared system of constraints. In any particular language, all the vocal sounds that are humanly possible are constrained to just a few score that are used in that language. Sound patterns constrain the manner in which sounds combine to form the sequences that are actually possible in the language. Lexical associations of form with meaning further constrain the set of minimal sound sequences to those that actually mean something. Finally, rules of grammar constrain the manner in which those minimal meaningful sequences combine to express larger thoughts. In fact, entire theories of language, such as Optimality Theory (Archangeli and Langendoen 1997), account for the surface forms in language in terms of constraint satisfaction. In the final analysis, it is the use of a shared system of constraints (or, a standard) that gives a speech community the freedom to communicate.

A shared system of constraints is what the linguistics community needs in order to develop the freedom it is ultimately looking for. The metaphor of "development as freedom" comes from the book of that title by the Nobel-prize winning economist Amartya Sen (1999). Whereas economists typically focus on issues like GNP growth or industrialization, Sen has distinguished himself by focusing on the social aspects of economic development. He argues that social development (including enhanced literacy, better health care, the empowerment of women, and the free flow of information) is the principal means of economic development. The expansion of such freedoms should also be the primary end of development, and as that end is achieved, it becomes the means for even further development.

What is the analogue of economic development for the linguistics community? The wealth of the community is its information. As linguists, we want to build an ever growing body of primary data encompassing every known human language. We want to analyze that documentary material to develop an ever growing body of secondary, descriptive data (Himmelmann 1998). We then want to mine that body of data about individual languages to build an ever growing body of frontier knowledge about the workings of language in general, and ultimately to refine that body of frontier knowledge to build an ever growing body of textbook knowledge on language and linguistics. Maximal freedom and wealth for a linguist would be to have all such known data and knowledge at one's fingertips in a form that could be queried and compared and repurposed. To achieve this we will need to embrace a full set of standards that will allow us to align all the puzzle pieces as discussed in the previous section.

Another concept that is central to Sen's work is that of individual agency — the ability to set and pursue one's own goals and interests. He argues that "development consists of the removal of various types of unfreedoms that leave people with little choice and little opportunity of exercising their reasoned agency" (Sen 1999:xii). If the ultimate goal of linguists is to participate in putting together the enormous puzzle of human language, and if the optimal approach is for each linguist to be able to see all the pieces and the progress being made by all other linguists, then what are the unfreedoms that prevent linguists from exercising their agency within this enterprise? For some it is still a lack of access to the web infrastructure for global collaboration. This is a problem whose solution lies outside the scope of the linguistics community; fortunately, the world around us is tackling this problem. For the linguists who do have access to the web, the unfreedoms are lack of access to information at all (because it is not in a digital form), inability to find relevant digital information (because it is not catalogued in a standardized way), and inability to compare information across languages (because it is not formatted in a standardized way or does not use shared terminology). The antidote to these unfreedoms is the development of standards within the community — shared constraints that will empower individuals to both contribute to and benefit from the information riches of the community.

7. Conclusion

Following community-wide standards involves good news and bad news. The bad news is that there will be times when the details of a standard lag behind the best current knowledge and will thus prevent linguists from being able to express what they really want to record in their digital data. However, the good news is that when a plethora of idiosyncratic practices gives way to one universally-shared practice, linguists will gain the freedom to access the global riches of information

248 Gary F. Simons

about languages and linguistics. It is the promise of this future that is motivating many linguists to participate in the process of developing and refining the standards that will empower us to act in community. When that infrastructure is in place, a new breed of twenty-first century linguists using new processes to collaborate with new players on a new global playing field will be able to achieve things we can only dream about today.

References

Archangeli, D. & Langendoen, D. T. 1997. *Optimality Theory: An Overview.* Oxford: Blackwell.

Bauer, H. H. 1992. *Scientific Literacy and the Myth of the Scientific Method.* Urbana/Chicago IL: University of Illinois Press.

Berners-Lee, T., Hendler, J. & Lassila, O. 2001. The semantic web: A new form of web content that is meaningful to computers will unleash a revolution of new possibilities. *Scientific American* 284(5): 34–43, May 2001. (Online: http://www.scientificamerican.com/article. cfm?articleID=00048144-10D2-1C70-84A9809EC588EF21&catID=2).

Bird, S. & Simons, G. F. 2003. Extending Dublin Core metadata to support the description and discovery of language resources. *Computers and the Humanities* 37: 375–88. (Online preprint: http://arxiv.org/abs/cs.CL/0308022).

Blaise, C. 2000. *Time Lord: Sir Sandford Fleming and the Creation of Standard Time.* New York NY: Pantheon Books.

Brandel, M. 1999. 1963: ASCII debuts. *Computerworld,* 12 April 1999. (Online: http://web.archive.org/web/*/http://www.computerworld.com/news/1999/story/0,11280,35241,00. html).

Farrar, S. & Langendoen, D. T. 2003. A linguistic ontology for the semantic web. *GLOT International* 7(3): 97–100. (Online: http://emeld.org/documents/GLOT-LinguisticOntology. pdf).

Farrar, S., Lewis, W. D. & Langendoen, D. T. 2002. An ontology for linguistic annotation, *Semantic Web Meets Language Resources.* In *Papers from the AAAI Workshop (Technical Report WS-02-16),* 11–19. Menlo Park CA: AAAI Press. (Online preprint: http://emeld.org/documents/AAAI-OntologyLinguisticAnnotation.pdf)

Friedman, T. L. 2005. *The World is Flat: A Brief History of the Twenty-First Century.* New York NY: Farrar, Straus, and Giroux.

Gordon, R. G., Jr. (ed.). 2005. *Ethnologue: Languages of the World,* 15th edn. Dallas TX: SIL International. (Online version: http://www.ethnologue.com/).

Grimes, J. E. 1974. *Word Lists and Languages* [Technical Report No. 2]. Ithaca NY: Department of Modern Languages and Linguistics, Cornell University.

Hendler, J. 2003. Science and the semantic web. *Science,* 24 January 2003, 520–1. (Online: http:// www.sciencemag.org/cgi/content/full/299/5606/520?ijkey=1BUgJQXW4nU7Q&keytype =ref&siteid=sci).

Himmelmann, N. 1998. Documentary and descriptive linguistics. *Linguistics* 36: 165–91. (Online preprint: http://corpus.linguistics.berkeley.edu/~ling240/himmelmann.pdf).

ISO, 2007. *ISO 639–3: 2007: Codes for the Representation of Names of Languages,* Part 3, *Alpha-3 Code for Comprehensive Coverage of Languages.* Geneva: International Organization for

Standardization. (http://www.iso.org/iso/en/CatalogueDetailPage.CatalogueDetail?CS-NUMBER=39534. Registration authority: http://www.sil.org/iso639-3/).

Kant, C. 2004. AAUP and academic freedom: A history. *The Alliance,* December 2004, page 1. Nevada Faculty Alliance. (Online: http://www.aaup.org/Com-a/Kantart.htm).

Lakoff, G. & Johnson, M. 1980. *Metaphors We Live by.* Chicago IL: University of Chicago Press.

Lakoff, G. 1995. Metaphor, morality, and politics, or, why conservatives have left liberals in the dust. In *Webster's World of Cultural Democracy.* Seattle WA: The World Wide Web center of The Institute for Cultural Democracy. (Online: http://www.wwcd.org/issues/Lakoff.html).

Lakoff, G. 1996. *Moral Politics: What Conservatives Know that Liberals Don't.* Chicago IL: University of Chicago Press.

Langendoen, D. T. & Postal, P. M. 1984. *The Vastness of Natural Languages.* Oxford: Basil Blackwell.

Langendoen, D. T., Farrar, S. & Lewis, W. D. 2002. Bridging the markup gap: Smart search engines for language researchers. In *Proceedings of the Workshop on Resources and Tools for Field Linguistics, Third International Conference on Language Resources and Evaluation (26–7 May 2002, Las Palmas, Canary Islands, Spain),* 24–1 to 24–9.

Polanyi, M. 1962. The republic of science: Its political and economic theory. *Minerva* 1: 54–73.

Rousseau, J.-J. 1762. *The Social Contract, or, Principles of Political Right.* Translated by G. D. H. Cole. (Web edition by the Constitution Society. Online: http://www.constitution.org/jjr/socon.htm).

Sen, A. 1999. *Development as Freedom.* New York NY: Anchor Books.

Simons, G. F. 1989. Working with special characters. In *Laptop Publishing for the Field Linguist: An Approach Based on Microsoft Word,* P. M. Kew & G. F. Simons (eds), 103–18. Dallas TX: Summer Institute of Linguistics.

Simons, G. F. 2000. Language identification in metadata descriptions of language archive holdings. In *Proceedings of the Workshop on Web-based Language Documentation and Description (12–15 December 2002, Philadelphia, PA),* 274–82. (Online: http://www.ldc.upenn.edu/exploration/expl2000/papers/simons/simons.htm).

Simons, G. F. 2002a. The electronic encoding of lexical resources: A roadmap to best practice, *E-MELD Workshop on Digitizing Lexical Information,* 2–5 August 2002, Ypsilanti MI. (Online: http://www.emeld.org/documents/roadmap.htm).

Simons, G. F. 2002b. SIL three-letter codes for identifying languages: Migrating from in-house standard to community standard. In *Proceedings of the Workshop on Resources in Tools and Field Linguistic, Third International Conference on Language Resources and Evaluation (26–7 May 2002, Las Palmas, Canary Islands, Spain),* 22.1–8. (Online preprint: http://www.sil.org/~simonsg/preprint/SIL language codes.pdf).

Simons, G. F. 2006. Ensuring that digital data last: The priority of archival form over working form and presentation form. *SIL Electronic Working Papers* 2006–003. (Online: http://www.sil.org/silewp/abstract.asp?ref=2006-003).

Simons, G. F. 2007. Doing linguistics in the twenty-first century: Interoperation and the quest for the global riches of knowledge. In *Proceedings of the E-MELD/DTS-L Workshop: Toward the Interoperability of Language Resources,* 13–15 July 2007, Palo Alto CA. (Online: http://linguistlist.org/tilr/papers/TILR Plenary.pdf).

Simons, G. F., Fitzsimons, B., Langendoen, D. T., Lewis, W. D., Farrar, S. O., Lanham, A., Basham, R. & Gonzalez, H. 2004a. A model for interoperability: XML documents as an RDF database. In *Proceedings of the E-MELD Workshop on Linguistic Databases and Best Practice,* 15–18 July 2004, Detroit MI. (Online: http://emeld.org/workshop/2004/simons-paper.pdf)

Simons, G. F., Lewis, W. D., Farrar, S. O., Langendoen, D. T., Fitzsimons, B. & Gonzalez, H. 2004b. The semantics of markup: Mapping legacy markup schemas to a common semantics. In *Proceedings of the 4th Workshop on NLP and XML (NLPXML-2004)*, G. Wilcock, N. Ide & L. Romary, 25–32. Association for Computational Linguistics. (Online preprint: http://emeld.org/documents/SOMFinal1col.pdf).

Sperberg-McQueen, C. M. & Burnard, L. (eds). 1994. *Guidelines for the Encoding and Interchange of Machine-readable Texts*. Chicago IL & Oxford: Text Encoding Initiative. (Online: http://www.tei-c.org/Guidelines2/).

Unicode Consortium. 2007. *The Unicode Standard, Version 5.0*. Boston MA: Addison-Wesley. (Online version: http://www.unicode.org/versions/Unicode5.0.0/).

CHAPTER 13

Sherwin Cody's school of English*

Edwin L. Battistella
Southern Oregon University

In this chapter Sherwin Cody's well-known correspondence course is analyzed within a historical context and according to the norms of the early part of the 20th century. Details of the course are summarized, and several notable examples are given concerning the prescriptive rules for pronunciation, practical grammar, and grammatical correctness. The course itself and aspects of the successful marketing campaign are discussed. Cody's prescriptivist and descriptivist approaches are evaluated according to early 20th-century society; it is argued that Cody's course was influenced by several, sometimes opposing, factors. The views of language experts of the day, including educators and linguists, are taken into account.

1. Introduction

Americans have always viewed skill in English as a means to financial and social success. In the 1800s many people relied on linguistic self-study through grammars, dictionaries and etiquette books. Even in the early 1900s as the work force was becoming more corporate and industrial, there were still relatively few Americans who completed high school. One result was that business education came to the forefront and publishers developed practical guides for speaking and writing. The most famous of these was Sherwin Cody's *100% Self-Correcting Course in the English*, a correspondence course taken by over 150,000 people in the years from 1918 to 1959. Cody's was one of the most durable courses and involved one of the longest-lasting print advertising campaigns of all time, an ad illustrated by Cody asking readers "Do You Make These Mistakes in English?" This essay looks briefly at Sherwin Cody's famous course and the ways in which he was engaged with linguistic issues of the day.

---

* This research benefited from a National Endowment for the Humanities summer research stipend, and from the help from a number of individuals, including Peter M. Cody of Maryland, Professor Gabrielle Hamilton Cody of New York, Aldus M. Cody of Florida, Rutgers University professor Carter A. Daniel and Anna Beauchamp of the Lenn and Dixie Hannon Library at Southern Oregon University. For a book-length study of Sherwin Cody, see my *Do You Make These Mistakes in English?* (Oxford University Press, 2008).

2. Sherwin Cody

In the 1890s, Sherwin Cody was working as a school-book publisher and a reporter for the *Chicago Tribune*. Correspondence education was coming into vogue at the newly-formed University of Chicago headed by William Rainey Harper, and the *Tribune* was offering home study courses as well. Cody, an Amherst College graduate, was put to work on a course on English. Of about a hundred courses offered by the *Tribune*, only two had any success, Cody's course and another one on bookkeeping, and Cody got the idea of republishing his course as a set of pocket-sized books called the *Art of Writing and Speaking the English Language*. With advertisements in magazines like *The System*, Cody's series sold well and he complemented it with a series of books on marketing, advertising and business practices. By 1910 he had nearly 100 publications to his credit and was becoming known in the American mid-west as a prolific writer of practical English books.

Cody was also involved in the efficiency movement in the American public schools. In 1915 he founded an organization called the National Associated Schools of Scientific Business to promote graduation standards in basic business skills and he began to develop a series of National Ability Tests that went along with the standards. He promoted the National Ability Tests as measuring the ability "to perform common operations in the business office" and as benchmarks for "the fundamental education which all office employment presupposes" (1919: 12). When the Gary, Indiana, school system hired superintendent William Wirt to reform their schools, Cody found an opportunity to test his ideas. In the spring of 1917 he piloted a grammar curriculum for about 1,000 students in both Gary and Racine, measuring improvement in spelling, grammar and punctuation. After about five weeks of drill, Cody found a 40–50% reduction in the number of errors (1919: 208). Cody later offered the tests in New York schools as well, and long after interest in Wirt's reforms had faded, Cody's experiences with the Gary schools would remain a running theme in his advertisements.

If students and workers were going to be tested for grammar and business ability, they would need efficient study materials. Here is where Cody's earlier work on speaking and writing the English language came in. The prospect of a correspondence version of his earlier English course developed from the idea that testing methods could be applied to English self-instruction. Cody's approach was to provide a system of grammar that was as simple and efficient as possible and that used examples and quizzes rather than theory to help students to overcome individual errors. For Cody, the course was part of his entrepreneurial vision as well. It would not only provide students with what they needed to speak and write appropriately, but would help them prepare for his National Ability Tests.

3. An advertisement that never changed

Part of the success of the *100% Self-Correcting Course* was due to the "Do You Make These Mistakes in English?" advertisement, and it is worth taking a closer look at its appeal. In a book called *How to Deal with Human Nature in Business*, Cody had suggested that "There is but one sane, salesmanlike way to begin a selling letter, and that is with the customer and his needs, his troubles, his fight for life and success." (1915:200). Cody's classic ad "Do You Make These Mistakes in English," was crafted by legendary ad man Maxwell Sackheim and the account later passed on to Sackheim's protégé Victor Schwab, who took particular pride in it as an example of the scientific approach to advertising. In an article for the industry journal *Printer's Ink Monthly*, Schwab referred to it as "An Advertisement That is Never Changed." Schwab's article gave a ten-year comparison of responses to the same ad with two different headlines—"Do You Make These Mistakes in English?" and "How to Speak and Write Masterly English." Schwab found that the cost-per-inquiry and the response rate were much better for the ad that asked speakers about their mistakes and offered an implied lesson.

Schwab emphasized the signature headline—"Do You Make These Mistakes in English?" It essentially offered a free lesson in English, by promising to explain *these mistakes in English*. The word *you* focused on the reader's needs rather than on Cody or the product, the word *mistakes* appealed the reader's insecurity, and, modified by *these*, implied specifics that would help readers to decide whether they need the product. Even the generality of the word *English*, as opposed to alternatives like *grammar*, *writing* or *speaking*, was designed so that readers could connect the headline with their own weaknesses.

The typical Cody ad copy led with examples of errors in English. Some were spelling and grammatical items while others were more esoteric (such as the claim that people should say "Have you heard from him today?" rather than "Did you hear from him today?"). The ad guided the reader along, moving from why people make mistakes, to Cody's credentials and the efficiency of the method and the results, and finally to action. It explained that Sherwin Cody discovered why people make mistakes by "scientific tests, which he gave thousands of times," and it assigned institutional blame to the schools. Shifting to the positive, the ad promised to be based in practice not rules, recounted Cody's successes in Gary to establish his credentials, and again invoked exclusivity in the form of the patented 100% self-correcting device.

The Cody ad ran widely, appearing in pulps, in glossy magazines and in the Sunday newspaper book reviews and magazine supplements. Cody's ads began appearing in the *New York Times* in 1919, and ran two or three times a year until

Figure 1.

1959, most often as a full-page on the back page of the book review or magazine. The peak years of *Times* advertising for Cody were the 1920s and 1930s. By the 1940s, ads were being run just three times a year and in the 1950s just twice a year, typically as school terms were beginning. Together with the Harvard Classics, the Book-of-the-Month Club, *The Book of Etiquette*, and *How to Win Friends and Influence People*, Cody's work stressed a transformational kind of self-improvement which encouraged consumers to improve themselves by developing the reading, language and interpersonal skills and habits of the successful.

Cody's audience included both those in the workplace and in the social world. He asked, "How can a carpenter, a machinist, a factory worker, use the English language to get ahead?" But he also gave the example of a newly-rich woman whose "murderous English" reveals her lack of education (1929:3–4). Cody linked slang, cursing, poor pronunciation and bad grammar with a lack of breeding and he invoked human nature to explain what happens if you don't try to improve your English. "How," he asked, "can anyone be other than critical of a person who does not seek to improve himself?" (1929:14)

4. The Cody course

For about $30, students received the full *The Sherwin Cody 100% Self-Correcting Course in English Language*—in 25 weekly installments. The weekly lessons were divided into five parts, one for each day of the workweek. Expression was on Mondays, spelling on Tuesdays, punctuation on Wednesdays, grammar on Thursdays, and conversation and reading on Fridays. The daily lessons were tied to other reference books by Cody: *Success in Letter Writing* was a reference for lessons in expression, *The Art of Speaking and Writing the English Language* and a book called *Brief Fundamentals* provided background on punctuation and grammar, and the Nutshell Library served as the supplementary text for conversation and reading. The basic plan of the course was for students to focus on the areas in which they had particular weaknesses. This entailed an assessment component—a self-test—and so lessons 1 and 25 included timed tests to allow students to see what they knew at the outset and what they had learned by the end of the course.

Cody's approach focused on proficiencies rather than content and reflected his interest in business testing, but it was also connected the philosophy of advertising that was so much a part of his thinking. A good English course, like a good advertisement or business letter, took the needs of the audience into account, and the most efficient way to do this, in Cody's view, was by guided self-assessment and self-correction.

The Tuesday through Thursday lessons focused on practical grammar and relied on various techniques—fill in the blank, choice among two forms, and even actual composition. The constant was Cody's avoidance of theory, definitions and lists of rules to memorize. The Tuesday lessons on pronunciation and spelling began with the difference between vowels and consonants and with an explanation of the syllable. Cody's definitions are understandable, though unsophisticated. Vowels are "the real sound letters" and consonants are sounds "which merely modify the vowels." The syllable, in turn, is "one vowel sound with consonants that can be pronounced with it" (1918: Lesson 2). Difficult pronunciations were also a Tuesday theme. Cody provided help on the pronunciation shibboleths of the day, especially spelling pronunciations or words that might mark someone as provincial. He noted that *Concord* should be pronounced *cong kerd*, not *con-cŏrd* and that *blackguard* is *blag gard* not *black-guard*. He warned against pronouncing *devil* and *evil* with the last syllable as *ill*, against pronouncing *iron* as *ī'ron* and *England* as *eng-land* (preferring *ing gland*). He indicated a length distinction between *there* and *their* as *thar* and *thār* and distinguished the pronunciation of *shone* and *shown*, as *shon* and *shōn* (1918: Lessons 4, 17, 13, 15). Cody included some general comments about American speech, criticizing the tendency of Americans "to pronounce all their syllables with great exactness." He cautioned therefore that "The largest number of mispronunciations comes from trying to enunciate obscure vowels accurately, as *or* at the end of *honor, favor, error*, where properly the sound in simply that of *er*."

Cody's discussion also demonstrated his understanding that pronunciation was informed by local standards. When authorities disagree, Cody wrote, students should follow regional fashion "if that fashion is recognized either as first or second choice." Either will be fine, he suggests, as long as a speaker is consistent and "does not make himself conspicuous by adopting a pronunciation that those he associates with will consider pedantic" (1918: Lesson 22). Pronunciation was best when it was colloquial—falling between the speech of vulgar and the pedantic and just as Cody warned against unrefined pronunciation, he also reminded readers that the pronunciations of *ask* with *ah* is an affectation. Implied in his advice is the understanding that speakers ought to meet the expectations of their audience, along with an increasing understanding of audience as neither unrefined nor over-refined.

Wednesdays dealt with punctuation: capitals, apostrophes, colons, semicolons, and even dashes and parentheses—which Cody cautioned against overusing. The main focus in punctuation, however, was on the use of the comma, which he saw as "nine-tenths of punctuation" (1918, Lesson 4). He gave comma rules for compound sentences versus compound predicates, for subordinate clauses, for nonrestrictive modifiers, for words and phrases in series, and for dates, addresses, and

Chapter 13. Sherwin Cody's school of English **257**

quotes. Cody's method was inductive rather than deductive—teaching punctuation by examples and exercises rather than rules and avoiding grammatical terminology. Punctuation, Cody thought, was a matter of usage that grew with experience as a reader and writer, not something than could be reduced to rule. In his *New Art of Writing and Speaking the English Language*, Cody was explicit about this, writing that "punctuation is as much an art as the choice and use of words. It is really a part of composition, for it is one means of attaining clearness and emphasis" (1938:75).

In the Thursday lessons on grammar, Cody shifted back from principles of composition to rules of grammar and the practical question of grammatical correctness. Lesson One was a self-assessment testing broad points of usage including agreement, verb forms, modification, pronouns, determiners, adjective and adverbs. Cody included fairly straightforward verb form errors such as *The bird has (broke–broken) its wing*, but tested less obvious verb agreement as well—to noun phrases quantified by *each* and *every*, to disjunctions (*The woman or the tiger*), and to corporate entities like *Montgomery Ward*. Cody also included a check of the agreement of the determiner with the head of the noun phrase (*that kind–those kind*) and of verbs between clauses such as *It had happened before I (saw–had seen) him*.

Other points of grammar were also tested, such as the distinction between objective and possessive case with gerunds, as in *What do you think of (me–my) going to town?* Cody quizzed students with examples of misplaced modification as well, asking them to select between *While sitting on my doorstep, a beautiful butterfly caught my eye* and *While sitting on my doorstep, I caught sight of a beautiful butterfly*. And finally, the self-test included questions distinguishing adverb and adjective forms such as *He feels (bad–badly) about it*. With a self-assessment as background, students began grammar lessons in week two. These started with the identification of basic elements such as subjects and predicates and with the identification of the nominative and accusative cases of pronouns. Cody's advice was often prescriptive, but he also frequently acknowledged language change and he consistently recommended colloquial usage to the extent that he deemed it respectable and reputable. For example, the note associated with *Whom will the paper be read by?* treated *whom* as awkward and pedantic and Cody suggested the alternatives *By whom will the paper be read?* or *Who is it the paper will be read by?* (1918, Lesson 3). Discussing *none*, Cody suggested that speakers not be misled by the etymology (derivation from *no one*), but rather follow the meaning of the noun phrase, and in Lesson 8, he gave 25 examples of the use of *none* to illustrate its variability, including *None of the men of our day (speaks–speak) so clearly as Wilson* and *None of the Fifth Regiment (were–was) wounded*. Cody elaborated on his reasoning in the *New Art of Writing and Speaking the English Language*, explaining that "In the past some critics have contended that *none* is always singular, since it is evidently derived from by a contraction of *no one*, but the best writers treat *none* as either singular or plural according as the writing is thinking of the last person or the last group of persons" (1938:32). And in the *New Art*, Cody commented on the "myth that the infinitive should not be 'split'" and the rule about not ending a sentence with a preposition, which "seems to have lasted far beyond its period of usefulness" (1938:49, 51).

Cody was however often dismissive of stigmatized forms. In Lesson 1 for example, he remarked that "'Ain't' is never a proper word to use." He gives the self-test item *I am going to have a piece of cake (ain't–aren't–what) I?* and rejects all of the options in favor of *am I not?* He was prescriptive as well in his discussion of the possessive, advocating its use for only for verbal nouns and for animate possessors (1918: Lesson 19). He gave the prescriptive rules for *will* and *shall* as well, writing that "In ordinary statements of fact in future time, use *shall* after *I* and *we*, *will* after other subjects. ... But if there is determination, of an exercise of will, reverse the ordinary usage, and say I or we *will*, you he, etc. *shall.*" Cody tempered this with a nod to usage for *should* and *would*, telling students to follow the same rules as for *shall* and *will*, "but observe that *would* after *I* and *we* is commoner than *will*" (1918: Lesson 14).

5.   Prescriptive or descriptive?

Cody was sometimes descriptive and sometimes prescriptive, but was above all a practical grammarian who wanted to help his students avoid error. He also emphasized that "'authority' in grammar is an old-fashioned but very poor thing to appeal to as compared with reason" (1918: Lesson 21). Like all practical grammarians, Cody had to balance the reality of language change with importance of norms, and he advised that it was sometimes better to be ungrammatical than rigidly proper. "Language exists for ideas," he said in Lesson 23, "not ideas for language" and the study of grammar is mainly to avoid the situation when the effect of language is lost because readers stop to criticize its form.

Cody's sentiments on language and grammar ran parallel to those of modern linguists. For linguists, standard language is a social construct rather than a unique medium for good thought, morals, and culture, and the view of grammar as a social necessity is one that Cody endorsed repeatedly. In *Commercial Tests and How to Use Them*, for example, Cody wrote that businesses expect employees to follow fashion in language as well as clothing and that one's English "should not be extreme to the point of being pedantic or affected." Rather one should be "correct without attracting attention, and so win the approval of educated people without

Chapter 13. Sherwin Cody's school of English **259**

raising the suspicions of the uneducated." (1919:51). In *The New Art*, Cody commented further on how this viewpoint was a break from the past:

> The standard of correct English usage has changed slowly but steadily since the opening of the twentieth century. In times past, the educational world has felt a necessity for teaching and trying to maintain the formal literary standard, according to which many common colloquial expressions are condemned.... The ordinary person is no longer misled into supposing that his everyday speech should conform to the rules of literary standards. (1938:3)

Cody also argued that teaching grammar as a system of rules was ineffective. In "Scientific Principles in the Teaching of Composition," he wrote that "we are actually teaching innumerable errors—we are condemning as improprieties the fundamental idioms of the language" (1912:162). Cody held to this position throughout his life, reiterating it in his advertisements and in his 1944 *Coaching Children in English*. The National Council of Teachers of English came to a similar conclusion and by 1936 its Curriculum Committee recommended that the teaching of grammar separate from writing be discontinued since there was no evidence that knowledge of grammar was useful (McDavid, *et al.*: 23). The conclusion that teaching grammar separately does not improve writing was sometimes misunderstood as the attempt to eliminate grammar, but this was not Cody's intent, or the intent of modern linguists. Rather, the common theme of Cody's courses and of the NCTE's linguistic researchers was to improve the teaching of grammar, not to eliminate it.

Though Cody embraced the importance of the colloquial standard, his ideas were not part of the academic discourse aimed at teachers, opinion leaders and scholars. Cody wrote primarily for businessmen, for home-study English students, and later for parents, and to the extent that he was noticed, he was dismissed as too practical in orientation or as rigidly prescriptive. In his condemnation of language purists, Sterling Leonard explained that English teachers overlook topics like organization and development in favor of "our weary preoccupation with a hundred mere insignificant conventions of wording and idiom." Noting that teachers were not the only ones misled by purism, Leonard offered a blanket condemnation of manuals of business English, writing that "Even more credulous iterations than ours of their worst misconceived dicta about usage are to be found in newspaper style sheets and in manuals of business English—places above all others where one would naturally look for guides to practically effective expression" (1918:295–6). Much later, Robert A. Hall, Jr., in his *Linguistics and Your Language*, took Cody to task explicitly. Hall began the chapter called "Right vs. Wrong" with a mock Cody ad, saying that: "those who talk or advertise in this way and offer to cure our errors in pronunciation or grammar are simply appealing to our sense of insecurity with regard to our own speech" (1960:9). Hall viewed purism as socially divisive and many prescriptive rules as misguided, and he advocated standardizing changes that had become widespread. At the same time, however, Hall acknowledged the social reality of norms:

> Often enough, we may find we need to change our usage, simply because social and financial success depends on some norm, and our speech is one of the things that will be used as a norm. (1960:29)

The irony of Hall's criticism is that he and Cody shared disdain for pedantic authority and both viewed language as a social and economic tool. In *Commercial Tests and How to Use Them*, for example, Cody had made the same point as Hall though in a more colorful fashion:

> The person who is a good talker and a correct writer will often pass for a college graduate, though only a high school graduate. On the other hand, what contempt people have for college graduates (of whom there are all too many) who can't write a decent letter, or who talk like baseball players, or beauty shop sales girls. (1919:13)

Like the linguists of the day, Cody aimed at giving people an awareness of the social role of language and the tools to be code switchers.

6. Nothing lasts forever

Cody's course was popular through the 1940s. Ads periodically updated the number of students served which grew to 150,000 by 1950. The success of the school was due to several factors, and certainly the advertising industry, the growth of correspondence education and the importance of book culture, magazines and the printed word were key elements. But the most important market condition in Cody's success was the long-standing American anxiety about correctness in language. When the course was sold after Cody's death, its buyer suggested that its decline was because "people don't want to speak good English any more. …. Now no one cares about grammatical errors" (Bart, 1962). Of course people did still care. Less than two years after Cody's death, *Webster's Third New International Dictionary* put the question of usage on the editorial and book review pages, and over the years new generations of grammarians would continue to decry the decline of grammatical standards. While it failed to outlast its originator, Sherwin Cody's course was a project that reflected the interests of average Americans in grammar and language as well as the linguistic perspectives of the first half of the twentieth century.

References

Bart, P. 1962. Advertising slogan is disappearing after forty years. *New York Times*. Feb 14:53.

Cody, S. 1903. *The Art of Writing & Speaking the English Language*. Chicago IL: The Old Greek Press.

Cody, S. 1906. *Success in Letter Writing: Business and Social*. Chicago IL: A.C.McClurg.

Cody, S. 1912. Scientific principles in the teaching of composition. *The English Journal* 1: 161–72.

Cody, S. 1915 *How to Deal with Human Nature in Business*. New York NY & London: Funk & Wagnalls Company.

Cody, S. 1917. *Brief Fundamentals*. Chicago IL: School of English.

Cody, S. 1918. *The Sherwin Cody 100% Self-correcting Course in English Language*. Rochester NY: The Sherwin Cody School of English.

Cody, S. 1919. *Commercial Tests and How to Use Them*. Yonkers-on-Hudson NY: World Book Company.

Cody, S. 1929. *How You Can Master Good English*. Rochester NY: Sherwin Cody School of English.

Cody, S. 1938. *New Art of Writing and Speaking the English Language*. New York NY: Sun Dial Press.

Cody, S. 1944. *Coaching Children in English*. New York NY: Good English Publishers.

Hall, R. 1960. *Linguistics and Your Language*. New York NY: Anchor Books.

Leonard, S. 1918. Old purist junk. *English Journal* 7:295–302.

McDavid, R., Gawthrop, B. Lightner C. M. Meyers D. & Russell, G. (eds). 1965. *An Examination of the Attitudes of the NCTE Toward Language*. Urbana IL: National Council of Teachers of English.

Schwab, V. 1939. An advertisement that is never changed. *Printer's Ink Monthly*, Sept. 1939: 10–11, 64–5.

Index

A
A and only B 16–18
abbreviation 214–16, 218, 220–2, 224
abstractness 91–2, 199, 211
acceptability xiv, 24, 48, 109, 125–7, 131–2, 187
advertising 251–60
agreement xiii, 11–12, 17, 32, 123, 124, 129–33, 135–7, 139, 141–2, 144–9, 257
Alexiadou, Artemis 93, 96–7, 99–102, 105, 107–12, 115
alternation 183, 212, 217, 220, 223, 231
ambiguity 45, 147
American English x, 184, 212
anaphor 4–6, 13, 30, 59, 108
Anderson, Stephen R. 19, 115
antireflexive context 24
approximative xi, 37–8, 40, 43–8, 50, 52
Archangeli, Diana x, xiii, 211, 246
Arg-S-Nominals 104–5
argument position 30, 32
Argument-Structure Nominals (AS-Nominals) 97, 98, 101, 102
articles, indefinite x, 38, 110, 112–13, 182, 190, 227, 231, 245
aspiration 210–12
atelic 108
attraction 124–6
automata xiii, 211, 211, 213, 220
automaton 213, 221–2

B
Baker, Mark 5, 33, 197, 209, 223
Basic Phonological Automaton (BPA) 215
Bender, Emily 93

binding theory 7
Bird and Ellison 211–12, 222
Bird, Steven 63, 163, 211–12, 222–3, 240
Borer, Hagit xiii, 91, 96–100, 103, 105, 107–9, 116
British National Corpus 38, 193
Business education 251

C
C-command 3, 5, 8–10, 12, 22, 27, 29, 32–4
cardinal 37, 43–4, 47–8
Carnie, Andrew 111
case marking xiii, 11, 142, 147
Channell, Joanna 44
children xii–xiv, 16, 122, 146, 153, 155–8, 161, 164–6, 168–70, 172, 179–87, 190–200, 202–3, 229–30
Chomsky and Halle 209, 211, 216
Chomsky, Noam ix, xiii, 4–5, 7, 27, 30, 32, 85, 92–6, 101, 106, 112, 115–16, 122–3, 151–2, 209, 211, 216, 228
Chumash 222
clitic xi, 15, 45–7
Cody, Sherwin x, 251–3, 255–60
collocation 44
Colloquial English, 256, 257, 259
complementation 213–14
Complex Shift 21
compound 45–6, 256
concatenation 213–14, 224
constraint 20, 27–8, 32–3, 56, 64, 68, 74, 80, 113, 158, 210, 221, 223, 246
coordination xi, xii, 121, 122, 151–2, 152–64, 166–72
Correspondence education 252
crossover phenomenon 5
Culy, Chris 223

D
derived subject 13
destructive processes 222
determiner xiv, 73, 108, 114, 141–2, 148, 178, 189–90, 192, 195–200, 257
deterministic 213
disjunctive 37, 39, 75
Distributed Morphology (DM) 101, 112
distributional regularity 212–13
distributional skewing 217
DNs 93–6, 100, 109, 111
do so 102, 108, 152, 158
domain of movement 96
Dutch 51, 137, 141–2, 145–6, 148–9

E
ECM constructions 110
education, English 245, 251–2, 255, 260
Ellison, T. Mark 211–12, 222
endocentric 46
English nominalization 92, 94, 101, 115
event structure 98
exemplar 44
exo-skelatal 98
Extended Projection Principle (EPP) 110

F
faithfulness 210–11, 221, 224
Farrar, Scott O. xiv, 241–2
finite state automata 211, 220
finite state automaton (FSA) 213
finite-state xii, xiii, 211, 222, 224
Finnish 51
flapping 212, 215, 217–20, 222–4
Fongbe 51
free morpheme 45

French 8–9, 18, 27, 32, 48, 104, 137, 201–3, 210, 212
frequency xiv, 177, 179, 181–2, 186–7, 193–5, 199–201, 212
Frozen Structure Argument 95, 110

G
generative phonology 222
generative semantics 58, 91–2, 107
Gerken, LouAnn 177, 196, 197, 201, 202
gerund 92, 111, 257
Golston, Chris 211, 221
Google 38, 103, 236, 238, 240
Grammar x, xi, 123, 158–9
grammatical encoding
grammaticality xiv, 4, 8, 10, 18–19, 23, 29, 32, 102, 106, 109–10, 113, 126, 129, 179, 181, 187
grammaticality judgments
Greenberg, Joseph 37
Grimshaw, Jane 97–9, 105, 115, 191
Gvozdanović, Jadranka, 37

H
Hall, Robert A., Jr. 259–60
Halle, Morris 209, 211, 216
Hammond, Michael, xii, xiii, 211–12, 221
Harley, Heidi x, 91, 93, 96, 101–2, 107, 110, 112–13
harmony 222
Harper, William Rainey 252
Heine, Bernd 37
hierarchical vs. flat structure, 123–6, 128–30, 132, 133
Higginbotham, James 115
Hooper, Joan 211
Hopcroft and Ullman 213–14
HPSG 222
Hurford, James R. 37

I
Idiosyncrasy Argument 94, 101
Internal-Structure Argument 95, 107
intersection 211, 213–14, 220–2, 224

intuitions 60, 64–5, 123, 179
inventory 211–12, 215, 219, 241
inverse reflexive 7, 31–3
Italian 9, 51, 137, 141, 145, 149, 203

J
Jackendoff, Ray 6, 29, 59, 91, 93, 108, 110, 114, 151, 178
Johnson, Douglas 28, 31, 152, 189, 192, 194, 202, 210, 243

K
Kahn, Daniel 212
Kaplan, Ronald 123, 210, 220, 222
Karttunen, Lauri 210–11, 222, 224
Kay, Martin 210, 220, 222
Kayne, Richard S. 48, 152
Klavans, Judith 46
Kleene star 213–14
Kleene, Stephen Cole 213–14
Koskenniemi, Martti 210

L
Lakoff, George 92, 102, 243
Lancaster/IBM Spoken English Corpus 179
Langendoen, D. Terence ix–xi, xii, xiv, 37–9, 91, 151–2, 170–2, 187, 228–9, 231–2, 235, 241–2, 244–6
language acquisition xi, xii, xiv, 151–9, 161, 164, 170, 172, 179, 183, 186–7, 189–90, 192, 194, 201, 228–30
language game 223
language production xiii, 124, 135–7, 139, 155, 172, 187
Lawson, Mark 213
learning 154, 177, 179, 182, 186, 190–5, 198–9, 203, 228–31, 237
Lewis, William D. 241–2
lexical entry 94, 220
lexical redundancy rule 93
lexicalist hypothesis 92–5, 110, 112, 115
lexicon 59, 93, 95, 98, 102, 105, 113, 171, 210–11, 219–21, 230
linguistic self-study/home

study 252
Long-distance reflexives 6
lower bound xii, 39–40, 52, 74

M
markedness 127, 129, 131–2, 136, 145, 210–11, 221, 224
McCarthy, John 223
McCulloch and Pitts 213
measurement 84
metathesis 223
Minimalist Program 91, 97
monostratal 211, 220, 222

N
National Associated Schools of Scientific Business 252
National Council of Teachers of English 259
natural class 212, 215–16
nominal
    argument structure 97
    complex event 97
    derived 93, 97, 101, 110
    eventive -er 105
    gerundive 92–3
    mixed 93, 100, 106, 109, 110, 112
    process 97, 99, 105
    referential 97
    result 97, 99, 100, 101
    zero-derived 113
nominalizations
    derived xiii, 93, 97, 101, 110
    gerundive xiii, 92–3
    mixed xiii, 93, 100, 106, 109, 110, 112
non-deterministic 213
nonlinear representation 221–2
noun phrases 95, 257
Noyer, Rolf 93, 110, 112–13
number, round 38–40, 44
numeral xi, xii, 38–41, 43–8, 50–2
    cardinal xi, xii, 38–41, 44–8, 50–1
    ordinal xi, xii, 38–41, 44–8, 50–1

O
odd (the morpheme), xi, xii, 38–52

Index 265

Optimality Theory (OT) x, xiii, 210, 221, 246
ordinal xi, 41, 46–8
outrank 31, 210
Oxford English Dictionary 38

P
particle 112–14, 193
Particle movement 96, 112
particle shift 112, 114
Pasiego dialect of Montañes Spanish 222–3
passive 9, 11, 13–15, 19, 22, 25, 26, 28, 32, 106, 110, 115, 181, 194, 231
patterns of alternation 212–13
phonological inventory 215
phonology xii–xiii, 56, 194, 210–12, 215–16, 218, 221–2, 224
practical grammar x, 256
prescriptive grammar 251, 257–60
Prince, Alan xiii, 210, 220
Principle A 4–11, 13, 18–20, 27–30, 32, 34
Principle C 5, 8, 27
prosodic morphology 223
prototype 39, 44
punctuation 183, 241, 252, 255–7

Q
quantifier 33–4, 48, 74, 77–8, 84

R
reduplication 26, 51, 223
Referential Nominals (R-Nominals) 97
reflexive xiv, 3–4, 6–34, 171, 171
register, spoken 43, 47, 201
register, written 43, 47, 201

regular expression 213–15
regular language 213–14
relative clauses 159, 179–80, 186, 231
  genitive 159, 179–80, 186, 231
  object 159, 179–80, 186, 231
  object of preposition 159, 179–80, 186, 231
  restrictive 159, 179–80, 186, 231
  subject 159, 179–80, 186, 231
Richness of the Base 221
Right Node Raising (RNR) 21
rule-ordering 210, 224
Russell, Kevin 61, 211, 221–2
Russian 50, 145, 149

S
Sackheim, Maxwell 253
Sag, Ivan 5, 57, 93, 123, 152
(un)salvageable, 20–4, 29, 30
Schwab, Victor 253
Scobbie, James 211, 222
semantic drift 107
Smolensky, Paul xiii, 210, 220
Spanish 137, 178, 212, 222
speech error 138
Spencer, Andrew 46
Stampe, David 211
Steriade, Donca 211
Sterling, Leonard 259
Subject 22, 57, 67
subject–verb agreement 135–7, 139, 141–2, 145–7, 149
subordination xi
suffix xi, 41, 45–9, 51, 93, 101–2, 106, 109, 146, 217, 219, 223
syllable 164, 193, 220, 256
syntax x, xi, xiv, 8, 47, 56, 98, 101–2, 107, 114, 116, 122–3,

132, 153–4, 161, 170–1, 179, 182, 186, 189–91, 230

T
telic 108
telic/atelic distinction 108
Tranel, Bernard 211
transducer 209–11, 220, 222
transduction xiii, 220, 222
Turing, Alan 213
two-level phonology 215
typology 49, 152, 171–2

U
Uniformity Hypothesis 4–5, 20, 22, 26
union 213–14, 219–20, 224
universal 4, 7, 10–11, 32, 152, 158–9, 191, 210–11, 235, 239
  formal 216
  substantive 216, 220
Universality Assumption 4–5, 7, 20, 28
upper bound xi, 39

W
Wachtel, Thomas 44
Walther, Markus 211, 222
Wasow, Thomas 92–3, 112
Wheeler, Deirdre 211, 222
Williams, Edwin 10, 21–2, 27, 29, 46, 57, 74, 104, 111, 114–15, 152
Wirt, William 252
word-formation rules (WFRs) 101

Z
zero-derivation 95, 99, 103

Linguistik Aktuell/Linguistics Today

A complete list of titles in this series can be found on the publishers' website, *www.benjamins.com*

140 **ROEHRS, Dorian:** Demonstratives and Definite Articles as Nominal Auxiliaries. xii, 191 pp. + index. *Expected March 2009*

139 **HICKS, Glyn:** The Derivation of Anaphoric Relations. xii, 306 pp. + index. *Expected February 2009*

138 **SIDDIQI, Daniel:** Syntax within the Word. Economy, allomorphy, and argument selection in Distributed Morphology. xii, 136 pp. + index. *Expected February 2009*

137 **PFAU, Roland:** Grammar as Processor. A Distributed Morphology account of spontaneous speech errors. xiii, 372 pp. *Expected January 2009*

136 **KANDYBOWICZ, Jason:** The Grammar of Repetition. Nupe grammar at the syntax–phonology interface. 2008. xiii, 168 pp.

135 **LEWIS, William D., Simin KARIMI, Heidi HARLEY and Scott O. FARRAR (eds.):** Time and Again. Theoretical perspectives on formal linguistics. In honor of D. Terrence Langendoen. 2008. xiv, 265 pp.

134 **ARMON-LOTEM, Sharon, Gabi DANON and Susan ROTHSTEIN (eds.):** Current Issues in Generative Hebrew Linguistics. 2008. viii, 393 pp.

133 **MACDONALD, Jonathan E.:** The Syntactic Nature of Inner Aspect. A minimalist perspective. 2008. xv, 241 pp.

132 **BIBERAUER, Theresa (ed.):** The Limits of Syntactic Variation. 2008. vii, 521 pp.

131 **DE CAT, Cécile and Katherine DEMUTH (eds.):** The Bantu–Romance Connection. A comparative investigation of verbal agreement, DPs, and information structure. 2008. xix, 355 pp.

130 **KALLULLI, Dalina and Liliane TASMOWSKI (eds.):** Clitic Doubling in the Balkan Languages. 2008. ix, 442 pp.

129 **STURGEON, Anne:** The Left Periphery. The interaction of syntax, pragmatics and prosody in Czech. 2008. xi, 143 pp.

128 **TALEGHANI, Azita H.:** Modality, Aspect and Negation in Persian. 2008. ix, 183 pp.

127 **DURRLEMAN-TAME, Stephanie:** The Syntax of Jamaican Creole. A cartographic perspective. 2008. xii, 190 pp.

126 **SCHÄFER, Florian:** The Syntax of (Anti-)Causatives. External arguments in change-of-state contexts. 2008. xi, 324 pp.

125 **ROTHSTEIN, Björn:** The Perfect Time Span. On the present perfect in German, Swedish and English. 2008. xi, 171 pp.

124 **IHSANE, Tabea:** The Layered DP. Form and meaning of French indefinites. 2008. ix, 260 pp.

123 **STOYANOVA, Marina:** Unique Focus. Languages without multiple wh-questions. 2008. xi, 184 pp.

122 **OOSTERHOF, Albert:** The Semantics of Generics in Dutch and Related Languages. 2008. xviii, 286 pp.

121 **TUNGSETH, Mai Ellin:** Verbal Prepositions and Argument Structure. Path, place and possession in Norwegian. 2008. ix, 187 pp.

120 **ASBURY, Anna, Jakub DOTLAČIL, Berit GEHRKE and Rick NOUWEN (eds.):** Syntax and Semantics of Spatial P. 2008. vi, 416 pp.

119 **FORTUNY, Jordi:** The Emergence of Order in Syntax. 2008. viii, 211 pp.

118 **JÄGER, Agnes:** History of German Negation. 2008. ix, 350 pp.

117 **HAUGEN, Jason D.:** Morphology at the Interfaces. Reduplication and Noun Incorporation in Uto-Aztecan. 2008. xv, 257 pp.

116 **ENDO, Yoshio:** Locality and Information Structure. A cartographic approach to Japanese. 2007. x, 235 pp.

115 **PUTNAM, Michael T.:** Scrambling and the Survive Principle. 2007. x, 216 pp.

114 **LEE-SCHOENFELD, Vera:** Beyond Coherence. The syntax of opacity in German. 2007. viii, 206 pp.

113 **EYTHÓRSSON, Thórhallur (ed.):** Grammatical Change and Linguistic Theory. The Rosendal papers. 2008. vi, 441 pp.

112 **AXEL, Katrin:** Studies on Old High German Syntax. Left sentence periphery, verb placement and verb-second. 2007. xii, 364 pp.

111 **EGUREN, Luis and Olga FERNÁNDEZ SORIANO (eds.):** Coreference, Modality, and Focus. Studies on the syntax–semantics interface. 2007. xii, 239 pp.

110 **ROTHSTEIN, Susan (ed.):** Theoretical and Crosslinguistic Approaches to the Semantics of Aspect. 2008. viii, 453 pp.